Pelican Books
Protest and Discontent

Bernard Crick and W. A. Robson are joint editors of the
Political Quarterly, which was founded in 1930 with
Robson and Kingsley Martin, who was soon succeeded
by Leonard Woolf, as joint editors. The *Political Quarterly*
has been an influential journal of public policy for forty
years, always striving to bridge the gap between theory and
practice, the specialist and the generalist, and the
universities and Whitehall.

Bernard Crick is Professor of Political Theory and
Institutions at Sheffield University and author of
In Defence of Politics and *The Reform of Parliament*
among other writings.

William Robson is Professor Emeritus of Public
Administration in London University and author of
Nationalized Industry and Public Ownership and
Local Government in Crisis among many other works.

Protest and Discontent

Edited by Bernard Crick and
William A. Robson for
Political Quarterly

Penguin Books

Penguin Books Ltd, Harmondsworth,
Middlesex, England
Penguin Books Inc., 7110 Ambassador Road,
Baltimore, Maryland 21207, U.S.A.
Penguin Books Australia Ltd, Ringwood,
Victoria, Australia

First published 1970
Copyright © *Political Quarterly*, 1970

Made and printed in Great Britain by
C. Nicholls & Company Ltd
Set in Linotype Times

In Memory of Leonard Woolf (1881–1969)

Contents

Preface

We dedicate this book to the memory of Leonard Woolf, who was joint editor of the *Political Quarterly* from 1932 until 1958, and then was literary editor until 1962. Active until the end, he suggested the basic idea from which this book arose. We thought it interesting for the last issue of the journal before its fortieth birthday to examine in a special number, having always been a journal of reform, the special quality of contemporary protest and discontent. As always in *Political Quarterly* we have cast our net wide, and different contributors take different points of view. But we have tried to offer a serious analysis of the character and conditions of contemporary troubles; we have not sought to give a platform to living examples of each and every kind of disturbance – this has been amply done elsewhere. And if some contributors are in a mood to answer back, perhaps it is about time that that happened. Our editorial tolerance rarely amounts to mindlessness. But one must be sure, above all, of what one is arguing about. This, then, is a symposium of some very different voices, but all directed to a common theme.

Twelve of these essays originally appeared in the October/December 1969 number of *Political Quarterly*, but most have been revised, some extensively; and contributions by Hanson, Rapoport, Taguchi and Swarup are wholly new.

Bernard Crick
William A. Robson

Introduction: A Time to Reason

Bernard Crick

'Which of us', said the Lord Hamlet, 'shall 'scape whipping?'
One of the contributors may have been too polite to mention
us as among the fossils of Social Democracy which seem inadequate to give a sense of purpose or direction to so many
radicals and socialists at the moment. The *Political Quarterly*
solidly and stolidly hoes a hard row: reason applied to practical social reforms; a desire to change, but to change by
political means; the illumination of desires to achieve a far
greater equality and social justice, but working with the materials that are at hand; so in this sense, perhaps, irredeemably
of the centre of the Left, but a centre that can, when stung to
life, be as truculent as any in its self-defence and advocacies
for the future. We believe, as the life of our late colleague
Leonard Woolf so well exemplified, both in reason and in
being reasonable; but it is never reasonable, hence the wasp-
ishness as well as the gentleness in Leonard Woolf, to compromise reason to forces of irrationality, whether of Left or Right.

There is no party line and only the occasional bracing whiff
of sectarian ferocity in this book: most of the contributors
share a recognition that these troubles are likely to be with us
a long time; that they are a mixed bag, some destructive,
some stimulating, some bewilderingly inchoate; and so they
had better be looked at coolly. Perhaps John Griffith provides
a provoking exception to this latter maxim, and Peter Sedgwick carefully and sympathetically attempts to sort out the
various schools of advanced socialist thought today, both from
each other and from the backsliders. But there have been many
symposia lately of exemplary writings of the radical protestors
(though more, it is necessary to remind ourselves, from the
Left than from the Right – however many stirrings are equally
apparent there, as James Jupp brings out in his essay on

youth). The views of the *enragés* and the *ultras* are not under-publicized. The general object in this book has been something more square and solid: to analyse critically.

Not everything has been covered by any means, and it is not claimed that the book is a fully comprehensive (or superficial?) international survey; some countries feature but not others, and we have neglected specifically nationalist influences even within the United Kingdom,[1] despite our deliberate concentration on our own immediate problems in Britain. Even so, 'what about the rest of us?', it may be asked. Protests of consumers, tax-payers, managers, professionals and the middle class are not without their interest and patronage; Young Liberals are a strange and interesting lot, worth treatment on their own; Michael Young's 'Open Group' has just rallied some of these inchoate forces into some kind of doctrinal utterance. And Edward Goodman's recent Acton Society pamphlet deserves close attention by any worried about both the technical and the qualitative problems of scale: his radical liberalism has many points of contact with those socialists who still think, or think again, of the small group as well as the central plan.[2] Obviously there is a danger in this book, as always, that in examining interesting extremes, one exaggerates their importance – as the Press has shown in building up a few self-styled student leaders and, more generally, in persistently referring to a very few extremists as 'the students', seeming to accept their own analysis that they are the leading point of a trend which only fails to touch the mass of students because of sloth and deceit. In fact, as Trevor Fisk brings out, students contain many sub-cultures; they are almost as mixed a lot as the rest of us; and many of the self-styled 'advanced elements' are in fact simply 'way out', sadly directionless and tragically lost.

Certainly the ideologies of the extremists are an extremely

1. But see in recent issues of the *Political Quarterly*, Cornelius O'Leary, 'Northern Ireland: The Politics of Illusion' (July–September 1969); E. Hudson Davies, M.P., 'Welsh Nationalism' (July–September 1968); J. B. Mackintosh, M.P., 'Scottish Nationalism' (October–December 1967).

2. Edward Goodman, *The Impact of Size: a study of human and economic values in modern industrial society*, Acton Society, 1969.

bad guide to the reasons why they suddenly appear to flourish. Their explanatory value is low and even their prescriptions have to be taken with some salt as a guide to the actual or probable behaviour of their advocates. They thrive not through their own merits, but by the prior failure of the established order of society to carry conviction. The revolutionary would not agree, but the theorist of the revolutions might, that it is the declining self-confidence of, and the growing internal discontent within, a governing order that create the conditions for effective revolutionary protest. Revolutions take place when governments break down, not just by purposeful and heroic struggles from below. And those who fortunately seize the chance of power are, certainly in their ideologies and their historical writings, far too obsessed with themselves and their opportunities to understand the basic reasons for the decline of the old order. Only if those are understood will 'the new men', if ever they come to power, cease to act so remarkably and depressingly like the old. I admire Peter Sedgwick's careful analysis of the varieties of current socialist thought, but I must remain more sceptical than he about both their novelty and, quite simply, their clarity and truth.

Certainly our times appear to be, now and rather suddenly, uniquely troubled: the students, eastern Europe, China, Vietnam, 'Biafra', Castroism, 'Black Power' and militant civil rights movements in the United States and now Northern Ireland, and, more humbly domestic but equally surprising, the sudden convergence of demands for reform of some of our basic institutions (Parliament, the Civil Service, Local Government, town planning, etc.) and some steps taken. It would be foolish not to see something unique in the convergence of so many currents, but it is possible – as Margaret Cole hints – to exaggerate the uniqueness of these events. So many of the young rebels have so little sense of history. The whole modern world has been turbulent and unsettled since the time of the French and industrial revolutions – if one defines modernity itself in terms of high rates of change of material environment and social values and, still more, in terms of a growing expectation of change. There is, by contrast, often depressingly little real change in the so-called 'development territories', but the expectations are great and men are governed by their expectations of what will happen quite as much as by their beliefs as to what is the case at the transitory moment.

During these times of great change, legality and constitutionalism have also made great strides, so that in Britain we now have a very low tolerance of disorder and public violence compared to our eighteenth-century ancestors (or, for that matter, to modern Americans). One has only to recall the lack of police in old London, the constant threats to the person in the street and the recurrent riots. The Gordon Riots were, after all, for a country at war, a remarkable event. And the conduct of elections right up until the 1890s, longer in Ireland, hardly shared the respectable dullness of today. Sometimes for 'student' one is tempted to read 'apprentice' and, recalling seventeenth- and eighteenth-century history, to murmur '*Déjà vu*'. Days of misrule and riots were once much more common and yet governments, let alone 'society', did not feel threatened by them in general, only particularly and personally. Would some of our political leaders who now deplore 'apathy' really like to have stood amid the shower of animal, vegetable and mineral matter of the nineteenth-century hustings? Perhaps for too long now we have become habituated to these forms of public participation turning entirely to football and scarcely even marginally to politics.

So let us beware, without becoming complacent, of exaggeration. Youth has usually been a somewhat nasty and threatening spectacle to middle age. The problem is not that of one generation supplanting another – unless some Rousseau-Herod were to arise, but is one, as David Rapoport argues so well, of the relationship between generations. And we are also apt to draw too sharp a line between order and violence. Politics is, in fact, rich with intermediate gradations between compliance and killing. Dr Johnson was going too far to say that behind every state must stand the public hangman (although the anarchists would agree with Duncan Sandys in this, at least); but equally rebellion usually has its limits, and its ritual. The eighteenth-century mob, for instance, smashed windows which were not illuminated in honour of popular heroes, but there is much negative evidence that the householders had due warning to get into the back rooms. Levels of violence can increase drastically, but usually violence is of specific kinds: it need not, as again the high Tory and the bomb-anarchist both believe, escalate comprehensively. Collective violence has far more tradition in its varied forms than the traumas of individual psychosis (which is one reason why psychoanalysis is a poor guide to history). There is a difference, after all, between assassination of individuals, terrorism against a class, and communal massacres – just as with individual political failure there is a difference between execution, imprisonment, exile, retirement and a seat in the Lords. Some of our worries arise because of an inadequate vocabulary to conceptualize modern politics: opinion, pressure, threat, strike, demonstration, parade, riot, rebellion, *coup d'état*, civil war and revolution all need distinguishing as, in some way, different forces with different conventions. Until we can be a little more precise in some of these respects, defenders of the *status quo*, reformers and revolutionaries all very often confuse and alarm themselves quite as much as their opponents. 'Revolution', or anything as clear cut, is simply not the issue in Britain, nor is it to be found in the cards before us and nor are there any but a handful of highly debatable and historically specific examples anywhere in the modern world.

What are typical of the modern world are not clear and unique threats or hopes, but the bewildering number of alternatives and the unprecedented intermingling of different time-scales of social and economic change. We all know now, thanks to television even more than the Press, 'how the other half lives'. *Seeing* how so many other kinds of people live, people conclude that things could so easily be different, here and there, were there a concerted will. So we all become disappointed, aggrieved and restless to an extraordinary degree: not just 'Youth', but even those older ones who see this Youth as either a UNIQUE PROMISE or a UNIQUE

THREAT. It was, after all, *The Times,* not the *Black Dwarf,* which had an editorial in May 1968 on 'The Sickness of a Capitalist Civilization'. It did not mean to imply that the disease was fatal, but it did assert that the sickness was radical: no amount of material prosperity could make up for what seemed to be a qualitative hole right in the heart of our culture. Some of us had heard that before, but not from such a quarter. And if the editorial writers of *The Times* had stayed a little frightened – which is, at times, a good stimulus to thought – they might have come to see that the problem of conflict between the generations, if such it is, is unlikely to be solved by playing-fields, adventure playgrounds, fresh air and the Duke of Edinburgh or even Prince Charles.

Even on the level of the consumption of goods, there is something both very enjoyable and plainly decadent in the prodigality of alternatives that our society showers upon us. It is becoming hard even to choose with any rational consistency – and most of the choices are trivial. Even 'fashionable' is now too rigid a concept for the trendy: the future is anticipated, but then neglected for yet another possible trend. And with ideas as for goods, everything is tasted but nothing is digested.

On top of these cultural tendencies, there is the greater uncertainty of the international situation. But, it is worth pointing out, there is also perhaps less real fear. The political events of 1956 meant the breakdown of the international Communist movement, or certainly of the Russian hegemony in it. Looking back to the 1945–55 era, this was a fantastic thing that no one dared to predict; and still more fantastic would have been the idea of a Russian–American 'understanding' growing out of mutual fear of China and distrust of the endless exactions of their own nominal allies. In the 'bipolar' world of the Cold War, there was the Great Fear of atomic warfare. The possibility remains, but – one dares to say, even to protesting Youth – the great and pressing fear has gone: the situation has now grown too complicated to think that there are any longer two clear sides of which one could knock out the other to ensure both world power and peace. But also, amid the great nuclear fear, there was a kind of clarity and, even if an unwanted certainty about where the world stood, a certainty nevertheless. Now that has gone. And, further, the break-up of so many international Communist parties released so many activists in so many different directions, but yet gave no focus to the generation just then growing up. If the youth of today had grown up in a world in which, as so very recently, the Communist Party dominated the Left, many would have looked at it eagerly, rejecting their present society as hollow or inadequate, but few would have joined it with its grim record of subservience to Russia and internal corruption. Those few, however, would have been the tough ones and their joining tended to push the rest, however uneasily, into organizations either specifically anti-Communist or lamely fellow-travelling.

Now a whole generation has grown up since 1956 into this fragmented and diffused stock of dissent. It was always easier to define one's enemies than one's concrete objectives; but, in the past, the objectives were provided either by the Communist Party or, in Britain, by the Labour Party – even if there had been for long a myth that Labour once had had genuinely socialist objectives away from which it was constantly backsliding but towards which it could be brought back again. Rebels were left without a cause, indeed. C.N.D. broke up as the Great Fear diminished, or rather grew so complicated; and suddenly the conviction grew that the real antagonisms were those of generation rather than of economic class, status or the possession of political power. Plainly there is something in this theory of generation conflict, but equally plainly it is, as both French and American experience suggest, a convenient doctrine for middle-class socialists rebelling against the gradualism and indulgence of their middle-class and socialist parents, as well as a side-effect of the fantastic concentration of commercial advertizing upon the teenage generation. There has been, as it were, a conspiracy of flattery that equates inexperience with political purity and urges the young to try, by deeds if not in years, to stay young forever. One feels as hypocritically sorry for the ageing revolutionary lecturer trying to keep up with his students as one does for the bank manager under orders to hook 'the spenders of tomorrow' however wobbly is their credit today.

In this context in Great Britain must be seen the colossal failure of the Labour Party in the 1950s to endure, at the very moment when the Communists had played into their hands, the verbal assaults of the Labour League of Youth and then the Young Socialists. So touchy were the Party leaders at internal criticism, so unperceptive were they of the consequences of 1956, that instead of pursuing a cynical or indulgent policy of letting little dogs bark, or of wading in and arguing with them, but keeping them in touch with the rank-and-file of the Labour movement at almost any cost, they took them at their word; even though they disbelieved in ideologies themselves, they rose to every verbal provocation and expelled them or murmured 'good riddance . . .' as they withdrew. And in power the Labour Government has done no better. Let us sadly admit an element of theatricality – almost of escapism – in the great youth causes of Vietnam, Cuba, Rhodesia and 'Biafra' (with no international brigades as for Spain in the 1930s, only weekend demonstrations under the tolerant eye of the London police); but none of the Labour leaders had even the most cynical perception of what even apparent concern for these problems might have done to mend their domestic political fences. Must the voice of Britain in foreign affairs always be so uniquely and deadeningly diplomatic? And must the deep concern of so many young people for international problems – as witnessed in the huge over-subscription for Voluntary Service Overseas, or membership of the United Nations Association – be steered only into such impeccably non-political channels? For there is now a Labour Party in Great Britain virtually without young members or influence on youth, and this is at a time when, even though let down by their Government, there is, at least, a great radical ferment among young people – but one going in fragmented and wildly disparate directions through lack of any intelligent and perceptive leadership (some even leaning more towards

Powell than socialism). The young will not thank the Government simply for giving them votes: they want something more compelling to vote about.

But see all this also in a still wider context. What price now the much-vaunted 'end of ideology'! It did not take C.I.A. money to make the regular contributors of *Encounter*, for instance, picture the cold war as a contrast between a practical-minded empiricism (or was it pragmatism?) and ideology. They already believed, as part of a Mandarin upper middle-class liberal culture, that positive beliefs were positively harmful. The polemic against ideology as something comprehensive and actually or potentially totalitarian was justified, but all forms of doctrine were then seen as ideological: the whole vast middle-ground of reform between empiricism (that is, acceptance of the present order) and compulsive, total alternatives was almost wilfully obscured. The effect of bad ideas in the 1930s and 1940s made men frightened in the 1950s and early 1960s of ideas at all – even the good revolutionary ideas of liberty, equality and fraternity as restated in Democratic Socialism. Moreover, philosophy, it was held, should not deal with value-questions, and social philosophy was a very funny kind of discipline at best concerned to stop one believing in anything. British academic philosophy is much to blame in helping to create that unnatural vacuum in education, an almost complete lack of challenge to the young or visible concern with the great issues of humanity, which both Ernest Gellner and Arthur Koestler discuss and deplore in different ways. So far from being at 'the end of ideology' we may hopefully be at the beginning of a revival of a recognition of the importance of social and political theory, both to show us how much we assume already (even the most practical of us) and to point new goals and new directions. We British have been blinkered empiricists for too long. Never has there been a time more ripe for constructive social and political thinking. As vast dogmatic alternatives collapse and as 'the merely practical' stands discredited, there is need to pick and choose rationally and qualitatively amid the debris and the mud (as the Czechs attempted so brilliantly and bravely in 1968 and, indeed – on the level of theory – succeeded: a true statement of the necessary relationship between freedom and economic planning). For any of us to talk of action and to reject rational understanding is madness, but for us to cultivate understanding and to divorce it from progressive action is wickedness.

If the effects of protest vary in each country and culture, it is hard to read, as here, of France, India, Japan and the U.S.A. (and we could well have added Germany and Italy too) without being aware of astonishingly similar forms but also, of much more significance, of broadly similar failures of the established régimes – failures so acute as to give the protests, often not so novel in themselves, both their unique opportunity and often their frustratingly irrational character. But in Britain, sad for the revolutionary and cold comfort for the reformer, we are not threatened with breakdown, simply with moral failure. It may almost be worse to have to go on living with ourselves than to fail after having tried for something radically better – this is plainly Professor Griffith's basic assumption: he comes to revolution out of pessimism, not from an impatient optimism. The protests of the moment arise from a society in which quality and quantity have become not conditions of each other, but bitter enemies. The scale and cynicism of things have grown too large to be endured. Revolutionary remedies are offered. But few of these would be listened to for five minutes if a reforming government had been able to carry conviction, even on certain elementary levels. 'Democracy' as well as 'technology' was one of Mr Wilson's catch-phrases in both 1964 and 1966. We have had a frustrated and hobbled phase of parliamentary reform, good words about 'openness' in the Civil Service, good words (in the Skeffington Report) about popular participation in planning. But the last mentioned is worth pausing upon – as does Professor Page – as a classic case of the Anglican grin of good intentions while the teeth remain *papier-mâché* or rubber. Democratic participation has degenerated into mere public relations. The trade union movement *should* so enter into management that industrial democracy would emerge – says a Labour Party policy statement. Would it not be nice, says the Skeffington report, if local authorities acted in all these new publicizing and participative ways? But it suggests not the slightest new power to Minister or inspectors to see that these good things are done. If the Joint Statement of the Committee of University Vice-Chancellors and the National Union of Students (October 1968), at one end of the scale, and the Plowden Report on Primary Schools, at the other, should also turn out to be 'polite, meaningless words', as may Parliamentary reform itself (which should tie all these things together), the fat may well be in the fire. Not the fire of revolution or even revolt, but of that utter cynicism and frustration which arises from glibly aroused expectations and results in exoticism, delinquency, decadence and decline of any concern for real public issues. There is no risk of revolution, only of a moral seediness, a collapse of civic spirit and political concern, and an ever-increasingly competitive materialism and a trivialized mechanism – nonetheless dehumanized for now operating in personalized or christian-name terms. 'Keep telling a man that he is nothing but an oversized rat', as Koestler puts it, 'and he will start growing whiskers and bite your finger.'

We have more time than we think if our nerves are strong, our sympathies eclectic and tolerant; but it is time that needs spending deliberately, visibly, energetically and sincerely to make the world better in such a way that the imagination of people is stirred to participate in politics in a freely moved and rational manner. We must no longer confuse social toleration with any unnecessary and self-destroying intellectual tolerance of nonsense – as Gellner argues so well; particularly, I would only add, when so much nonsense gets written, not even in plain English for ordinary people, but in the barbaric abstractions of the dialectic (*le mot juste*?) fusion of American social science and an equally abstract translator's Marxism. (What is clear can be said clearly.) To hold strong views and to remain silent is not to be especially tolerant: it is to be peculiarly foolish or cowardly. Intolerance arises from the manner in which we act, not from action itself.

The time has come to argue back against irrationalism of

both Right and Left, and to change the conditions in which it can flourish. Have we grown too frightened of the worst in men any longer to dare to call forth the best? And are the Left doomed to quarrel amongst themselves forever more effectively than they can persuade the others? This I will not believe – whatever the present facts.

In the Past

Margaret Cole*

When beginning to write, as I have been asked to do in this essay, a kind of historical curtain-raiser to the present-day problems of discontent and unrest, there are two questions one must be prepared to answer – what do you mean by the words? and, what period do you propose to cover? On the first point, I think one can distinguish, broadly, two kinds of discontent: first, the protest which is *specific*, directed to some ascertainable and presumably attainable end, like the rehabilitation of Dreyfus or the repeal of the Corn Laws, and secondly the kind of 'protest movements' which are so large and so ill-defined that the complainants could scarcely be satisfied without a revolution or at least a major change. Of this latter kind were the complicated masses of grievance which foreshadowed the French and Russian revolutions, or in this country the aspirations of the working classes during the Owenite and Chartist times. One has also to consider what I may call the 'setting' of discontent: it is possible to observe combinations of social, economic, and political conditions which make it fairly obvious (at least in retrospect) that demands for change will arise, and, by contrast, other situations in which there is no very patent cause for dissatisfaction, but in which a good number of people are plainly unhappy and dissatisfied and one has to look for less obvious reasons. These two sets of conditions often shade into one another, as indeed do the two kinds of protest, since sociological generalizations are always imprecise; but I believe it is possible to see a difference.

As to the period covered, 'protest', like the poor, is always with us; and it would be possible, no doubt, to go back to the

* President of the Fabian Society and author of many works of politics, history and biography.

Black Death, or to Domesday. But it would not be very interesting or enlightening; and I think the best point at which
to start is round about the turn of the century, the time of the
Diamond Jubilee and the South African war, when what has
been called the Victorian Compromise or the Heyday of Empire – or you can take your choice of a number of other de-
scriptions – showed signs of coming to an end. (Some quote
Kipling's *Recessional* as evidence of changing mood: myself,
I find that famous lyric more of a literary exercise in gloom,
with its reference to the boastings of the Gentiles – were
the 'Gentiles' in question German or French?) We can thence
proceed to the Great Unrest of the years immediately preceding the 1914 war, then via the wartime troubles and those of
the first half of the twenties and – a fairly different prospect –
those of the thirties, and so to the 1945 election and what came
after – with this proviso always, that so brief a look at so com-
pressed a history is bound to be selective and to reflect, to
some extent, the personal outlook of the writer.

To begin, then, with the late nineties. At first sight that
decade would not seem to have been fertile ground for unrest;
almost everything, including Ireland, was fairly quiet. The
country had recovered, economically, from the bad years –
but not to such an extent that the 'industrious classes' were
uncomfortably demanding; there were no more Great Dock
Strikes, and the mid-century fears of the mob were dying
away. The Commune was a long time ago, and the Socialists,
Blatchford's *Clarion* and the I.L.P. notwithstanding, did not
appear to be increasing their appeal; indeed, various pieces of
social legislation were surely mitigating the unpleasing conditions which Charles Booth's studies of London had uncovered.
Local government had been nicely tidied up in a series of
Acts of Parliament, and outside the island shores there did
not seem much to worry about, once the unsavoury little epi-
sode of the Jameson Raid had been cleared up.

Nevertheless, there was a perceptible uneasiness beginning
to grow underneath, born partly of a desire for a more 'permissive' society – and of a parallel fear, showing itself in the
outburst over Oscar Wilde and reactions to the reported be-

haviour of the Prince of Wales and his wealthy friends, that a more permissive society might turn out horridly vulgar – partly of the undermining, by Huxley and others, of the foundations of revealed religion, and partly of a feeling among the more percipient that the splendours of empire and of the capital city rested on some pretty noisome foundations.

All this discomfort was enormously increased, quite suddenly, by the outbreak of the Boer War, or rather by the development of a 'necessary' disciplinary operation into a real and highly damaging war; it became manifest, first, that the British Army was performing disgracefully, secondly, that Britain was appearing to most of the world in the image, not of a headmaster like Thomas Arnold, but of a Flashman-type bully egged on by money-grabbers, and thirdly, that a sizeable number of Britain's own citizens shared the opinions of the outsiders. The Government did, of course, win the 'khaki' election; but it is not always remembered that that election was nothing like that of 1918, or 1931. Only three seats were gained on balance, and that to the accompaniment of some shocking hysterical demonstrations. The treatment of the pro-Boers is an indication of the amount of hysteria which lay ready for tapping, the more particularly as it was not confined to one side; the eulogies which persons of advanced libertarian views poured out on the Boer farmers (forgetting, of course, the native Kaffirs) must be re-read to be believed today; and Hilaire Belloc produced some nasty anti-semitic verse.

A disquieting sight, and the disquiet did not end when the war ended. The final months and the aftermath provided unpleasant revelations – about the physical condition of recruits and rejects, about sickness in the field and sickness in the 'concentration camps' – inefficiency rather than inhumanity, but that made little difference. Then came Chinese labour on the Rand, to stagger the humanitarians. Then the Government managed to outrage sturdy Liberal nonconformists by trying to cure the muddle in public education (which had started a scare that better-trained German clerks were going to hamstring Britain's foreign trade) by ignoring the sensible Bryce proposals for secondary education in favour of reform mainly administrative – which, whatever its merits, outraged the enlightened spirits who sat on the London School Board, and handed large dollops of public money to the Anglican Church. Then came Chamberlain and his Tariff Reform, scandalizing the Liberals, scaring the working classes, splitting the Tories. The House of Peers took an unexpected judicial hand and in Taff Vale served notice to the unions that it would pay them to spare a little sustenance for the weak little Labour Representation Committee – this when the rise in wealth per head had almost come to a stop and wages were starting to lag behind prices.

So it is easy to watch the climate of dissatisfaction changing steadily into something like a real demand for change, a lot of change. One overt sign was the election to Parliament of Will Crooks and Arthur Henderson; and it may have been a dim consciousness of what was happening that induced the dispirited Liberal Party to stop squabbling and make Campbell-Bannerman their leader in an election which, as far as my childhood recollection of the street posters goes, was fought on a splendid bag of mixed issues. They did not say 'Balfour Must Go'; but that was what they meant; and they produced a landslide in which, as Robert Ensor wrote nostalgically nearly thirty years later, 'Radicals and Socialists alike, released from the suppression of two decades, were radiant with sudden hopes of a new heaven and a new earth.'[1]

For two or three years they thought they were getting it. After the Trade Disputes Act had put paid to Taff Vale, there followed a whole list of measures-for-mitigating-the-condition-of-the-poor – old-age pensions, feeding of hungry school children, Trade Boards; there is no need to list them for anyone who knows any history at all. They were crusts, no doubt, from a *laissez-faire* capitalist table, which the table could well spare; but they were quite solid crusts. Moreover, the next instalment of reform, as asked for by the Radicals, was really quite mild and could, one thinks, have been given without much difficulty. To take the three major issues of the

1. Ensor, *England, 1870–1914*, Oxford University Press, 1936, p. 391.

Great Unrest which blew up into so great a storm: the Irish Home Rulers, at that date, were asking for little more than a glorified county council for Ireland; the women agitators, again at that date, would have been satisfied with the enfranchisement of a quite small number of respectable middle-class women; the industrial workers were aiming at no more than a much-needed improvement in wages and conditions – such as a fair settlement of the 'abnormal place' problem in the coal mines – and the recognition by employers as well as the law that trade unions had a right to exist and to receive fair treatment. All very reasonable; nor did anybody, except perhaps Mr H. G. Wells, who had launched a furious but unsuccessful attack on The Faults of the Fabian before the new government had even got into power, appear to be in a violent hurry. People seemed to realize that even huge majorities cannot produce new heavens and new earths in a day; and the explosive storming of Victor Grayson from Colne Valley into the House of Commons, demanding instant justice for the unemployed, could be regarded as an aberration. *Someone* is always sure to be discontented, and the Labour Party rejected Grayson. Yet so short a time later, there was turmoil all over the country, with massive strikes, law-breaking, arson, threats of civil war, and a discontent, in the minds of those not directly affected by any of these, a discontent with the 'achievements of civilization' that even seemed to welcome the prospect of war itself.

'Likelier', Chesterton had written in *The Napoleon of Notting Hill*,

> Likelier the barricades shall blare
> Slaughter below and smoke above,
> And death and hate and hell declare
> That men have found a thing to love.

And Henry Newbolt – no red revolutionary – had lamented that he could find

> no more defeat, faith, victory – O no more
> a cause on earth for which we might have died.

Readers of the mid-thirties derived a good deal of the impressions of this period from George Dangerfield's book, *The Strange Death of Liberal England*, published in Canada twenty years after it was all over[2] – a brilliant though rather over-written book. 'Liberal England' did not die, even if momentarily it looked as though it were determined on suicide; it is in fact very arguable that if one regards the picture all round and in all parts of the realm England today is much more 'liberal' than in the time of Edward VII, which has inspired so much nostalgic reminiscence: it was not Liberalism but the Liberal Party which then entered upon a long decline. Nevertheless, a great deal of Dangerfield's picturesque detail is true enough.

It is easy to see some perfectly prosaic and valid causes for the Great Unrest. We may note the determination of Lloyd George in the Budget to take away some of the wealth and obsolescent privilege of the House of Lords, and to do it in so provocative a way as to goad them into challenging the Commons, with the inevitable result of the comparatively mild ball-and-chain of the Parliament Act. We may then observe that the indifference of the English electorate – or perhaps the persistent affection of Englishmen for lords – resulted in the stalemate whereby neither the Irish nor Labour could hope to get what they wanted – Home Rule, the eight-hour day, the reversal of the Osborne Judgement – except by maintaining the government in office and therefore acquiescing in a number of things which they did not like at all; and we can guess without surprise that neither Redmond's followers in the country nor MacDonald's would be likely to regard this state of things with understanding acquiescence. Finally, we should take note that in a time of fairly good trade real wages were steadily falling, this with a government in power that had been regarded as the workers' friend, and that unemployment, the Poor Law and the workhouse (for conditions in which see George Lansbury's reminiscences) were waiting round the next corner. The extreme heat and drought of the Coronation summer may have added some-

2. Reissued in England in 1966.

thing; but I doubt that it made very much difference. There was reason enough for discontent and even for anger; but the eventual explosion was much angrier than might have been foreseen.

What happened after 1909 was a combination of two different things. The first was the treason – I use the word advisedly – of the Tory leaders in revenge for the Budget and the Parliament Act. The whole course of action of Carson, Smith, Bonar Law and their supporters, from the decision to 'play the Orange card', as Randolph Churchill had called it twenty years before, and the determination of owners of southern Irish estates like Lansdowne not to let the fires die down in Ulster, to Bonar Law's quoting of Marlborough's betrayal of James II, the Curragh mutiny and the gun-running at Larne, all hangs together. So does the violently abusive language employed in Parliament and outside – Kipling publicly calling Rufus Isaacs 'Gehazi' because of mildly smelly behaviour over Marconi shares is an extreme case; and Garvin in the *Observer* went to almost the same lengths. Those Unionist leaders were in febrile fear, not of the mob, or of Catholics as such, but of losing privileges to the lower classes; and it is not surprising that they elicited a response in kind from Irish Nationalists, and from some of the English strike-leaders.

The case of Labour was, however, different. Essentially, the mood derived from a sudden realization that the worsening conditions (felt, if not specifically stated) were closely connected with a denial of personality rights to a great part of the nation – that part which could be discarded by an employer who had no immediate use for it like any other unwanted tool, and when savings were exhausted could look to the Poor Law at the clear price of losing any claim to citizenship in the community. Robert Tressell's *Ragged-Trousered Philanthropists*, with its contemptuous picture of the workers in the building trades who are deluded enough to make money for their masters at the expense of their own humanity, put the point clearly; so did Chesterton in his *Song of the Wheels*, written in August of 1911:

> All the wheels are thine, master, tell the wheels to run . . .
> We are only men, master, have you heard of men?

It is worth remembering in how large a proportion of the strikes of 1910 to 1914 a part of the demand was for recognition, carrying with it an implication of security and the right to a life of one's own, to get drunk, like Driver Knox, when off duty – this coincided with, but was not caused by, the visions being concurrently preached of peace, freedom and prosperity to be found in a world where the workers' organizations, having come to power through strike action, would use it to run industry, and society as a whole, more efficiently than their masters, without profit and without exploitation. But the visions did contribute a great deal. It is not likely that many of the individuals who downed tools in South Wales, in Dublin, in Liverpool, in port after port, and on the railways, had ever heard of Sorel or studied the 'myth' of the General Strike, or even read S. G. Hobson's denunciation of wage-slavery in the *New Age*. But many of them had heard Lloyd George denouncing oppression (before he had discovered in the Insurance Acts how to induce the working classes to pay for part of the security for which they longed), and they could now hear Tom Mann, Ben Tillett, Larkin, Connolly and others urging them, in the name of syndicalism, industrial unionism, or later Guild Socialism, to take matters into their own hands. It may be noted, however, that though the 'unrest' and the strikes were of course a working-class movement, the movement was not treasonable nor nearly as violent in its expression as was the other side. The *Don't Shoot* leaflet, for which Tom Mann and others were very promptly sentenced, was quite exceptional, and Tillett's 'God strike Lord Devonport dead!' was hardly a serious attack. Even the *Daily Herald* was ebulliently rampageous rather than really revolutionary – savage though some of Will Dyson's cartoons might be – and certainly not nihilistic.

The 'self-expression' of left-wing Labour could be called extravagant and utopian; it could not be called hysterical. The same could not be said of the women's agitation – on either

side: the difference was brought out clearly when Sylvia
Pankhurst was disowned by her mother and sister for over-
much concern with the problems of working women. The two
conspicuous militant personalities, Emmeline Pankhurst, with
her gift for capitalizing on her personal sufferings in the Cause
and her shrewd instinct for hitting her adversaries where it
hurt most (in arson and destruction of property) and Christa-
bel, the beautiful and autocratic virago, were no doubt exceptional; but the fierce language and inordinate claims of their
followers and their literature were the product of the long
history of the Subjection of Women coupled with the conviction now reached that the barrier was insurmountable, that
a society organized by men, whatever individuals might say –
or, if they were in power or seeking it, promise – simply would
not give women votes. The women felt themselves to be as
firmly held down as the subjects of the Tsar, and with as little
hope of legitimate escape; hence the wild words about White
Slave Traffic and man as the source of all disease – words
matched with equal fury by the other side, in, for example,
the furore which raged round *Ann Veronica* and the attempts
to label the militants 'drug fiends' – a term now obsolete. This
fury was partly stimulated by a dim realization that some
social emancipation was in fact happening; clothes, however
odd they seem today, *were* becoming less constricting, and a
handful of women were making their appearance in fields
hitherto unknown. This added to the feelings of blind resentment, which were further reinforced by minor explosions on
the literary and artistic scene – Wyndham Lewis's *BLAST*,
for instance, Signor Marinetti, and the Cubists.

Looking back, nevertheless, there seems to have been a certain innocence – possibly a dangerous innocence – about all
this violence of expression and action, born in a Britain which
appeared basically secure. Those Carsonites who were declaring that they would rather live under the Kaiser did not really
mean it; nor, in the other strain, did Robert Blatchford or
even the *Daily Mail* really want to go to war with Germany.
Chesterton did not *want* bloodshed in the streets of London;
the young who went about chanting *When ther Revolution*

comes, ther bluddy Revolution did not expect to see it; that monster of 1913, the Triple Alliance of miners, railwaymen, and transport workers never took the first steps to make its organization fit for an industrial battle of American type.

After August 1914, the picture changes, and in many ways simplifies. The passions of which I have written in the preceding paragraphs apparently disappeared. There was a fairly brief period of hysteria, signalled by rumours of 'War Babies', i.e. bastards born to the wives of serving soldiers, by white feathers handed out to men not wearing uniform and by persecution of those who had German surnames. But the 'unrest' which began to grow after 1916, the Somme battles and the Russian Revolution, had clear and evident causes. War-weariness, of the kind that we had not then learned to call 'normal', was combined with an optimism arising largely from the remarkable results of which effort harnessed to na-tional ends was showing itself capable. The insurgency of shop stewards' committees, the burgeoning idealism of the Guild Socialists and similar groupings, the many plans for Post-War Reconstruction – all these flourished in the inflated conditions of wartime – inflated in much more than a purely monetary sense. Failure to recognize this inflation for what it was pro-duced in its turn the disillusion and disappointment of the early twenties, when the bubble burst and 'workers' control' went down the drain with all, or nearly all, the proposals of the Ministry of Reconstruction. There is no need to discuss this phase in detail; only to note that its discomforts have recently tended to be minimized by writers who were barely adult when the war ended and seem in their reminiscences to see it as a second Golden Age – in Oxford, at all events. But that the feeling was disappointment, not despair, is seen in the resilience with which people recovered – the trade unions picked themselves up after the disastrous experience of the General Strike, and the electorate perked up enough to kick the Tories out of office three years later. Those who had re-joiced in the Russian Revolution were not yet finding cracks in it; their League of Nations friends noted happily that a puffed-up Italian organ-grinder had been pushed out of Corfu. Furthermore, 'emancipation' and experimentation was on its way all round. D. H. Lawrence was an exciting writer who shocked the old and prejudiced: not as yet an obsession. The war was really over – so far in the past that one could even again read about it – in *Farewell to Arms, All Quiet on the Western Front, Journey's End* – with horror indeed, but with a basic and comforting conviction that it could not come again.

But it could; and in the files of the *New Statesman*, well recalled in the second volume of Kingsley Martin's own autobiography, one can read what chaos, what bewilderment was created in the minds of the intelligentsia – a group becoming more numerous as educational opportunity very slowly increased – as they came gradually to realize that it could, and as the thirties drew to a close, that it *had*. Besides the obvious and melancholy ending of bright hopes, besides the feeling of guilt among those of middle age at having somehow let down their juniors and a parallel (though not widespread) indignation among those juniors, what contributed most to the bewilderment was the sickening discovery of what 'democracy' could do. It could turn its back, deliberately, on what had been called 'civilized' values; it could *vote* itself into chains and under jackboots, and be acclaimed in some quarters for so doing. What happened in Britain, in 1931, was only a pale semi-copy of what was happening elsewhere. If one adds to this shock the new 'horror stories' produced by the peace parties, in books like *What Would be the Character of a New War?*, of imminent physical destruction and mental demoralization, it is all too easy to understand. Bevin's brutal description of Lansbury 'trailing his conscience round from conference to conference asking to be told what to do with it' in part sums it up.

In part only, though. For the dilemma of 'Hitler and Rearmament' was not the whole of the story. To be set against it, preventing demoralization on a national scale, there were two factors. The first was a growing and comparatively uncomplicated indignation at the state of society at home. In a book called *The Condition of Britain*, G. D. H. Cole and I put together the shaming facts which stared one in the face –

about unemployment and the unemployed above all, but also about health, housing, public education, etc. – and this was reinforced and amplified in many other publications, some from such respectable sources as Boyd Orr and the B.M.A. The point is that the feeling of shame affected all classes, not merely those who bought the red-covered publications of the Left Book Club. 'Involvement' was the catchword of the time; and those who were 'involved' were indignant at the stark nonsense of 'starving in the midst of plenty', and were sustained by a conviction that these things need not be, that they could be remedied by application of Marxism, humanism, Keynesian economics, or science (mixture compounded according to the personal taste of the prescriber). There was little really overt opposition; the frustrations which enraged the many protesting groups – Popular Fronts and the rest of them – lay rather in the lumpish inertia of the mass – particularly of the Labour Party. This inertia, due partly to plain fear of the future, was the second factor; it did not prevent the intelligentsia feeling, as a young relative of mine born in 1922 put it, that 'Until after Spain we knew where we were; we knew more or less which was Left and which was Right, and that Right was Wrong'; but it did prevent society coming to pieces. And when society did make up its mind, after Munich, the result was a solidarity of purpose which banished 'unrest' almost completely for some years. 'War hysteria', as experienced in 1900 and 1914, was negligible in 1940. The place was taken by the deep and for long hardly noticed conviction that the 'Condition of Britain' must never be like that again. ASK YOUR DAD, said the posters of 1945.

So came the 1945 election – 1906 over again, with the like high hopes, disappointed more quickly, for those who had not noticed the mushroom cloud, by economic conditions, by the American Loan, the Cold War, the savage post-war rationing. These, off-setting things like the fulfilment of Labour promises, the Health Service and social security, and the freeing of India, shook the Labour Government to its fall, with cruel irony, just on the brink of an economic revival that would have enabled it, and not its enemies, to say, 'You never had it so good'. There is nothing difficult to understand about the desire for a let-up (which the Labour Government was actually preparing, just before its fall, in the Festival of Britain) which let in the Tories in 1951 and kept them there until 1964 – nor about the two following elections, when the winds of change were really beginning to blow and the *Recessional* becoming cold fact, as the far-called navies melted away. But since then ...?

Since then, in the last couple of years, there has developed a condition of confused and fragmented discontent and resentment which reminds me of 1911 rather than 1931. 1911, because it is made up so largely of angry disappointment that things which ought to have turned out good have turned out all wrong, and there is nothing comfortably defined to blame and fight against – rather, a combination of evil. Cobbett, a hundred and fifty years ago, called it The Thing: Ibsen's Peer Gynt saw it as the Great Boyg who conquers but does not fight: Nekrassov, in nineteenth-century Russia, thought it was Tsardom, which might perhaps be ended by assassination but in no other way. In Britain, the words 'the Establishment' were used at the outset; but rather more than that seems to be meant today. It is not only the social and political institutions; it is the whole technological 'triumph' which is declared to be dust and ashes. (See a very penetrating – and pessimistic – analysis by Richard Lowenthal in *Encounter*, which appeared just after my original article was published.[3]) I am not sure how long-lasting this mood is going to be; its emphasis shifts from month to month; student bodies change their notions about the meaning of 'participation'; vandals transfer their attentions from telephone kiosks to football trains – and where next? Battered Babies, poisoned seabirds and child-kidnapping provide headlines in turn. What happens next is matter for prophecy – and for other contributors to this book. I only reflect that, supposing my comparison with 1911 to have any validity, the Great Unrest only came to an end, abruptly, on 4 August 1914. Which is small help for prophets.

3. 'Unreason and Revolution', *Encounter*, November 1969.

Rebellion in a Vacuum*

Arthur Koestler†

Hoping to discover at long last what the verb 'to educate' means, I turned the other day to the Concise Oxford and was amused to find this definition: 'Give intellectual and moral training to'. And further down, to drive the nail home: 'Train (person) ... train (animals)'. I would not be surprised to see, when the next rioting season starts, a bonfire of C.O.D.s; and that definition, with its Pavlovian echoes, certainly deserves no better. But I am doubtful whether much would be gained by replacing the offensive term 'training' by 'guidance'. That sounds nice and smarmy, but it begs the question. Guiding, by whatever discreet methods, always implies asserting one's mental powers over another person's mind – in the present context, a younger person's. And the ethics of this procedure, which not so long ago we took for granted, is becoming more and more problematical.

My own preference is for defining the purpose of education as 'catalysing the mind'. To influence is to intrude; a catalyst, on the other hand, is defined as an agent that triggers or speeds up a chemical reaction without being involved in the product. If I may utter a truism, the ideal educator acts as a catalyst, not as a conditioning influence. Conditioning or, to use Skinner's term, social engineering through the control of behaviour, is an excellent method for training Samurais, but applied on the campus it has two opposite dangers. It may lead to a kind of experimental neurosis in the subjects, expressed by violent rejection of any control or influence by authority. On the other hand, it can be too successful, and

* This is a revised version of a paper read at the Symposium 'The University and the Ethics of Change' at Queen's University, Kingston, Canada, November 1968, reprinted with permission of the University.

† The author is a Hungarian-born English writer, living in London.

create the phenomena of conformism, with a broad spectrum ranging from a society of placid yes-men manipulated by the mass media to the totalitarian state controlled by the Thoughts of Chairman Mao.

The alternative to conditioning is catalysing the mind's development. I can best explain what is meant by quoting a passage from a book I wrote some years ago on creativity in science and art.

To enable the student to derive pleasure from the art of scientific discovery, as from other forms of art, he should be made to re-live, to some extent, the creative process. In other words, he must be induced, with proper aid and guidance, to make some of the fundamental discoveries of science by himself, to experience in his own mind some of those flashes of insight which have lightened its path. This means that the history of science ought to be made an essential part of the curriculum, that science should be represented in its evolutionary context – not as a Minerva born fully armed. It further means that the paradoxes, the 'blocked problems' which confronted Archimedes, Copernicus, Galileo, Newton, Harvey, Darwin, should be reconstructed in their historical setting and presented in the form of riddles – with appropriate hints – to eager young minds. The most productive form of learning is problem-solving. The traditional method of confronting the student not with the problem but with the finished solution, means to deprive him of all excitement, to shut off the creative impulse, to reduce the adventure of mankind to a dusty heap of theorems.

Art is a form of communication which aims at eliciting a re-creative echo. Education should be regarded as an art, and use the appropriate techniques to call forth that echo – the 'recreation'. The novice, who has gone through some of the main stages in the evolution of the species during his embryonic development, and through the evolution from savage to civilised society by the time he reaches adolescence, should then be made to continue his curriculum by recapitulating some of the decisive episodes, impasses, and turning points on the road to the conquest of knowledge. Much in our textbooks and methods of teaching reflects a static, pre-evolutionary concept of the world. For man cannot inherit the past; he has to re-create it.[1]

This is what I meant by education as a catalytic process. But now comes the rub. Assuming we agree that the ideal method of teaching science is to enable the student to rediscover

1. *The Act of Creation*, Huchinson, London, 1964, p. 265 ff.

Newton's Laws of Motion more or less by himself – can the same method be applied to the teaching of ethics, of moral values? The first answer that comes to mind is that ethics is not a discipline in the normal curriculum, except if you specialize in philosophy or theology. But that is a rash answer, because implicitly, if not explicitly, we impart ethical principles and value-judgements in whatever we teach or write on whatever subject. The greatest superstition of our time is the belief in the ethical neutrality of science. Even the slogan of ethical neutrality itself implies a programme and a credo.

No writer or teacher or artist can escape the responsibility of influencing others, whether he intends to or not, whether he is conscious of it or not. And this influence is not confined to his explicit message; it is the more powerful and the more insidious because much of it is transmitted implicitly, as a hidden persuader, and the recipient absorbs it unawares. Surely physics is an ethically neutral science? Yet Einstein rejected the trend in modern physics to replace causality by statistics with his famous dictum: 'I refuse to believe that God plays dice with the world.' He was more honest than other physicists in admitting his metaphysical bias; and it is precisely this metaphysical bias, implied in a scientific hypothesis, which exerts its unconscious influence on others. The Roman Church was ill advised when she opposed Galileo and Darwin, and from a rational point of view was lagging behind the times; but intuitively she was ahead of the times in realizing the impact which the new cosmology and the theory of evolution was to have on man's image of himself and his place in the universe.

Wolfgang Köhler, one of the greatest psychologists of our time, searched all his life for 'the place of value in a world of facts' – the title of the book in which he summed up his personal philosophy. But there is no need to search for such a place because the values are diffused through all the strata of the various sciences, as the invisible bubbles of air are diffused in the waters of a lake, and we are the fish who breathe them in all the time through the gills of intuition. Our educational establishment, from the departments of physics through biology and genetics, up to the behavioural and social sciences, willy nilly imparts to the students a *Weltanschauung*, a system of values wrapped up in a package of facts. But the choice and shape of the package is determined by its invisible content; or, to change the metaphor, our implicit values provide the non-Euclidian curvature, the subtle distortions of the world of facts.

Now when I use the term 'our educational establishment', you may object that there is no such thing. Every country, every university and every faculty therein has of course its individual character, its personal face – or facelessness. Nevertheless, taking diversity for granted, and exceptions for granted, there exist certain common denominators which determine the cultural climate and the metaphysical bias imparted to hopeful students practically everywhere in the non-totalitarian sector of the world, from California to the East Coast, from London to Berlin, Bombay and Tokyo. That climate is impossible to define without oversimplification, so I shall oversimplify deliberately and say that it is dominated by three Rs.

The first R stands for Reductionism. Its philosophy may be epitomized by a quotation from a recent book in which man is defined, in all seriousness, as 'nothing but a complex biochemical mechanism, powered by a combustion system which energizes computers with prodigious storage facilities for retaining encoded information'. This is certainly an extreme formulation, but it conveys the essence of that philosophy.

It is, of course, perfectly legitimate to draw analogies between the central nervous system and a telephone exchange, or a computer, or a holograph. The reductionist heresy is contained in the words 'nothing but'. If you replace in the sentence I have just quoted the words 'nothing but' by 'to some extent' or 'from a certain angle' or 'on a certain level of his many-levelled structure', then everything is all right. The reductionist proclaims his part-truth to be the whole truth, a certain specific aspect of a phenomenon to be the whole phenomenon. To the behaviourist, the activities of man are *nothing but* a chain of conditioned responses; to the more rigid variety of Freudian, artistic creation is nothing but a substitute for goal-inhibited sexuality; to the mechanically oriented biologist the phenomena of consciousness are nothing but electro-chemical reactions. And the ultimate reductionist heresy is to consider the whole as nothing but the sum of its parts – a hangover from the crude atomistic concepts of nineteenth-century physics, which the physicist himself abandoned long ago.

The second of the three Rs is what I have called elsewhere the philosophy of ratomorphism. At the turn of the century, Lloyd Morgan's famous canon warned biologists against the fallacy of projecting human thoughts and feelings into animals; since then, the pendulum has moved in the opposite direction, so that today, instead of an anthropomorphic view of the rat, we have a ratomorphic view of man. According to this view, our skyscrapers are nothing but huge Skinner boxes in which, instead of pressing a pedal to obtain a food-pellet, we emit operant responses which are more complicated, but governed by the same laws as the behaviour of the rat. Again, if you erase the 'nothing but', there is an ugly grain of truth in this. But if the life of man is becoming a rat-race, it is because he has become impregnated with a ratomorphic philosophy. One is reminded of that old quip: 'Psycho-analysis is the disease which it pretends to cure.' Keep telling a man that he is nothing but an oversized rat, and he will start growing whiskers and bite your finger.

Some fifty years ago, in the heyday of the conditioned reflex, the paradigm of human behaviour was Pavlov's dog salivating in its restraining harness on the laboratory table. After that came the rat in the box. And after the rat came the geese. In his recent book *On Aggression*, Konrad Lorenz advances the theory that affection between social animals is phylogenetically derived from aggression. The bond which holds the partners together (regardless whether it has a sexual compontent or not) is 'neither more nor less than the conversion of aggression into its opposite'. Whether one agrees or disagrees with this theory is irrelevant; the reason why I mention it is that Lorenz's arguments are almost exclusively based on his observations of the so-called triumph ceremony of the greylag goose, which, in his own words, prompted him to write his book. Once more we are offered a *Weltanschauung* derived from an exceedingly specialized type of observations, a part-truth which claims to be the whole truth. To quote the Austrian psychiatrist, Viktor Frankl: 'The trouble is not that scientists are specializing, but rather that specialists are generalizing'.

A last example for the second R. About a year ago, a popular book on anthropology was heading the bestseller lists in Europe and America: *The Naked Ape – A Zoologist's Study of the Human Animal* by Dr Desmond Morris. It opens with the statement that man is a hairless ape 'self-named *homo sapiens*. . . . I am a zoologist and the naked ape is an animal. He is therefore fair game for my pen.' To what extremes this zoomorphic approach may lead is illustrated by the following quotation:

The insides of houses or flats can be decorated and filled with ornaments, bric-à-brac and personal belongings in profusion. This is usually explained as being done to make the place 'look nice'. In fact, it is the exact equivalent to another territorial species depositing its personal scent on a landmark near its den. When you put a name on a door, or hang a painting on a wall, you are, in dog or wolf terms, for example, simply cocking your leg on them and leaving your personal mark there.

To avoid misunderstandings, let me emphasize once more that it is both legitimate and necessary for scientific research to investigate conditioned reflexes in dogs, operant responses in rats, and the ritual dances of geese – so long as they are not forced upon us as paradigms for man's condition. But this is precisely what has been happening for the best part of our middle-aged century.

My third R is randomness. Biological evolution is considered to be nothing but random mutations preserved by natural selection; mental evolution nothing but random tries preserved by reinforcement. To quote from a textbook by a leading evolutionist: 'It does seem that the problem of evolution is essentially solved. . . . It turns out to be basically materialistic, with no sign of purpose. . . . Man is the result of a purposeless and materialistic process ...'[2] To paraphrase Einstein, a non-existent God playing blind dice with the universe. Even physical causality, the solid rock on which that universe was built, has been replaced by the driftsands of statistics. We all seem to be in the condition which the physicist calls 'Brownian movement' – the erratic zigzag motions of a particle of smoke buffeted about by the molecules of the surrounding air.

Some schools of modern art, too, have adopted the cult of randomness. Action-painters throw random fistfuls of paint at the canvas; a French sculptor achieved international fame by bashing old motor-cars with a demolition machine into random shapes; others assemble bits of scrap iron into abstract compositions, or bits of fluff and tinsel into collages; some composers of electronic music use randomizing machines for their effects. One fashionable novelist boasts of cutting up his typescript with a pair of scissors, and sticking it together again in random fashion.

These schools of contemporary art seem to derive their inspiration from the prevalent bias in the sciences of life – a kind of secondary infection. Randomness, we are told, is the basic fact of life. We live in a world crammed full with hard facts, and there is no place in it for purpose, values or meaning. To look for values and meaning is considered as absurd as it would be for an astronomer to search with his telescope for Dante's heavenly paradise. And it would be equally absurd to search with a microscope for that ghost in the machine, the conscious mind, with its ghostly attributes of free choice and moral responsibility.

Let us remind ourselves once more that the essence of teaching is not in the facts and data which it conveys, but in the interpretations that it transmits in explicit or implied ways. In terms of modern communication theory, the bulk of the information consists of interpretations. That is the core of the package: the data provide only the wrappings. But the recurrent, embittered controversies in the history of science prove over and over again that the same data can be inter-

2. G. G. Simpson, *The Meaning of Evolution*, Newhaven, Connecticut, 1949.

preted in different ways and reshuffled into different patterns. A minute ago, I quoted a distinguished biologist of the orthodox neo-Darwinian school. Let me now quote another eminent biologist, C. H. Waddington, who, based on exactly the same available data, arrives at the opposite view:

To suppose that the evolution of the wonderfully adapted biological mechanisms has depended only on a selection out of a haphazard set of variations, each produced by blind chance, is like suggesting that if we went on throwing bricks into heaps, we should eventually be able to choose ourselves the most desirable house.[3]

One could go on quoting such diametrically opposed conclusions drawn by different scientists from the same body of data. For example, one could hardly expect neurophysiologists to belittle the importance of brain mechanism in mental life, and many of them do indeed hold that mental life is nothing but brain mechanism. And yet Sherrington was an unashamed dualist; he wrote: 'That our being should consist of *two* fundamental elements offers, I suppose, no greater inherent improbability than that it should rest on one only'. And the great Canadian brain surgeon, Wilder Penfield, said at an interdisciplinary symposium on 'Control of the Mind' at which we both participated: 'To declare that these two things [brain and mind] are one does not make them so, but it does block the progress of research.'

I quote this, not because I am a Cartesian dualist – which I am not – but to emphasize that the neurophysiologist's precise data can be interpreted in diverse ways. In other words, it is not true that the data which science provides must automatically lead to the conclusion that life is meaningless, nothing but Brownian motion imparted by the random drift of cosmic weather. We should rather say that the *Zeitgeist* has a tendency to draw biased philosophical conclusions from the data, a tendency towards the devaluation of values and the elimination of meaning from the world around us and the world inside us. The result is an existential vacuum.

3. In The *Listener*, 13 November 1952.

At this point I would like to quote again Viktor Frankl, founder of what has become known as the Third Viennese School of Psychiatry. He postulates that besides Freud's Pleasure Principle and Adler's Will to Power, there exists a 'Will to Meaning' as an equally fundamental human drive:

It is an inherent tendency in man to reach out for meanings to fulfil and for values to actualise. In contrast to animals, man is not told by his instincts what he must do. And in contrast to man in former times, he is no longer told by his traditions and values what he ought to do.... Thousands and thousands of young students are exposed to an indoctrination along the lines of a reductionist concept of life which denies the existence of values. The result is a world-wide phenomenon – more and more patients are crowding our clinics with the complaint of an inner emptiness, the sense of a total and ultimate meaninglessness of life.[4]

He calls this type of neurosis 'noogenic', as distinct from sexual and other types of neuroses, and he claims that about 20 per cent of all cases at the Vienna Psychiatry Clinic (of which he is the head) are of noogenic origin. He further claims that this figure is doubled among student patients of Central European origin; and that it soars to 80 per cent among students in the United States.

I should mention that I know next to nothing about the therapeutic methods of this school – it is called Logotherapy – and that I have no means of judging its efficacity. But there exists a considerable literature on the subject, and I brought it up because the philosophy behind it seems to me relevant to our theme. However that may be, the term 'existential vacuum', caused by the frustration of the will to meaning, seems to be a fitting description of the world-wide mood of infectious restlessness, particularly among the young and among intellectuals.

It may be of some interest to compare this mood with that of the Pink Decade, the 1930s, when the Western world was convulsed by economic depression, unemployment and hunger marches, and the so-called Great Socialist Experiment

4. In *Beyond Reductionism – The Alpbach Symposium*, edited by A. Koestler and J. R. Smythies, London, 1969.

initiated by the Russian Revolution seemed to be the only hopeful ideal to a great mass of youthful idealists, including the present writer. In *The God That Failed*, I wrote about that period:

Devotion to pure Utopia and rebellion against a polluted society are the two poles which provide the tension of all militant creeds. To ask which of the two makes the current flow – attraction by the ideal or repulsion by the social environment – is to ask the old question whether the hen was first, or the egg.

Compare this with the present mood. Today the repellent forces are more powerful than ever, but the attraction of the ideal is missing, since what we thought to be Utopia turned out to be a cynical fraud. The egg is there, but no hen to hatch it. Rebellion is freewheeling in a vacuum.

Another comparison comes to mind – another historic situation, in which the traditional values of a culture were destroyed, without new values taking their place. I mean the fatal impact of the European conquerors on the native civilizations of American Indians and Pacific Islanders. In our case, the shattering impact was not caused by the greed, rapacity and missionary zeal of foreign invaders. The invasion has come from within, in the guise of an ideology which claims to be scientific and is in fact a new version of Nihilism in its denial of values, purpose and meaning. But the results in both cases are comparable: like the natives who were left without traditions and beliefs in a spiritual vacuum, we, too, seem to wander about in a bemused trance.

It is, of course, true that similar negative moods can be found in past periods of our history, variously described as *mal de siècle*, romantic despair, Russian nihilism, apocalyptic expectations. And there have been Ranters, Messianic sects and Tarantula dancers, all of whom have their striking contemporary parallels. But the present has a unique and unprecedented urgency because the rate of change is now moving along an ever steeper exponential curve, and history is accelerating like the molecules in a liquid coming to the boil. There is no need to evoke the population explosion, urban explosion and explosion of explosive power; we live in their midst, in the eye of the hurricane.

This brings me back to my starting point. The ideal of the educator as a catalysing agent is for the time being unattainable. Exceptions always granted, he has been a conditioning influence, and the conditions he created amount to an explosive vacuum.

I do not believe that the crisis in education can be solved by the educators. They are themselves products of that *Zeitgeist* which brought on the crisis. All our laudable efforts to reform the universities can at best produce palliatives and symptom-therapy. I think that in a confused way the rebellious students are aware of this, and that this is why they are so helpless when asked for constructive proposals, and why no proposed reform can satisfy their ravenous appetites. They are, simply, hungry for meaning, which their teachers cannot provide. They feel that all their teachers can do is to produce rabbits out of empty hats. Up to a point the rebels have succeeded in imparting this awareness to society at large; and that, regardless of the grotesque methods employed, seems to me a wholesome achievement.

Why We Need a Revolution

J. A. G. Griffith*

It is the scale of the failure that is so impressive. 'Something must be done' shouts one Prince of Wales across 35 years to his successor. But it won't be, because, as we shall see, it cannot. On the face of it, Western scientific man has a passion for the irrelevant. He is the original gadgeteer. He makes toys while his friends and relations die of starvation. He fiddles while napalm burns. But the face of it is not the whole of it. The Western man cannot be explained away as a clever thoughtless child. When you meet him he doesn't look like that.

The failure is to be fighting in Vietnam, not to stop the war in Nigeria, to be unable to blockade Rhodesia, to invest in South Africa, not to prevent starvation in Bihar; but it is also the poverty in our own cities, homelessness, and inadequate care for the deprived child, the old, and handicapped, and the mentally ill. In 1967 there were 3·9 million families in Britain with two or more children. Of these, 345,000 families with 1,100,000 children had initial resources which were less than those provided under supplementary benefit scales. If one-child families are included the number of children in poverty increases to 1,250,000.

To all this the sophisticate may shrug his shoulders and say it was ever thus or it is better than it was or this is the nature of man; or he may say that life is a harsh competitive existence in which some go to the wall and that this is the price to be paid for human discovery and invention. It is true that we still cannot control all natural calamities but it is also true that poverty and disease in the Western world are mostly acts of man rather than of God. The failure is the inability to

*The author is Professor of English Law in London University.

prevent the preventable, to remedy the remediable. Which is why man probably will destroy himself.

But this is not all. The ways we are going, the systems which control us, are continuously reducing the spiritual (choose your own word) quality of our lives. Our existence is becoming more pre-packed and processed, while at the same time our physical movements are becoming more and more confined. Television, with its desperate need to fill hour after hour with moving pictures of some kind, is obliged to become repetitive because human creativity cannot meet its requirements; and, in any event, repetition is cheaper. New stereotypes are emerging and becoming accepted as normal reactions, normal behaviour, normal people. H. G. Wells wrote a short story called *The Obliterated Man* in which a news reporter was suddenly made a theatre critic and found himself using (consciously but against his will) the dramatic voices and language and gestures of those whom he was obliged to write about each day. Television also produces this world of its own and its addicts would become unhappy without the identical stimulant and so the teletypes of speech and action become more deeply embedded. So also it looks as though the automobile has defeated us. Buchanan was not, after all, the beginning of new thought but the twitchings of a dying culture. And more houses are to be destroyed in London to provide more roads.

The assumption is often made that all these questions – what should Western man do about Vietnam, Nigeria, Rhodesia, South Africa, starvation, homelessness, poverty, the care of the old and the infirm, the processing and the closer containment of action which mark the increasing deprivation of liberty – are questions about policies and priorities, about choices, about what we in Britain can and cannot do, about first getting the balance of payments 'right' and then we shall see what is to be done. To keep the illusion of choice is sometimes necessary for sanity – 'I will do such things. What they are yet I know not; but they shall be The terrors of the earth' – but the true possibilities of alternative action may be very small or non-existent. I do not mean because of lack of national resources or because of treaty obligations or other external influences. I mean because the system of politics and economics determines not only the range of choices but often the choice itself.

This determinism is very close, as I understand him, to Professor Oakeshott's pursuit of intimations.[1] Political activity to him is what springs from the existing traditions of behaviour and 'the form it takes, because it can take no other, is the amendment of existing arrangements by exploring and pursuing what is intimated in them'. To those who found this 'meaningless in respect of every so-called "revolutionary" situation and every essay in so-called "idealistic" politics', Oakeshott replied that he was neither intending a description of the motives of politicians nor of what they believed themselves to be doing, but of what they actually succeeded in doing. In this way, Oakeshott is not only a philosopher of conservatism, but also an apologist for conservative politics. He is giving a philosophical basis and justification for a system of politics and economics which determines the limits of what is politically and economically possible. Now I think that Oakeshott would reply to this by saying that it is not a system of politics and economics but the nature of the society itself which is the determinant. 'Politics is the activity of attending to the general arrangements of a collection of people who, in respect of their common recognition of a manner of attending to its arrangements, compose a single community.' If I am right in this, then the difference between us is real and important – which confirms both my intimations and my disposition. For a radical change in a system of politics and economics is for him literally preposterous. Conservatism, on this view, is a necessary as well as a desirable philosophy and when faced with an unjust world we can proceed only very slowly, with great care, with all our antennae quivering and with an intention to withdraw at once if we feel ourselves to be going against our traditions. My view is that our present institutions and ways of proceeding are heading us more and more towards greater injustice and inhumanity and

1. See *Rationalism in Politics and other Essays*.

that only by radical change can we hope to avoid catastrophe.

If it is true either that the nature of the society largely determines the system of politics and economics or that the system
of politics or economics largely determines the nature of the
society, then gradualism leading by an accumulation of reforms to radical change is wholly evitable. To this I will return.
First I wish to look more closely at the reasons for the failure
of the political and economic system to begin to solve the
problems of our society.

Our present political arrangements emerged out of that
period of mid-Victorianism which we are still struggling to
understand. At the party level it had to do with the infighting
that led to the franchise reform of 1867. At the industrial
level it had to do with the joint stock company and the
struggles for better conditions in the factories, the mills and
the mines. At the administrative level it had to do with Chad-
wick and all those professional men who followed him and
who created the basis of the regulatory state. By way of explanation to their contemporaries and, less happily, to us,
J. S. Mill, Bagehot and Dicey provided their commentaries.

Out of all this came liberalism and parliamentary democracy and representative government as-we-know-it-today. The
impact of these ideas and political practices on those who
lived between 1870 and 1914 seems to have been considerable
and largely subterranean, because those who profited from
them did not question them greatly and those who did not
profit from them accepted parliamentarianism as the way of
reform.

Today this same system of government is one hundred years
old and looks its age. We are left with a device for replacing
one set of political leaders with another set who are barely
distinguishable. Within the system there is much to be said
for the threat of loss of personal power to one group of individuals, but the life has gone out of the struggle except for
those who directly participate in it. It is difficult to be enthusiastic about the rival merits of Mr Wilson and Mr Heath,
not because they themselves are inconsiderable men (for they
are at least the equals of most of their predecessors in this

century), but because for the mass of the electorate life is not changed and is not likely to be changed in the future by their relative success or failure at the polls. The answer to the question 'why apathy at local elections?' is not to be explained in terms of the quality of candidates. It is simply that the local electorate believes that it does not matter whether X or Y succeeds nor whether X party or Y party has control. And very largely the local electorate is right so to believe. General elections continue to attract support and interest but the urgency has gone, the light has failed, and present-day interest is taking on the interest which those who never go to a racecourse indulge in on the occasion of the Derby or the Grand National. Moreover, the games played on television have enhanced this interest in the spectacle, at least in the early stages. But the recognition that, as between the Conservative and Labour parties, the number of genuinely alternative proposals for the solution of national problems is very small, has been greatly increased by the adoption during the last three years of measures which are difficult to distinguish seriously from those which would have been adopted by Her Majesty's Opposition. Once the Labour Party under the pressure of the electoral system abandoned its belief in the class struggle and abandoned its role as representative of the industrial working classes, this near-identification with Conservative policies became inevitable. The system of politics and economics operates to force a common course of conduct on the politicians who form the administration. Certainly, differences remain. But the fact that a Labour government is more likely than a Conservative government to seek to impose an Industrial Disputes Bill underlines the similarity of approach.

The conversation about politics fortifies the myth that ordinary men and women participate in political power and can share in deciding what shall be done. The art of politics is to persuade people that they make decisions while ensuring that they do not. The paraphernalia of party conferences and trade union congresses, the ballyhoo of general elections, 'juries' on television, everything that seems to involve people in the decision-making process conduces to this illusion. And as media of communication become more and more wide-spread so the illusion can be made stronger.

At the same time the control over political comment and criticism grows tighter. The powers exerted over the Press and television by owners, editors, governing bodies and advertisers are being extended. This is particularly apparent in the content of television programmes. The disappearance of hard-hitting political satire from B.B.C. T.V. will continue to be regarded as politically inspired until much better evidence to the contrary has been presented. The influence exerted by some Ministers over the content of television programmes in which they appear, the power of the Prime Minister to appoint to senior positions in the B.B.C. and I.T.A., the opportunity which senior Ministers use to make life more, or less, difficult for political commentators, the working of the lobby, the strict libel laws – all these and other factors confine freedom of political comment.

The view that all is not well with government in Britain – essentially a very different statement from that which I am making – is now become fashionable. When Professor Brian Chapman's comparative *British Government Observed* was published in 1963, it brought down on its learned author's head a torrent of dignified criticism (or trenchant abuse, depending on your observation point), although in fact he did know a great deal more about other systems of government than most of his critics. Probably he should have adopted a different style. But not so many years later the first chapter of the Fulton report was much more savage (though differently phrased) and hardly documented at all. Yet although it was criticized, this was more in sorrow than in anger. Times had changed.

But although the machinery of government question has been much debated of late, it seems to me that no one has been able to develop any very helpful ideas. The recent Political and Economic Planning (P.E.P.) pamphlet called *Renewal of British Government* and put together by a group 'which includes two Vice-Presidents of P.E.P. together with distinguished Members of Parliament from both major parties, public administrators, academics and publicists' had this approach:

To bring out a recent evolution of British opinion from a state of reluctance and confused recognition that all is not well with the nation, through a spasmodic and chaotic series of attempted *ad hoc* remedies, towards a more fundamental and comprehensive awareness of a new new need to examine our worn and often ineffective institutions as a whole, in the light of new social and economic conditions and a dawning new relationship between government and governed.

That is, indeed, one hell of an approach. The remit cannot be accused of lacking in ambition.

The pamphlet does not pretend to give solutions but only to raise questions. Its function is to select the right questions. The interest (to me) is that by adopting a reformist and not a revolutionary analysis, it fails (as I would say it must fail) to do more than represent the old problems most of which have been long debated, some of which have been tried, and none of which begins to uncover the roots of the present discontents. What we are told about are problems of ministerial responsibility and public accountability; the function of the Cabinet; the need for a smaller number of central departments and drastic devolution; the hiving off to public boards; more regionalism with more powers to the regions; reform of the finance of local government; the control of public expenditure and Parliamentary Committees; subordinate legislatures; the role of the Second Chamber; the need for a system of public law and its relationship to parliamentary questions; a Bill of Rights.

The intractability of the present constitutional set-up, the reason why nothing short of a revolution will do the trick, is evidenced by the pamphlet's argument about the need for Parliamentary Committees to be more independent of the executive. The defects are seen to be appointment by the Whips and the Government's power of patronage. 'Overnight, an effective and independently minded M.P. may become a member of the executive and, more than once in the last few years, a government has laid itself open to the charge of using its patronage to maintain its parliamentary power rather than to select the best Ministers.' So the argument runs that M.P.s need a counter-attraction to ministerial office and that this could be provided if Parliamentary Select Committees had as many teeth as the committees of the U.S. Senate and if members of such committees were paid with the chairman receiving 'almost as much as a Cabinet Minister'.

This seems to me to be one modest way in which the present system could be usefully improved. But we know it won't happen. And it won't happen because it could happen only with the Government's positive sponsorship and that will not be given because the main purpose of the reform is to strengthen the House of Commons in its relation to the Government and so to weaken the Government. Governments are the least masochistic of institutions. They have their grip on the House of Commons and from this grip comes their most important power, that of legislation; and their second most important power, that of being able, not wholly but largely, to decide the terms within which they can be criticized. It is now over 50 years since M.P.s began to argue the need for more efficient Select Committees. The other day a small experiment was tried and within months the Government began to dismantle it. Politics is not a game; it's a harsh business because it is about power and money. And you don't find people who like power and money relinquishing their control over these commodities.

The authors of the pamphlet believe that 'the State is evolving into a mechanism for self-government. We are becoming a self-governing society and we must renew our institutions to reflect this change. Government must show that it belongs to the people.' All this I most clearly do not believe. I feel less self-governing every day.

So far I have been talking about politics without explicit (though I hope not without implicit) reference to the economic structure. If any of my Marxist friends have read this far, I apologize to them now. I have also avoided the shorthand 'capitalist' and have preferred the clumsier 'political and economic' system. Marxism is the most important philosophical and practical influence of our time, and its literature is deep and rich, both in the scrolls and in the commentaries. And 'capitalism' as a word is capable of embracing a great range of meanings. I mean range, not variety. It may include only the citadel of the system. But it may be used to include what are seen by Marxists to be the connected ramifications and ramparts of that citadel. In this latter and wider sense it embraces the whole structure of the State.

We live in a society which pays great material rewards to those who acquire economic and political power. Power and the money that goes with it bring (apart from more power and more money) entry into small circles of men whose influence in all important matters is crucial. I have no wish to sound conspiratorial. There is, after all, no need for a conspiracy. It is only when you are conspiring against the King that you need to look under the bed. Conspiring with the King is a much more open affair although there may well be many occasions when a little modest privacy must be insisted on.

When we speak of a State being capitalist we are drawing attention to a very considerable concentration of power in the hands of those who control the large industrial companies. These men employ and can dismiss a huge labour force. Their decisions about future development, about the extent of investment, about where to expand and where to restrict, about automation, will affect the lives of millions of men, women and children. The primary duty of those who exercise this control is, over the short and long run, to maximize profits. That is why shareholders have invested their money in these particular companies. It is no part of their duty to consider whether their commodity serves any useful purpose but only whether it can be sold in the 'right' quantities at the 'right' time at the 'right' price.

But there is also the public sector, embracing the activities of government departments, nationalized industries and other public corporations, and local authorities. Here also we have employers on a very large scale whose decisions will vitally affect the future of thousands of employees. The structure of all these public bodies has more similarities to than differences from those in the private sector. Ministers will come and go more frequently than chairmen of companies and local authorities are elected. They do not, however, exist with the main purpose of making money but of providing services.

Now it seems to me to be both misleading and a gross simplification to assume, as some Marxists do, that the public sector is trapped within and exists to serve the private sector; and that the power of private industrial capital is so great that all other centres of power must or wish to bow before it. I would need many more words than are available here to spell this out. But I am not arguing for the doctrine of countervailing power. And I am not denying that the activities and purposes of private industrial capital are the strongest determinants of government action. I am saying that, when we look to see who it is that manages the political and economic system, we must include politicians, industrialists, civil servants and all those others who at a senior level are the effective decision-makers. The fact that at times their immediate interests seem to be in conflict is not important. They all exist to make the system work and the fundamental assumptions which they have in common are far more significant than their marginal differences.

I find no evidence in recent developments to suggest, in the words of the P.E.P. pamphlet, that 'the State is evolving into a mechanism for self-government' or that 'we are becoming a self-governing society'. On the contrary, it seems to me that we are daily becoming less so and that the growth of authoritarian, totalitarian power in both the economic and the political spheres is remarkable and is becoming more blatant. Even the attempts to conceal this growth of power are becoming more and more perfunctory. The students' protest is a recognition of this not primarily in their demands for more representation on the governing bodies but in their much more important and fundamental insistence on the reshaping of their courses. The response of de Gaulle to the events of May and June in 1968 was to call for more participation in industrial and academic affairs. This is an old response and is unlikely to satisfy but it is a recognition of some part of what the students and the workers were demanding.

This demand is unlikely to be met because there are no ways of meeting it within the political and economic system. More and more power is being concentrated in fewer and fewer hands as the large industrial complexes extend their empires and as the electorate has less and less say (not that it ever had much) in the political decisions of governments. Not only is there no will in those having authority to share it more widely (why should there be such a will?) but there are no means by which this sharing can be insisted on. The politicians have no motive which would encourage them to seek this kind of industrial reform and even if they had the motive they have not the power to effect this change. The politicians themselves cannot be required to share their power.

Essentially the difficulty faced by those who believe that it is possible within the existing political and economic system to introduce reforms which will enlarge individual freedom, and make possible a more just society, is that the system itself operates precisely to exclude those reforms. Those who exercise authority within society, in both the political and the economic spheres, must in their own self-interest prevent radical change the purpose of which is to reduce that authority. The enlargement of individual freedom must be at their expense. It must reduce their power. This is why the Rhodesia blockade will fail, why trade with South Africa will continue, why arms were to the end supplied to both sides in Nigeria. It is the political and economic system which prevents the elimination of the housing problem, which results in widespread poverty in the affluent society, which ensures that the poor countries become poorer, the rich countries richer.

When the excitement of the moon landing has subsided, will the question begin to be asked why, if technological achievement has reached such heights, it should still be necessary for so many to live in slums or below the starvation line? The gap between those things which our political and economic system chooses to produce and those which it chooses not to produce widens. Will the question begin to be asked why this should be? And if these disparities seem to be irremovable by ordinary political and economic measures because the system cannot operate to implement those measures, will there not be those who will seek a new system?

In the old days, when I was a young man, the case for revolution was that radical changes were desirable in order that utopia might come more quickly. Now only revolution is likely to save us from a degeneration which will embrace us all. It is not that the world is becoming a worse place to live in, though, for all save a few, this is so. It is rather that the worsening is the consequence of the economic and political system which Western man has constructed and which must therefore be changed if the degeneration is to be halted. Revolution looks more and more to be necessary not as a reaction to the evils of the time, not as a leap away from the course of contemporary events into the darkness of the unknown, but as the only alternative now that reformism has not simply failed but has been shown to be incapable of success.

What is and what is not utopian as a way of thinking is a profitless argument. I have a disposition to be utopian. Professor Marcuse has written: 'What is denounced as "utopian" is no longer that which has "no place" and cannot have any place in the historical universe, but rather that which is blocked from coming about by the power of the established societies.' That degree of optimism I can admire but not share.

The bringing nearer of a better world is not to be seen as the removal of blocks. It is not that established societies impede our progress to a new heaven and a new earth. Rather is it that those societies have created and will increasingly create the conditions in which the world worsens. We are not struggling towards the summit, impeded by those who wish to prevent us from reaching it. We are struggling to avoid slipping even further down the slope. Our immediate aim is limited: it is not to hear all the trumpets sounding for us on the other side, but to escape from the city fathers who are bent on destruction.

Varieties of Socialist Thought

Peter Sedgwick*

Winding up the last of the volumes that comprised his *History of Socialist Thought*, the late G. D. H. Cole added, shortly before his death in 1959, a short personal credo: 'I am neither a Communist nor a Social-Democrat, because I regard both as creeds of centralization and bureaucracy.' Such a statement, at the time it was written and for decades previously, could be no more than a solitary confession of faith, from a maverick thinker who could gain a footing in public politics only through his high personal integrity and the connexions he still maintained with the official party of Labour. To be a Socialist – and at the same time to be out of sympathy with the ideologies offered within the Communist and the Social-Democratic parties – was an extraordinary position, requiring a special explanation. Today, Cole's declaration could be inscribed on a banner to which tens of thousands of young Socialists, not only in Britain but in France, in Germany, in the United States, would willingly rally. To these – as well as to hundreds of thousands more in their generation who have rejected conventional party appeals without defining their own political alternatives – it would be the Social-Democratic or the Communist Party politician who was the oddity, the sectarian of moderation whose ideas lay outside the common currency of the expressible. The agencies which manufacture and maintain new critical approaches to capitalist society, which form and transmit the perspectives of a further and better social order, which, in short, make Socialists, have passed outside the grasp of the two great international machines which dominated the Left for most of this century.

This movement of the 'extreme' into the 'consensus', and

*The author is Lecturer in Politics at the University of York, and a member of the editorial board of *International Socialism*.

conversely of the Centre into the defensive fringes, has not proceeded through competition or debate, that is, through the canvassing of rival theoretical constructs and the emergence of one complex of opinion as that which has rebutted its intellectual challengers. It is rather that systematic Socialist debate takes place today *within* the boundaries of rejection defined by Cole, while the main concepts of political theory which carried gradualist Socialism or Comintern Marxism from the thirties into the fifties have dropped out of anybody's argument. It goes beyond the scope of this essay (which will be limited to developments in Britain) to take full account of the international Communist crisis; suffice it to say that the breakdown of Stalinist orthodoxy, with the appearance of separate national Communisms in Eastern Europe, Latin America and Asia, has not resulted in the formation of any fresh political synthesis from writers in the British Communist Party. Its few remaining productive intellectuals gain their standing as participants in the general forum of the 'New Left', not as Party spokesmen. Since 1956, the Communist Party of Great Britain has been obliged to follow and adapt to initiatives, whether of theory or of campaigning, which have sprung from the newer sources of the Left. On the Social-Democratic side, we are faced with an actual disappearance of any sustained intellectual work since the early sixties. It may be said, of course, that this is only a short interval, and that in any case opposition provides better scope for reformist rumination than does the stressful activism of office; but what is striking is not the time-span of the interval so much as the total rupture of continuity between the gradualist theorizing of the fifties and the preoccupations of the intelligentsia in and around the present Government. What was said then is not revised, or rationalized, or even made into a ritual of paraded ideals (the usual options for a disappointed ideology); it is simply left unsaid, and appears to be unsayable. It requires, in fact, a real effort of historical detachment even to recall and to locate the writing of Labour Party theoreticians from the period 1956–62; but this work of excavation is a necessary prelude to any account of subsequent Socialisms, and it is here that we shall begin.

Social Democracy

'Today, we are not putting our politics in a sufficiently philosophical form, which is why people are cynical.'
Mrs Barbara Castle (*Sunday Times*, 27 July 1969)

Reformist Socialism, especially in Britain, has so often been at pains to distinguish itself from the tenets of Marxism that the similarities between the two itineraries of social change are usually ignored. In reviewing the theoretical documents of the Labour Party during Mr Gaitskell's leadership, we are now likely to be impressed by their strong flavour of historical materialism, of an evolutionary, optimistic rationality based on the conviction that social development proceeds by distinct stages; and that socio-economic laws applicable to the more contemporary of these stages may be grasped by means of political reasoning. As in Marx, our epoch forms a moment of junction between historical phases, between an outmoded era of parasitism and irrationality and an imminent or incipient age of reasonable and just social distribution; as in Lenin, a political party, armed with this knowledge and drawing upon what is best in modern scientific and organizational technique, can master the blind, unconscious elements of a competitive economic system and oversee the installation of co-operative, egalitarian and expansionary values at essential switchpoints within the social mechanism.

Texts:
Anthony Crosland: *The Future of Socialism* (1956); *The Conservative Enemy* (1962).
John Strachey: *Contemporary Capitalism* (1956).
Douglas Jay: *Socialism in the New Society* (1962).
Richard Crossman: *Labour in the Affluent Society* (Fabian pamphlet, 1960).
The Labour Party: *Signposts for the Sixties* (policy statement, 1961).

Within the different and often mutually hostile traditions of Socialism, there is of course wide variation in the description of the relevant stages, agencies and objectives of the transformation. 'Monopoly capitalism' expresses a view of current unreformed reality which has little in common with, for example, 'the Tory Windfall State'. Strachey's 'last-stage capitalism', which only awaits the 'countervailing pressures' of 'democracy' to be pushed 'out of existence', is a different creature from Lenin's 'highest stage of capitalism' which awaits 'the smashing of the bourgeois state machine'. Marx's tense disjunction between 'private appropriation and social organization' in production is at best tangential to the Galbraith–Crossman 'private opulence, public squalor'. Crosland's socially responsible stratum of corporate managers, freed from the private appetites of shareholding, is an agency for the realization of the common good which stands apart from almost all other perspectives of Socialism – though it is remarkably close to Saint-Simon's old appeal to a class of technocratic savants who will ally with the workers to squeeze out the useless rich.[1] But if the means of transition in Socialism vary – from Parliament to syndicates, from taxation to expropriation; if the locus of the 'new society' sometimes lies before us, in 'workers' power' to be won or 'commanding heights' to be stormed (and sometimes behind us, in long-achieved conquests of rationality through Keynesian planning and welfare legislation), there is still an essential core of agreement which separates all these views from a Conservative philosophy (the art of good government) or from a Liberal (the optimum mix of freedoms and desires). All Socialisms have been founded on some belief in historically phased movement of social and technical relationships around industry. For anti-Marxists no less than for Marxists, the mode of production is 'the base' which sets the terms for analysis and prescribes the opportunities for action.

The severest test which now confronts any future definition

1. The connexion between Gaitskell's disciple and Marx's precursor is not entirely fanciful. Professor Sheldon Wolin (in the final chapter of his *Politics and Vision*, 1963) has noted the facility with which neo-Saint-Simonian ideas have taken root, in the form of modern 'organization theory', within the technocratic soil of the United States: and it is precisely this variety of organizational theory (Berle, Burnham, Galbraith), which has formed the premiss for the British 'revisionist' re-definition of capitalism.

of Social-Democratic theory lies in the loss of its evolutionary vision. The practice of the Wilson Government has imposed stress upon a number of the particular concepts created
within the 're-thinking' phase of opposition: Strachey's be-
nign 'countervailing power' of trade unionism has become a
malignant 'wage-drift' (and none of Labour's thinkers in this
period even posed a trade-union problem). The trust-busting
ethos of 'the democratic diffusion of power' has given way
to the Industrial Reorganization Corporation's search for the
giant conglomerate and the pushful merger. The synonym
of 'planning' with 'expansion' has been sundered by a whole
series of planned deflations. But the most serious theoretical
effect of the Government's performance is likely to be more
gross, more diffuse and more deadly.

For, whatever justifications the sympathizers of Mr Wilson
may offer for his record over the last five years, the doings of
the fourth Labour Government have not the remotest connexion with the minimum logical presuppositions which, we
have suggested, must guide any formulation of the Socialist
project. Technical command over the economy no longer
forms the instrument for realizing Socialist values: Labour
in office relinquishes the economic sphere to the operation
of restrictive (and traditionally Tory) mechanisms, with
catastrophic consequences for the belief-system which has
guided the party over decades. Indeed the very success of the
pre-1964 rhetoric of Labour's technological revolution', in
cementing and rallying a divided party, bears witness to the
importance of the sense of historical movement, within the
terms of technical-evolutionary reason, not only for the
party's morale but also for its basic rationale. The writings of
Labour's old theoreticians, whether 'revisionist' or growth
enthused, must now stand convicted not for their complacency, empiricism and evasion (the most common charges
against them from the 'Clause Four' Left of its day), but
for their sweeping rationalism, their confidence in the period-
ization of history and their utopian vision of a world controlled.

It remains to be seen whether any further variant of Social-

Democratic theory can be reconstructed, after the revelation that a Labour Government does not after all have access to the levers of social regulation under capitalism. The indications are that, on the contrary, the ambitions of history-making and of cohesive social analysis are being abandoned, in favour of the propagation of 'radical' virtues which require for their theoretical groundings only an ethical commentary on contemporary manners. As some sort of compensation for the loss of public control, parliamentary time is accorded more willingly to the reforming Private Member: economic constraint is offset by legislation for permissive mores. The 'end of ideology' attained by continental Social-Democracy ten and more years ago appears at last to have struck its British section. Reason and its historic project have succumbed to a rootless reasonableness.

Welfare and Equality

'I don't see a future of achieving our social objectives by constantly shifting resources from the private to the public sector so that people have a less and less proportion of their income to spend as they choose.'

Mr Roy Jenkins (*Guardian*, 21 July 1969[2])

The first wave of Labour Party theory after the war (Crosland and Strachey) was an attempt to come to terms with the apparently permanent conquest of economic stability in Britain and the West. From 1956 onwards, new origins of discontent compelled the formation of a Socialist intelligentsia: the rupture of bipartisan unity following the Suez invasion; the self-

2. This revealing interview (headed 'The Radical Creed of a Civilised Man') documents, more tellingly than my own arguments, the decline of equality as an official Labour Party ideal. Mr Jenkins, it will be recalled, was the author of the section on 'Equality' in the *New Fabian Essays* of 1952. His current aversion to redistribution is made quite explicit: 'To a greater extent now than in 1952 I believe that a generally rising standard of living, which of course is tied up very closely with economic growth, is an important equalizing factor. It is incomparably easier to open up new windows to new groups of people on the basis of a rising standard of living than in a purely redistributist framework.'

consciousness of a generation of 'scholarship boys' who had risen from their communities with the 1944 Education Act; and the shattering of the Stalinist intellectual mould with the Twentieth Russian Party Congress and the Hungarian revolution. Until the middle sixties, a highly articulate but organizationally loose grouping, known to itself and to the world as 'the New Left', flourished in association with Centre and Left writers from the Labour Party: a catalogue of contributors to New Left publications from this period would reveal among them the names of Barbara Castle, Thomas Balogh, Judith Hart, Richard Crossman and John Strachey. There was also an interesting alliance with a vanguard of redistributive Fabian theory (Titmuss, Townsend, Abel-Smith), though it is probably safe to say that the identification was largely one-way, with the New Left mentally co-opting the distributists rather than vice versa. A number of writers had already turned to the literary or sociological investigation of the quality of life in working-class localities and among the 'submerged' poorer groups who had been left out of the calculations of official welfare. While the early work of Hoggart and Michael Young's Institute of Community Studies of Bethnal Green avoided any direct programmatic relevance, the whole line of inquiry reinforced the subsequent sharper critique of the norms of resource-distribution in Conservatism's 'Opportunity State':

Texts:

Richard Hoggart: *The Uses of Literacy* (1957).

Brian Abel-Smith and Peter Townsend: essays in *Conviction* (1958).

Richard Titmuss: *The Irresponsible Society* (Fabian pamphlet, 1960).

Audrey Harvey: *Casualties of the Welfare State* (Fabian pamphlet, 1960).

Dorothy Wedderburn and John Saville: essays in the *Socialist Register* (1965).

Richard Titmuss, John Westergaard, Perry Anderson and Robin Blackburn: essays in *Towards Socialism* (1965).

Peter Townsend: *Poverty, Socialism and Labour in Power* (Fabian pamphlet, 1966).

The New Reasoner and *Universities and Left Review* (1957–60).

Our texts here form a natural coalescence. Distributive injustice was experienced as much in the forms of working-class
cultural deprivation as in the bare statistics of low incomes.[3]
Observed inequalities of human destiny, however minutely observed in immediate behavioural terms, were seen to proceed
from a 'deep structure' of inequality in the differentiation of
classes around the ownership of wealth and the enjoyment of
education. (Titmuss's *Irresponsible Society* is strikingly clear
in taking matters to this level of analysis.) The last statements
of this consensual position on the roots of British inequality
occur in the *Towards Socialism* essays of 1965 cited above.
While only a few of these contributors were members of the
Party's 'Welfare brains trust' with an influence on policy, the
general tendency of writing reflected the aspirations of a
Labour intelligentsia who expected some serious results to
emerge from their critique once Wilson's team got into office.

Such, at least, is the conclusion that one is entitled to draw
from the virtual obliteration of this approach, as a developed
and developing variety of social theory, since the Government's arrival. Peter Townsend, it is true, sounded an alarm
for the future of the tradition in his pamphlet of 1966. It is
evident, however, that the current reforming definition of inequality, among both Ministers and academics, has moved
from the structural (involving the analysis of power and
wealth) to the marginal (involving the identification of special
target groups of the under-privileged). The new status of pressure groups (for the disabled, for large families, for hospital
patients), pushing for ministerial and back-bench attention
and drawing sustenance from the research projects and the
journalism of institutional and welfare reform, is a token of
the shift; as is the official concern with the selective pinpoint-
ing of problem areas in the cities (Plowden areas, Crossman
areas). However more rewarding these separate concerns may
prove to be, they mark a distinct retreat from the political at-

3. The boundaries of class division could be traced in the defensive
barriers of localized consciousness that surrounded the communities of the
poor, whether in the genteel submissiveness of the Tory working man
(Ralph Samuel, 'The Deference Voter', *New Left Review*, January–February
1960) or in the close corporate life of Covent Garden porters (Lindsay
Anderson's 'Free Cinema' film of 1957, *Every Day Except Christmas*).

tack upon the foundations of inequality suggested even five years ago. Even those social security benefits and pensions provisions, which are the centrepiece of the Government's intended welfare legislation, reinforce the trend; for the redistribution they envisage is far less between the social classes than between the spells of working life (from health to invalidity, from earning to retirement) with class, as it were, held constant.[4]

The neglect of central politics by the welfare reformers has, in the end, frustrated the attainment even of their limited local objectives. The master-forces of our social system prevail very easily against the gains registered by the single-issue campaigner. Indeed, much evidence suggests that the burden of increase in the Labour State's revenue is falling disproportionately upon the lower-income groups, with regressive and direct forms of taxation (insurance contributions, local rates and expenditure taxes) expanding steadily. The facts on these matters are always late in coming: they are given in John Hughes' calculations for 1964–6, cited conveniently in Peter Wilsher's preface to Ferdinand Lundberg's *The Rich and the Super-Rich* (1969), and are taken to 1967 in James Kincaid's survey in *International Socialism* (June–July 1969). Some of the more recent pension and taxation provisos may somewhat redress the balance; but the general run of increases in retail price indices, expenditure taxes and interest rates for housing is likely to set it swinging with a further inegalitarian bias – inegalitarian, that is, as compared with the structure of real income and taxation for the years of Conservative rule.

These empirical considerations are by no means out of place in an analysis of Socialist ideological developments. Facts, here again, test theory, and test it to the point where certain

4. For a critique of this scheme, see the section 'Pensions: New Deal or Stacked Deck?' in J. Kincaid, 'Social Policy and the Labour Government', *International Socialism*, April–May 1970. Kincaid's work, within an explicitly Marxist conceptual framework, remains the only comprehensive criticism of Labour's performance in the social service field. The silence of Labour's welfare-academics has been loudly broken in 1970 by Peter Townsend on behalf of the Child Poverty Action Group: the isolation and specialism of this protest both bear witness to the exhaustion of Social-Democracy's own welfare tradition.

key concepts and concerns apparently 'drop out' under pressure. The gradualist–egalitarian tradition that was so formative in an earlier period has not been renewed: it has patently failed to enter the recommendations of the Prices and Incomes Board, so permissive towards the income expectations of the higher managerial strata, so exigent and strict with the claims of manual workers. Even the 'wealth tax' advocated in recent years by the Party's residual Left (a modest enough proposal, which would at least provide some evidence of a continuing Labour concern with inequality) has been abandoned as a firm commitment in the new programme *Agenda for a Generation* – with scarcely a murmur of opposition from any quarter. Without the development of a fresh structural perspective upon the generation of wealth and poverty, the seventies must see the finale of redistributive gradualism. The old motto of the Fabian Society – 'When I strike, I strike hard' – will have to be taken up by those who are actually prepared to strike.

Social-Democratic Marxism

'Onions can be eaten leaf by leaf, but you cannot skin a live tiger paw by paw; vivisection is its trade and it does the skinning first.'
R. H. Tawney, 1934

At the official level of conference speeches and policy statements, the Labour Party's momentous commitment to incomes policy in 1963 occurred with scarcely any theoretical preparation. However, in the immediately preceding and subsequent years, an elaborate political case for incomes planning was set in motion by several economic writers who, although Party members, stood well outside the leadership's channels of influence. Of some interest is the fact that here, for the first time since the Socialist League's propaganda of the late thirties, a demand for a new orientation in Party policy was made in a language which formally united Social-Democratic with Marxist terminology.

Texts:

John Hughes and Ken Alexander: *A Socialist Wages Plan* (New Left discussion booklet, 1959).

Henry Collins: *An Incomes Policy for Labour*, *Views* (Summer 1964).

Michael Barratt-Brown and Royden Harrison: articles in *Tribune* (8 January and 5 February 1965).

(See also the polemic between Bob Rowthorn and Hughes, Alexander, Barratt-Brown and Harrison, in *New Left Review* (November–December 1965, March–April 1966 and May–June 1966).)

The source in Marx's own career for this aspirant Social-Democratic Marxism (or 'revolutionary reformism' as some of its proponents called it) can be identified with some confidence as the period of the 1860s when the great revolutionary, along with other radical and Socialist ideologues, joined the counsels of the International Working Men's Association, in fruitful conjunction with the expanding trade-union organization of Britain.[5] How often, indeed, during the Left's debates on incomes policy, were watchwords drawn from Marx's endorsement of parliamentary labour legislation thrown out to rally us: 'the victory of the political economy of labour', and so forth.

Some of us, however, even then did doubt whether slogans deriving from Marx's association with a simple trade unionist like George Odger were applicable to present-day encounters with a slippery technocrat like George Brown (just as we would resist the common tendency to fight the old battles of the First International over again, by summoning Marx's diatribes against Bakuninist putschism as material in the discussion of modern student grievances). But, apart from its theoretical embedding, the Left theory on incomes policy rested on hopes and anxieties that were specific to the pre-devaluation era: anxiety lest straight 'money-wage militancy' might neglect opportunities for legislative reform in industrial

5. I say 'with some confidence', because two of these writers were concurrently immersing themselves in just this phase of labour history with their notable contributions to the growing library of Marxology: Henry Collins in *Karl Marx and the British Labour Movement* (jointly with Chimen Abramsky, 1965) and Royden Harrison in *Before the Socialists* (1965).

conditions, and hope for the evolution of an agreed wages policy between unions and government, to uplift the lower–paid and feed into the processes of enlightened planning.

Other writers again saw the arrival of incomes policy not so much as a good in itself, but as an opportunity for raising urgent matters for debate among trade unionists. Conditional or hypothetical support of wages planning, rather than out-right rejection, was therefore recommended. (This mode of thought was expressed, again within an explicitly Marxist frame of reference, by Ken Coates and Tony Topham.) The quest for a trade union strategy within which specific demands would trigger off larger and larger instalments of political-industrial radicalism was typical, indeed, of a cluster of thin-kers on the Left who owed much to the Continental theorists Ernest Mandel and André Gorz. (Gorz's essays in the 1965 *Towards Socialism* and the 1968 *Socialist Register* are the most accessible examples of this approach.) Within this pers-pective, a programme of 'transitional demands', 'structural reforms', or Gorz's 'intermediary objectives' would enable workers to contest centres of capitalist decision-making either within the firm or on the national level, by insisting, for in-stance, on the disclosure of company secrets or by raising de-mands about civic planning. Interest in these possibilities among Continental writers has waxed with the expectations of the 'opening to the Left' in the Italy of the early 1960s, and waned again with the closure of the *apertura* and the ap-pearance of much more explosive and 'unmediated' working-class manifestations (without the benefits of a strategically guided training in encroachment) in France and Italy over the last couple of years.

In Britain, the deflationary propensities of the Wilson Cab-inet, and its determination to constrain 'wage-drift' and 'money–wage militancy' along lines unacceptable to the union leaderships, has removed from incomes theorists of the Left the essential condition which they associated with their ad-vocacy of wages planning – that is, a government–union alliance for economic expansion. Their focus has now switched to a multitude of issues which are summed up in the slogan of 'workers' control'. Over some dozen years among the 'little Left' of small journals and meetings, there has been something of an 'underground' tradition of interest in the ideas of shop-floor democracy first fostered by the syndicalists, Marxists and Guild Socialists of 1910–20; and this current has now partially surfaced, in a manner so far widely attractive to trade unionists, with the foundation of the Institute of Worker's Control. Ken Coates' and Tony Topham's historical reader *Industrial Democracy in Great Britain* (1968) and Walter Kendall's astounding re-creation of an older upsurge, *The Revolutionary Movement in Britain 1900–1921* (1969), are the more important contributions by writers from this Institute. At a lower level of synthesis, there has been much elaboration of blue-prints for factory democracy in different industries, but this is now taking second place to the problems posed in the many local struggles over productivity bargaining: a defensive workers' control against the stop-watch and the small print in the package deal is beginning to replace the 'strategic' preparation of an ideal and overall offensive – the political agency for which is plainly lacking.[6]

Culture and Socialism

Texts:

Raymond Williams: *Culture and Society* (1958); *The Long Revolution* (1961).

Perry Anderson: 'Mr Crosland's Dreamland: A Study of Sweden', *New Left Review* (January–February and May–June 1961).

Perry Anderson and Tom Nairn: essays in *Towards Socialism* (1965).

E. P. Thompson: *The Making of the English Working Class* (1963); 'The Peculiarities of the English', *Socialist Register* (1965).

6. Once again, the Left's relaxation of interest in central politics, in favour of more evident local tasks, has considerable dangers. Fundamental to the whole ideology of 'productivity bargaining' – even in the more militant version propagated by the trade union leaders (Jones, Scanlon) who are associated with the Institute – is the effective liquidation of those traditional arguments for pay increases (rising cost of living, comparison of rates for those doing similar work) which do not hinge on extra output.

(See also Perry Anderson's reply, 'Socialism and Pseudo-Empiricism', *New Left Review* (January–February 1966).)
Ralph Miliband: *The State in Capitalist Society* (1969).

The range of preoccupations in Raymond Williams's work – however much his specific judgements were challenged – shaped the consciousness of a generation of Socialist intellectual writers, and virtually redefined the subject-matter of political inquiry. The nub of Williams's method was an acute sensitivity to the interplay of cultural cross-currents, and especially of rival value systems, within British literary and public life. An early implication of the approach was a critical analysis of the values propagated in the mass media: an implication which Williams himself has continued to pursue in his proposals for the reorganization of cultural agencies under the control of their working staff. Owing to various blows of fortune – chiefly the exhaustion of the 'Old New Left' in the decline of C.N.D. in 1960–62 – the only present-day continuation of this particular critical tendency lies in the group of Catholic-Marxian writers around the journal *Slant,* published by Sheed and Ward.

The habit of intensive cultural investigation in traditionally political areas was taken forward, with some crucial modifications, by the team of younger writers who assumed the direction of *New Left Review* after 1961. Thus we already find, in Perry Anderson's brisk but reflective study of Sweden, published in that year, the beginnings of that cultural perspective, stemming from but also revising Williams's orientation, which henceforth characterized the review's editorial policy. Labour 'revisionism' (notably Crosland's) had placed the axis of social class-division at the inequality of mobility or opportunity; the elder New Left had tended to insist that class was also an inequality of power; but Anderson, in analysing Social-Democratic Sweden, fastened on the deeper dislocations of common living, in intimate areas of culture and work, which Scandinavian reformism had failed to touch. Class is '. . . a universal loss. There is one human need it violates in all members of society, oppressors and oppressed alike: the need of men for each other.' The task of theory was now to create 'a characterology of class' in which the special inner universes inhabited by the superior and subordinate groups of the society would be explored; this analysis had to be located in a synthetic portrayal of the society's 'totality', its specific aggregate of mutually conditioning parts. In strong contrast with Raymond Williams's conception of working-class culture as the bearer of a collective, democratic value-system, encircling and probing into the strongholds of capitalist morality, the writers of the 'New New Left' assigned little political weight to the communal traditions of working-class life. Instead, drawing upon Gramsci's concept of 'hegemony' – the expression of class-dominance in ideological and cultural spheres – they sought the formation of a radically detached Socialist intelligentsia which would play a key role in formulating the programme of an ascendant 'historical bloc' uniting workers and salariat.

At first, the Labour Party was cast in the role of the potential 'hegemonic party' which could rally and fuse these myriad cultural aspirations. Heralding the arrival of the Wilson Government, Perry Anderson and Tom Nairn published a vast and brilliant historical panorama tracing back the crisis of the British economy over three centuries of incomplete and broken bourgeois revolution. English capitalism had repeatedly surrendered to the counter-challenge of an aristocratic tradition: in the conjuncture of 'a supine bourgeoisie' with a 'subordinate proletariat', the prime default lay in a nerveless intelligentsia which had produced neither the enlivening Jacobinism of a Continental-style bourgeois revolution nor an indigenous Marxism to service and guide the Labour movement. In the clash of personalities and programmes that marked Wilson's ascendancy, new options of hegemony were possible: 'the unfinished work of 1640 and 1832 must be taken up where it was left off.'

The project of a 'characterology of class', paying close attention to the nationally peculiar structural complexes defining the social 'totality', was carried through steadily in the work of New Left Review during the next years: its Asian, African and Latin American material has been particularly rich, although it is to be noted that the accounts produced for these areas are typically grounded in the structural inter-relation of economic, political and military variables, and hazard much less cultural and psychological intuition than does the Anderson–Nairn *schema*. For Britain, the review's series of reports on 'Work' (now collected in two Penguin paperbacks edited by Ronald Fraser) has captured the pheno-menon of class in a local, direct and subtle manner that puts to shame much academic sociological discussion of 'aliena-tion'. The larger thesis on British society has proved much more controversial. Edward Thompson undertook a long and vigorous critique of the whole *schema* querying the validity of all the propositions outlined above; Anderson's defence and counter-attack was no less strenuous. It is impossible to summarize briefly the contentions of both parties at all ade-quately or even impartially: the exchange is closely argued, and spaced with frequent polemical arias, themselves of a high dia-lectical power. The level of the debate itself, however, indicates that sensitivity to cultural nuances and to historical points of choice has become a major factor among the British Left in determining general attitudes towards political events.

Edward Thompson's more strictly historical work has thus become indispensable for any revaluation of Socialist theory. He has insisted that any definition of class 'can be made only in the medium of *time* – that is action and reaction, change and conflict', and can be refined only by evidence drawn from the intentional, subjective world of social actors. This would seem to suppose a method of history-writing (and, for those inclined, of history-waging) which is 'Marxist' in so far as the class struggle is its vital theme, but not Marxist in that the old distinction between 'base', 'superstructure', 'social being' and 'social consciousness' finds no room within it; and a method in which 'economic history' no longer exists as a separately demarcated area.[7]

7. Thompson's criticism of the methodology of George Rudé and Eric Hobsbawm, working within a more 'quantitive' frame for *Captain Swing*, is interesting in detail. See his review of the book in *New Society*, 13 February 1969.

Perhaps the widening perspective of militant Socialist theory can best be illustrated by a comparison of the two influential books by Ralph Miliband. *Parliamentary Socialism* (1960) represents the union of two critical traditions. The Labour-Left Marxism of Harold Laski (Miliband's friend and mentor) and the extra-parliamentary politics of the burgeoning New Left meet here in an analysis which permits itself still some glimmer of hope for the Labour Party. In his recent *The State in Capitalist Society,* the parliamentary arena diminishes to pin-size as broader sociological and cultural vistas come into view: the communications media, the power-structure of local communities, the class biases of education and the psychology of senior civil servants. Increasingly, the role of the committed intellect is seen as one transcending the modest Marxist lobby within conventional channels, typified by a Laski; it reaches instead towards the task of universal cultural renewal propounded by a Gramsci. If not 'hegemony' (an aim that would be modestly disclaimed by most of these theorists), at any rate an unmistakable seriousness and depth is with us.

The Extra-Parliamentary Opposition

'The bureaucracy will hold the machine; but the New Left will hold the passes between it and the younger generation.'
E. P. Thompson, 1959

With a few exceptions of individual intransigence, all the trends of critical thought that we have so far discussed invested psychologically and intellectually in the prospective victory of the Labour Party in 1964. By 1967, disillusionment and disgust with the turn of the Government's policies had impelled a number of these writers to issue, collectively, *The May Day Manifesto* (later expanded into a Penguin Special, 1968) – a ringing indictment of Labour's participation in 'the managed politics' of a technocratized capitalism: 'we are faced with something alien and thwarting: a manipulative politics, often openly aggressive and cynical, which has taken our meanings and changed them, taken our causes and used them; which seems our creation, but now stands against us, as the agent of the priorities of money and power.' (The cadence here suggests the hand of Raymond Williams.) In calling for a 'new, prolonged and connected campaign' for the definition and assertion of Socialist objectives, the Manifesto summoned a cause which its authors could no longer implement. The ground of militant, anti-capitalist thought and action was now to be occupied in Britain by a variety of organizations and journals which owed nothing to the Social-Democratic heritage. Some of these intellectual tendencies gained their force from older revolutionary traditions which had long rejected the perspectives both of the Comintern and of Socialist parliamentarianism: the small, tenacious grouplets of Trotskyist and anarchist provenance. Others grew up in post-Fabian years, situated in a rebellious youth culture which could see the reformism of its elders seated in office and sinking into a quagmire of national and foreign commercial pressures. During 1968, a weighty train of cultural influences, propagated in the main by international example (the fighting martyrdom of Guevara, the paralysis of the U.S. army through the N.L.F.'s Tet offensive, the rising in May of the French students and workers) converged upon Britain to create a large and homogeneous revolutionary milieu, whose amplitude can best be judged from the scale and spirit of the Vietnam demonstration in London on 27 October of that year. 'STREET POWER' began the briefing to the marchers: '*We Take The Street.... We Go The Whole Route.* (If anyone at all should try to divert us, *we simply move forward along the whole route, sweeping aside obstacles, giving obstructors no time for violence*).... *We Hold Our Ground.* . . . VICTORY TO THE NLF AND THE VIETNAMESE REVOLUTION!' The organizers claimed 100,000 for this march, which was graced by no careful parsons, no Members of Parliament, no liberal angels. Even on a lower estimate, this was the largest demonstration under overtly revolutionary slogans that Britain had seen since the days of the Chartists: *New Society*'s survey of the demonstration, published

immediately afterwards, revealed that the bulk of the participants believed that they were marching against capitalism. An
international causality of revolutionary thought and action
was operating, it seemed, to annul the boundaries that separated Saigon from Paris, Frankfurt from Washington, Prague
from London.

All the same, the very ease with which the ideas and styles
of revolution captured the accessible young from country to
country determined the limits of the upsurge. The force of
international example can enter the consciousness only of
those whose mental processes are already somewhat detached
from the immediate nexus of national and local influences:
that is to say, students and to some extent working-class youth.
It is the very same set of causes – namely, the crisis of a world
economy whose growth is constrained by national frontiers,
oppression of backward regions, and the loss of control by
private or State decision – makers and enforcers – which produces the sit-in of the student nurse, the raid of the peasant
guerrilla, the undergraduate's disillusionment with official
creeds, the trade unionist's sudden strike and the drug addict's
precipitate death. Yet in the case of those who are socialized
into the subordinate levels of production and social reproduc-
tion – the vast majority of workers and housewives – these
causes usually have to be experienced with an immediate,
personal impact, in the form of a cut in real wages, say, or a
brutal act of oppression by boss or landlord, before a reaction is evoked. Sheer exposure of the bankruptcy of a prevailing belief, or of the illegitimacy and stupidity of an authority
figure (which may well represent the same causation working
on a more abstract plane), will be enough to spur into action
those who happen to be engaged in a crucial intellectual task
of personal or social self-definition. The N.L.F.'s Tet offensive
immediately 'enlarged the field of possibility' (to quote
Sartre's handy phrase) of the radical or liberal student, but
there is no pressing reason why it should have been felt by the
mass of the population in France or Britain to enlarge the
field of *their* possibilities. The instant 'detonator' of Student
Power does not generally keep time with the slow-burning

fuse of popular grievance; and this is one detonator that may get damped through the knowledge of previous failures to synchronize with the real explosive. In Britain particularly, 1968 was a year of spectacular student protest, but with scarcely any serious industrial trouble. 1969, with little in the way of campus 'unrest', saw large tenants' demonstrations and widespread strikes both from customarily militant and previously untried sections of the labour force – one of the most interesting manifestations being the May Day strike against anti-trade-union legislation, remarkable as both a political and (in the main) an unofficial stoppage, which brought out nearly a quarter of a million workers.

The shrinking of the revolutionary Left's base among student youth (the 'Vietnam mobilization' of November 1969 could scarcely muster two thousand demonstrators) has been accompanied by a more visible ideological differentiation within its ranks. This move towards theoretical (and often sectarian) divergence in fact marks some improvement on the frenetic activism of Guerrilla Year: positions are now taken up more coherently and clearly, and the Left can claim less indulgence for the looseness of its answers to the problems of theory and organization which at first overwhelmed it. Before specifying the main characteristics of the newer 'varieties' (a full catalogue of which would outnumber the range advertised by Messrs Heinz), it will be as well to stake out the common ground held by all elements of the anti-Social-Democratic, anti-Stalinist opposition. The development of further intellectual differentiation has proceeded upon this common basis, which has been derived in great measure from the international and personal experience of the years 1967 and 1968. One difficulty, indeed, which the revolutionary Left may increasingly meet, is that of presenting its theories to youngsters whose political involvement first occurred outside the confrontation atmosphere of 1968. There are signs of rapid obsolescence, of an inability to 'make the scene' any longer, among those Left forces who have invested their commitment too exclusively in the mood-politics of a year or two ago. This is no new phenomenon, as survivors of the transient myriads of C.N.D. and the Committee of 100 will testify; it need not be fatal to the revolutionary groupings, provided that they can step back from the fading panorama and engage with the more liberal and more localized (but also more substantial) eruptions of the more recent period.

Here, then, is a minimum description of that extra-parliamentary opposition which not long ago could be observed at most points between Grosvenor Square and the pavement around the Eros statue, and which in mid-1970 can still be seen mixing in with the throngs of Student Christians, Young Liberals and voting-at-eighteen Labour electors outside (or inside) the Springboks' stadiums, vainly trying to get everybody to link arms to stop the fuzz from singling out victims: Existing society is intelligible, for those, as a structure which, both as a whole and in every one of its separate dominant institutions, has two main elements: the powerful few and the powerless many. The element which is the many can be further sub-divided: there are those who competitively aspire towards the positions occupied by the few, or those who accept the subordination of their own relation to the few as a reciprocal sacrifice, in the cause of a perceived unity holding few and many together; and then there are those who aspire to and believe in the values of democracy, of freedom, of community, but say that they are not realized in the present structure, and that the prevailing institutions which claim to realize them are a sham. To be able to describe the existing society in this fashion is at once to conceive of an alternative form of social existence, in which the few–many relationships of superiority and subordination, competition and deference are absent. In this other society, relationships between individuals would manifest equality, love, fun, and the production and enjoyment of art.

These views plainly do not entail the adoption of any political perspectives of any description. A fair number of the new critical generation feel it to be possible to construct an 'alternative society', expressing the social and aesthetic values they affirm and rejecting the structures of the dominant order, simply through living their lives in a freely chosen manner.

This set of choices is expressed, and continuously reinforced, by the 'underground' magazines (*Oz* and *International Times*, for instance); through the thematic content, both words and music, of many popular songs, and by the maintenance of friendships based on common refusals and affirmations. This culture is not entirely separate from the world of oppositional politics;[8] but the political critics acknowledge a different relationship between the existing, dominant social order and the alternative society of equal human living. For the political, the construction of such an alternative lies on the other side of a future transition involving the entry of the presently powerless many into the structures controlled by the few, in a seizure that will annihilate these structures and fashion new ones based on co-operative goals and democratic voting. The ultimate political perspective is, in short, one of revolution, of the communitarian, mass-rising variety that is exemplified in the Russia of 1905 and 1917, the Spain of 1936, the Hungary of 1956 and the France of 1968.

In analysing the separate kinds of revolutionary ideology that now exist, it must be admitted that no completely new distillation has emerged in Britain during these last years. The trendy thinkers listed in the colour supplements do not represent genuine trends of thinking. Marcuse, for instance, has had little or no influence on any section of the revolutionary movement here (though his term 'repressive tolerance' is sometimes used as a convenient description of the authorities' technique of smothering discontent by a simulated assent or attention). Apart from the publication of *King Mob Echo*,

---

8. My own suspicion is that any connexion between the 'underground' and the political Left is maintained almost exclusively by a few key persons, basically politicos, who happen to have a ticket of entry into the hippy kingdom. The occupation of 144 Piccadilly seems to have been led, for example, by a small hard core of young anarchists, who worked nearly to death keeping some minimum technical and military discipline going among the stoned and hung-up multitude. Yeats's stark choice – perfection of one's life, perfection of one's work, but never both – is probably unavoidable: the Life-perfecters of pot and pad have to call in the Work-perfecters from the traditional Left creeds if they want a rational statement written or a demonstration organized.

which has little currency outside the metropolis and scarcely any following even there, we see no evidence of a successful British importation of Situationism, that baffling (but after three or four readings, dazzling) reconstruction of Marxism for advanced capitalist societies produced by the Strasbourg student commune. The Revolutionary Socialist Students Federation (now a rump central apparat) never produced any speakers or writers outside the established political-group circuit. (Here, the students' juniors within the schools action movement made a far better showing, with their excellent journal *Vanguard*.) The fortnightly *Black Dwarf* started as a simple meeting-ground for diverse ideologies (*New Left Review* Third-Worldists, the International Marxist Group, International Socialists, anarchists and dissident C.P. members); but it has since then split following a tussle between the *Red Mole* faction of 'youth vanguard' post-Trotskyism and those who wished to keep the paper as a broad forum mixing underground display style (poetry, posters, pictures) with general political commentary and reportage. Any real innovation on the British Left today should be seen in terms of presentation and medium rather than of ideas, with the present phase characterized by an expansion of combative journalism (with the International Socialist weekly *Socialist Worker* overtaking the Old Left's *Tribune* and the Socialist Labour League's daily *Workers' Press* moving in to compete with the *Morning Star*) and of communication by drama (with the Ciné-Action group of strike-servicing film-makers and the various street theatre troupes like the Cartoon Archetypal Slogan Theatre and the Bread and Puppet Players). Many towns now have their own local radical news-sheet, operating within the broad framework of revolutionary ideology that we have sketched.

Varieties of Revolutionary

In listing the differences that provoke active debate on the far Left, two main classifications are at once obvious. Revolutionaries differentiate themselves (i) in terms of the importance that they attach to student radicalism, as compared with the more traditional agency of Socialism, the working class; and (ii) in terms of the degree of looseness or tightness that they feel to be indispensable in a properly conducted Socialist political organization. Associated with this latter organizational variable, we also find theoretical differences in the analysis of the regimes (Russia, China, Cuba, North Korea and Vietnam and the East European States) which combine a state-owned economic structure with a proclaimed allegiance to Marxism. On the whole, it is those who are most sympathetic to the Socialist pretensions of any or all of these regimes who are also most inclined towards a tight, centralized framework for their own (ideal or actual) political organizations; conversely, a penchant for organizational looseness goes with a reluctance to consider these states as representing any form of Socialism. This correlation, however, is so approximate that it might well decline to insignificance if an actual sample were taken. The exceptions to it are striking: anyone who knows the contemporary Left will be familiar either with the hairy hash-inhaler, libertarian in his personal life and creed to the point of downright indiscipline, who will blench and bridle at any suggestion that Ho Chi Minh was other than a kindly uncle, or at the other extreme with the stern denouncer of all existing governments as State–Capitalist tyrannies, who is still ready to expel any of his comrades and peers at the drop of a deviation.

The case for regarding student rebellion as the vanguard of modern revolution was put, frequently and persuasively, in the wake of the French upheaval of May 1968. The writing of Tom Nairn (himself a participant in the superb occupation of Hornsey that summer, and later victimized) is the most persuasive summary of this position.[9]

According to this view, late capitalism, through its dependence on the forces of 'mental production' in the era of its advanced technology, itself creates in the student body, like

9. We refer to Part Two, 'Why It Happened' in his Panther paperback *The Beginning of the End* (1968) and to the anonymous collective production *The Hornsey Affair* (Penguin Education Special, 1969), in which his formulations may be detected at a number of points.

Frankenstein, a monster – an anarchic 'social brain' or 'mental surplus' which oozes impetuously beyond the careerist confines imposed on it by the system, and which 'arises as the potential unity of society, the prefiguration of the classless social body, the transcendence of the split between manual and mental labour (which could only occur under the emergent dominance of the latter).' Already in the post-mortem volume on the Hornsey defeat, this analysis was being modified to take cognizance of the systematic weakness of the student Left in this country (although even here, *The Hornsey Affair* commented 'it is hard to see what other force than the student movement could serve as the lever of change in Britain'). Few Socialists today would venture to ascribe such a degree of primacy to the explosions on campus. At the most it is suggested, by the theoreticians of the 'international youth vanguard' such as Ernest Mandel and his co-thinkers in the International Marxist Group, that the militant student should seek to secure himself a 'mass base' among his fellows on the campus *before* he turns to Socialist activity outside the institution (advice which will keep him waiting a very long time indeed in most British universities before he makes contact with the town).

Even fewer Socialists, on the other hand, would today urge a policy of abstention upon student and academic issues. The derisory showing of the French Trotskyite *groupuscule*, who ordered their followers to absent themselves from the heroic 'Night of the Barricades' – denouncing as a student 'adventure' action which soon sparked off a strike of millions of workers – has formed an urgent cautionary tale influencing the behaviour of the younger Left. There is general agreement on the existence of some important side-effects – often delayed, and tending towards imitation rather than hostility – which explosions in educational institutions have brought to bear on some sections of the working class. An extended analysis of the political sociology of student radicalism in Britain, mainly cautious though breaking into over-optimism in some passages, can be found in *Education, Capitalism and the Student Revolt* (International Socialist booklet, 1968).

On the organizational front, we may characterize the main present tendencies, in a roughly ascending order of centralism, as follows:

Anarchists. The theory of anarchism has changed little, if at all, since the time of Kropotkin and Bakunin. Anarchists reject all external authority, and favour the re-organization of society through the voluntary federation of local communes, accompanied by the destruction of such institutions as private property, the authoritarian family, prisons, the army, etc. The main anarchist organ, the weekly *Freedom* (founded by Kropotkin himself in October 1886) provides a lively libertarian commentary on current politics (though it is rather weak on industry); and the monthly *Anarchy* has a solid record of publishing special issues and articles in such areas as criminology, progressive education and anarchist history. Crime seems to have an unusual fascination for anarchist writers, whether through moral identification with the under-dog or the belief (curious, in view of the notorious conservatism of this class) that criminal offenders are potential revolutionaries. Two common (and opposite) tendencies distinguish anarchists, in my own experience: first, a belief in efficient *confrontation* – for anarchists, unlike Marxists, view the police as the base, not as the superstructure, and therefore conduct operations against police with more skill and seriousness than the Left can usually manage; secondly an acceptance of *marginal reform* – for anarchists, who must be bound to view all past and present societies as almost unrelievedly reactionary in the light of their own absolute criteria, tend (among some of their membership, at least) to be thankful for small improvements, islands of libertarian principle, which others would dismiss as irrelevant palliatives.

Solidarists. This is the term once bestowed by the *Daily Mail* on the small and interesting group that publishes the monthly *Solidarity*, and forms a parallel to the French journal *Socialisme ou Barbarie* (discussed at some length in George Lichtheim's *Marxism in Modern France*, 1966). *Solidarity*'s

contents are usually made up of local reports of factory disputes or college confrontations, though the group has also
produced some good documentary pamphlets on the libertarian
opposition to Bolshevism (for example, on Kronstadt, the
'Workers' Opposition', and a forthcoming one on Bolshevik
policy towards factory committees in 1917). This intense
localism derives from the theoretical perspective propagated by
the group, drawing chiefly on the work of their French mentor,
Paul Cardan. In Cardan's opinion, the economic contradictions analysed in capitalism by Marx have now been superseded, since the system has permanently solved the problem
of securing growth: the major contradiction in society is now
one that operates at the level of institutional confrontation
between the holders of authority and their subjects. A model
of class-differentiation developed originally for Stalinist Russia (based on the notion of a bureaucratic stratification of
power) is thus applied to Western societies: the revolutionary
process is engendered now by the continuous contradiction
between 'those who receive, and those who give, orders'.
Solidarity, as distinct from most of the anarchist publications,
believes that a revolutionary political organization must be
created for Socialists, on very loose and decentralized lines
that will mirror the structure of the future society of workers'
councils; and as distinct from most Marxists, it refuses to call
for a new party (still less a 'vanguard'). At the moment it is
expanding by sub-division into several different journals (all
called *Solidarity*), so that it is rather difficult for the outsider
to keep up with what the group is saying.

Maoists. Propagation by sub-division is taken to much greater
extremes by the British followers of Chinese Communism,
most of whom acquired their political identity during the
period 1963–7. There are about a dozen Maoist groups in
Britain, publishing small journals and engaged in what is often
pragmatically sensible industrial work. Paradoxically, the very
generality and abstraction of 'Mao Tse-Tung Thought', along
with its repertoire of homespun adages invoking the priority
of local experience, has made it easier for its followers to

strike out a modestly independent path: despite appearances, nobody was telling them what to do. The Maoists appear to be extraordinarily contented with the tiny, local scale of their work, and show no interest whatever in fusing their forces. It would be misleading to call most of them Stalinists (though they share the Communist Party's suspicion of anything that can be remotely seen as 'Trotskyist'). In the main, they are best thought of as incomplete anarchists, and the mustachioed ikons of Russia's old butcher that they insist on carrying in demonstrations have no greater diabolical significance than the British worker's habit of writing 'Joe for King' on munitions during World War Two.

International Socialists. A grouping (the largest of these fragments) very difficult to describe partly because the writer has been in it for some years, and partly owing to the complex heterogeneity of views, from semi-anarchist to orthodox-Trotskyist, represented within it. Originally a splinter-group from Trotskyism (a number of its founder members were expelled from the official British 'Fourth International' section for simultaneously denouncing America and Russia in the Korean War), it rapidly discarded a number of traditional theories, including both the Leninist concept of 'the labour aristocracy' (with its implication of a revolutionary mass of workers beneath the thin crust of bribed traitors) and the 'State ownership' criterion for determining the existence of a Workers' State or Socialist Country. (I.S. is often nicknamed the State Capitalist Group owing to its theory of the class-nature of Russia.) These developments were in retrospect important only in so far as they facilitated the group's later interest in working-class oppositional behaviour in the Western and Sino-Soviet blocs. Influenced chiefly by the two main I.S. economists, Tony Cliff and Michael Kidron, International Socialists draw a distinction between the working-class consciousness engendered in unfavourable economic conditions and that associated with strong bargaining power: the consciousness of the pre-war depression was that of a weak working class which looked to agencies outside itself (Labour politicians, or Russia if you were militant) to act for it; but post-war economic expansion, a conjunction of affairs resulting from the global effects of arms expenditure rather than from Keynesian wisdom, has encouraged workers in a buoyant ' do-it-yourself reformism' of local bargaining through Britain's dense network of shop-stewards. The experience of local wage-gains – still thriving despite frantic governmental attempts to check the process – helps to weaken the worker's sense of dependence on parliamentarians. A parallel network of politically sophisticated rank-and-file militants, educated in revolutionary-Socialist appraisal, now has a base.

The main emphasis of the I.S. weekly *Socialist Worker* and of its seventy-odd branches, is therefore on industrial-political propaganda and basic Socialist education among workers. The position of the group is argued in detail in Tony Cliff and Colin Barker's *Incomes Policy, Legislation and Shop Stewards* (1966), Kidron's *Western Capitalism Since the War* 1968; revised as a Penguin, 1970), and in Cliff's *The Employers' Offensive* on productivity deals. The influence of the group's internationalist and Marxist principles may also be discerned, along with the contribution of his own powerful talents, in the analyses of British politics published by Paul Foot (Penguins on racialism, Enoch Powell and Harold Wilson; the *Anti-Cameron Report*; and articles for *Private Eye* and the I.S. press).

Trotskyists. A number of propositions advanced by Leon Trotsky, and propagated by him and his isolated following in years when the advocacy of 'Trotskyism' courted excommunication, and sometimes physical violence, from the dominant forces of the Left, have now become widely accepted in the newer revolutionary generation. The identification of Social-Democracy as an anti-working-class, pro-capitalist force, and of Stalinism as the expression of the conservative, nationalist backwardness of Moscow's rulers; the refusal to countenance united fronts with the bourgeois parties, strong and treacherous in the advanced countries, weak and treacherous in the backward; and a firm commitment to the development of revolutionary politics conducted outside the framework of Stalinism and Social-Democracy and necessarily on an international scale: these are the classic positions of Trotskyism. And inasmuch as modern New Lefties accept them, we are all Trotskyists now. However the terms 'Trotskyism' and 'Trotskyist' are often used in a more circumscribed sense, as applying to those members of the far Left who claim a lineal descent, in organization and ideas, from the 'Fourth International' founded by Trotsky in 1938 in an attempt to build national sections of his followers upon a pyramidal structure of 'democratic centralism' working from the top (i.e., the International Secretariat or Executive). No less than four rival organizations exist in the present-day world as pretenders to the succession of the original Fourth International, and two of these have a significant following in Britain. The International Marxist Group (the British affiliate of the Paris-based Fourth International) emphasizes the role of the 'colonial revolution' in the Third World; it entertained particular hopes for Socialist advance from Ben Bella's Algeria and has included Castro's Cuba in the pantheon of 'workers' States'. The International Marxist Group, like most of the other Paris Fourth International affiliates, has effectively postponed any activity among industrial workers until it can build up an adequate 'youth vanguard' of students. The other main Trotskyist group, the Socialist Labour League (the main component of the London-based Fourth International), is industrially oriented, and for some years has run a fairly successful youth section (the Young Socialists) which can regularly turn out around a thousand young workers on its own demonstrations. The S.L.L. has extraordinary energy (testified by its production of the *Workers' Press* daily), a unique degree of spleen against all other Left forces, and a high membership turnover; all these factors derive from its economic perspective, usually very cataclysmic, and from its willing acceptance of the conviction that the working class is situated in a 'crisis of leadership' where sectarian in-fighting is at a high premium. Except for Peter Fryer's fairly staid *The Battle of Socialism* and Tom Kemp's monograph *Theories of Im-*

perialism (1967), not a single book, or even any original and lengthy pamphlet, has been produced by any member of a British Trotskyist section since the thirties.

The Future of Socialist Thought in Britain

The extreme fragmentation and frequent incoherence of the British revolutionary Left should not be permitted to obscure the fact that, for the first time since 1910 or so, militant Socialist propaganda and analysis, free from Labourite apologetics and from Comintern zig-zags, is being carried forward seriously in the main industrial and academic centres of these islands. ('Islands' has to be in the plural, since the revival of Connollyite Socialism around the People's Democracy and Left Republicans in Ulster must also be noted.) True enough, the newer opposition may have its own apologetics and its own zig-zags to answer for. The British New Left has, however, avoided most of the more outstanding lunacies of its American and Continental counterparts; its present limited retrenchment after 1968 is but a slight recession (chiefly affecting college politics) compared with, for instance, the decline of the anti-nuclear movement in the early sixties; and it has no rival ideologies which could move up to influence the neo-liberal protesters if these should decide to look at society as a whole rather than at separate issues. The landscape of Socialist theory, in short, is populated exclusively either by dead ducks or by live fledgelings: and the latter abound in sufficient genetic variety, surely, to ensure the survival of a hardy species.

The Discontents of Youth

James Jupp*

A quarter of a million young people gathered in Hyde Park in July 1969 to commemorate the death of Brian Jones, a former Rolling Stone. No other political, civic or religious event could hope to attract such an audience. A debate between Harold Wilson and Ted Heath, presided over by the Archbishop of Canterbury, might just fill the Albert Hall. But the average age of the audience would be in the forties and fifties, while the Stones' followers are rarely over thirty and frequently under twenty. A youth movement has grown up in Britain, as in most other advanced industrial nations, which creates more active enthusiasm and participation among its members than the adult religious and political groups which once monopolized mass mobilization.

Nor can this increasingly powerful youth movement be dismissed as an offshoot of the entertainment world, as serious as a Cup Final crowd and as easily dispersed. Youth has its own publications, not simply in the mass circulation musical weeklies, but also in papers like *International Times* and *Oz*, which, incomprehensible though much of their material is to anyone over thirty, have enthusiastic readerships as large as most of the adult, serious weeklies. One is much more likely to see 'I.T.' on sale on street corners than *Tribune*, which partly accounts for it having nearly twice the circulation. The Roundhouse attracts larger audiences than its near and much smaller neighbour, Unity Theatre. Above all, pop music has a massive, well-informed and actively participating following of millions, rivalled only by football in the adult world and possibly surpassing it in terms of live, as opposed to television audiences.

* The writer is Lecturer in Politics at the University of York and author of *Australian Party Politics*, *Arrivals and Departures*, and *Political Parties*.

The whole Western world is experiencing a phenomenon which had its origins in the United States, the creation of an autonomous 'youth culture'. The basic features of this culture are: that it rejects the adult world; that it is confined effectively to those between puberty and thirty; that it creates its own leaders and symbols; that it demands 'liberation'; that it requires less and less adult co-operation for its sub-society to function; that it frightens the adult world to death, and that it is basically harmless despite a dangerous and even self-destructive aspect.

To say all this is not to argue that the youth culture embraces the whole of its potential following. Electoral research in Britain suggests that half the new voters between eighteen and twenty-one may vote Conservative. The Labour Party may well founder on the teenage vote as the Liberals did on the women's vote (among other things). While voting Conservative is not completely inconsistent with supporting some aspects of youth culture, it may generally be taken as accepting adult leadership, social hierarchy and stability. Thus at least one-half of adolescents are probably still immune to critical, let alone revolutionary, influences. Like their counterparts in the United States, Australia or Scandinavia, they are conformist, conservative and respectable. The only element of revolt may be in rejecting the Labour politics of their parents. Indeed, voting Labour may be even more conventional when that party is in power.

In varying degrees that part of youth, still a minority, which rejects parental values and the adult world, tends to look to its own age group for leadership and inspiration. Adults are often seen as ridiculous, or simply as failures. The Second World War, which dominates the thinking of most parents in the Western world, is so remote and boring that small sections of young people, particularly in the United States, became Nazi admirers a few years ago, wearing German uniforms and saluting pictures of Hitler without necessarily subscribing to fascist views. This craze did not last long. But the much stronger movement of sympathy with China and Cuba may also be traced to a desire to annoy and reject parental values.

No two countries are more hated and feared in the United States. Because of the dominant influence of the U.S.A. over Western youth, the cults of Castro, Guevara and Mao have spread from California and New York to European states where these leaders have no relevance to local politics at all. The current revival of Trotskyism and anarchism among students in Britain, France and the U.S.A. may also be evidence of a search for leaders who have not been sullied by the adult world. Thus an adult world hero like Dubcek attracted little support among youth because of his strict adherence to conformist methods of resistance and protest.

Political protest is, of course, a minor strand in the general rejection of the adult world, and one largely confined to students who make up at most one in ten of the relevant age group. A more widespread if less publicized form of rejection is the adoption of activities and cultural forms which are foreign to the adult world and largely outside its comprehension. At one extreme this involves immersion in cults of drug-taking and pseudo-Eastern mysticism, with their adherents often ending up destitute on the doorstep of the British embassies in Kabul, Teheran or Katmandu. But in general there is a fairly harmless search for distinctiveness in dress and music.

The development of teenage 'gear' had its origins in the American revolt against school uniform, in the bobby-soxers of the 1940s. For young people to build up a distinctive wardrobe of their own, which cannot be worn in the adult-controlled worlds of school or work, involves financial independence from parents. In Britain this was not generally possible until the Teddy Boy era of the early 1950s. Since then dress has gone rapidly through phases which are shortlived enough to support the growing teenage clothing industry. By the early 1960s in Britain, Australia and other urban industrial nations, clothing had become a mark of distinction, not merely between youth and adults, but between the two major classes of adolescents known as 'Mods' and 'Rockers'. These corresponded roughly to the two major social classes of grammar and modern school educated, with university students left outside in a group which can only be termed 'scruffies'. The seaside battles of Margate and Brighton some five or six years ago probably mark the height of sartorially based gang warfare. The 'Skinheads' and 'Hell's Angels', found on opposite sides of the squatters' barricades in Piccadilly in 1969, continue the Rocker tradition to some extent.

Generally speaking Mods were smart, scooter riding, rather snobbish and clean, while Rockers were leather jacketed (an American-inspired uniform as contrasted to the 'British' effeteness of the Mods), rode motorbikes, were proletarian and dirty. But both had in common the wearing of clothes which appeared absurd (*pace* one or two Anglican clergymen) when worn by adults. Today this basic characteristic still holds, even when the strict divisions have gone. As the adolescent clothing boom merged with the music boom, the pop singers began to set trends which had previously been inspired from America. On the whole the Mods came off best, with leather jackets retreating to such cultural deserts as Greece or Sunderland. But the variety of clothing became greater and a person's social class was no longer clear from what he wore. This trend corresponded with rising incomes among manual workers, with spreading tertiary education and with the consolidation of a new youth leadership in pop music and fashion.

Clothing today reflects individual aspirations to a greater extent than previously, despite uniformities among minority sub-cultures. Thus the politically active went through a phase of forage caps and zipup jackets which could, if necessary, be worn in the Sierra Maestra. John Lennon caps or Mick Jagger flowered shirts denoted loyalty to a musical cult, while the student anarchist became hairier and dirtier every year. Caftans and dark glasses became uniform among the drug-taking minority. Some of these uniforms were constructed from cast-offs. The industry in general, which became increasingly under the financial control of young people, sold Carnaby Street and King's Road to those who were too fastidious to patronize Portobello second-hand stalls.

Most of these trends spread outward from London, even as

far as Europe and the United States. They can be studied, like so much else in youth culture, by looking at the Beatles over seven or eight years, from their leather-jacketed past to their bizarre and flowered present. There is no way of prophesying where fashion trends will move next, only that they must, by the logic and economics of the industry, keep moving and that they will continue to aim at distinguishing youth from adults. The same explosive situation holds in pop music. For despite its contempt for commercial values, the youthful audience is captured by dynamic industries. The Beatles need never make another sound for their investments to expand ever more rapidly. Indeed, their seemingly desperate attempts to run companies like Apple into the ground may indicate a reaction against the Frankenstein of success.

The irony of the youth revolt in clothes and music is precisely that it cannot but create an expanding financial empire. Without high incomes independence from parents is either impossible or produces starvation. Behind many a starving hippy there is a parental cheque-book. A community of several thousand young people live in West-central London without regular jobs or permanent addresses, precisely because, as in Greenwich Village or Haight-Ashbury, there are affluent parents or friends around if absolutely necessary. Among the much wider adolescent world, cultural independence must be paid for by high wages and low commitments. Thus in the working class the culture of youth cuts out at marriage in the early twenties, while in the middle classes, and particularly at universities, one can be young for rather longer. But both groups must be aware that the free world of youth will be snatched away fairly soon. It is this transience of the whole movement that gives point to demands for 'total liberation'. 'We Want the World and We Want it Now', as walls proclaim from San Francisco to Notting Hill.

The general contours of the developing youth culture are fairly plain. It dresses its adherents differently, gives them different music and different gods. But to what extent does all this denote protest, rather than simply a drawing together in the temporary phase of adolescence? To what extent do young people have different ideas, as well as different habits? Here the difficulty is that most overtly political protest among young people is dominated by, and largely confined to, students who are a small minority. Even among students it seems likely that most of those in strictly vocational fields, from law to teacher training, are fairly conventional and see themselves as preparing for adult life rather than revolting against it. It is that section of students who cannot see their lives so clearly mapped out that form the spearhead of political protest. If we accept that in most advanced industrial societies only one in ten are actively interested in politics, then it is not surprising that among young people the proportion is no higher. It is the intensity of involvement, not its scope, which differs markedly.

The Press tells us that Marcuse is the main influence on protesting youth and this is believed by Governor Reagan in Marcuse's home state. Yet Marcuse is extremely difficult to read, combining Freud and Marx in his own even more opaque version of German-English. It seems unlikely that he *converts* any but a small minority of arts and social science students. What he does is to echo feelings and sentiments which are widespread, but are incoherently expressed by millions. These are basically: that modern society is a confidence trick offering high standards of material comfort in exchange for slavery to the industrial machine; that modern learning has acceptance of this situation as its main goal; and that the only sections likely to revolt against this are the unbribed poor, racial minorities and youth.

The basic ideas here are quite simple, despite Marcuse's elaboration. The sense of being tricked caters to youth who are frustrated and annoyed for many reasons, but who see themselves surrounded only by the kindly faces of liberal parents and teachers. The aggressiveness aroused by kicking against open doors is often vented against authority in ways specifically designed to provoke counter-violence. This is the Marcusean way of proving that violence lurks behind the liberal façade. All it really proves is that if you kick a policeman he will kick you back. But in permissive and liberal societies like Britain the 'anti-fuzz' protest gives at least some sort of link with youths tackling more fearsome opponents in the United States, France, Japan or Latin America.

This Marcusean tactic of 'ripping the mask from violence' satisfies the youthful desire to fight. It gives intellectual justification for the kind of behaviour long found among adolescents at football matches and on Glasgow housing estates. The battles between Mods and Rockers have been replaced by those between 'the fuzz' and the forces of good. Where violence is directed against the sort of forces which strafe American campuses from helicopters, Marcuse has opened a window on truth. But where, as so often in Britain, the fight is deliberately provoked to prove a point, then he has simply licensed the creation of a public nuisance.

Having 'proved' that violence is the basis of society, the next puzzle is to explain why so many people, including the poorest, seem unaware of this. Here 'false consciousness' steps in.

The Marxist notion that men are often unaware of their true situation is the basis of much of the modern sociology of knowledge. Unfortunately, in the hands of Leninists (and of Marcuse) the corollary is acceptance of an enlightened élite who really *do* know what the real situation is. Hence the great appeal of Marcuse to university students, always the most insecurely arrogant section of youth. They are flattered into believing that they can see what is hidden from the bus driver or the Co-op shopper. These latter are being fooled and exploited in the very act of watching television or buying a new car. Giving them material goods involves a surrender of economic and intellectual freedom.

The idea that youth is both enlightened in this respect and capable of liberating at least itself, is irresistible. It justifies any rejection of the adult world, any form of violence against it, alliance with any group or nation which also seems to be fighting the conformists. It breeds sympathy with Black Power extremists who want to 'burn America down'. The political danger of such a position is, of course, that it can lead anywhere except towards constructive work in established political institutions. As all such institutions are by nature corrupting, association with them will also corrupt. This rejection helps to explain the unbridgeable gap between formal adult radicalism and the youth revolt in most advanced countries. In strict logic it leads more directly to fascism than to communism, even if all the heroes of the movements are on the extreme Left. Fortunately, strict logic rarely applies.

The acceptance of the Marcuse–Cohn-Bendit amalgam by wide sections of university students is easily explained by the failure of adult radicalism in the West since 1945. Communism, except in its chaotic Cuban or Chinese variety, simply rationalizes a vast industrial bureaucratic empire, whose only attraction is that America hates it. Social-democracy has become liberalism, most hated because gentlest of all the rationalizations for capitalism. The underdeveloped world disappoints everywhere except where, as in Southern Africa, it still fights against colonialism. Thus most of what still seems progressive to the adult world has become reactionary to the young. Their main enemy is often the Berkeley–Harvard–Essex permissive liberal, who *pretends* to like them.

It is almost impossible to assess the extent to which this rather sophisticated rationalization is accepted outside the universities. Even within the universities movements like Oxfam and UNSA testify to the survival of 1950's liberalism. In Britain the largest political demonstration conjured up by Tariq Ali did not exceed 50,000 and was a tedious farce. The three most influential semi-political journals circulating among under-thirties, *Private Eye, International Times* and *Oz,* sell about 100,000 copies between them, while no one seems to know whether Tariq Ali's *Red Mole* is likely to prove permanent. But even these figures, when placed beside comparable indices of adult political involvement, are fairly impressive.

The chief agency for spreading views of society among the young is still probably the pop singer. Some have been overtly ideological like Bob Dylan (who denies it) and Cliff Richard (on behalf of God). The Beatles and Rolling Stones are ambivalent. John Lennon currently sees himself as devoted entirely to urging peace, although his methods of propaganda have become increasingly bizarre and, one would have thought, ineffectual. Most pop singers advocate peace and permissiveness but whether they are moulding or reacting to the opinions of their audiences has not been measured. The few like Joan Baez who deliberately take part in political protest are greatly outnumbered by the many who get rumbled for smoking hash and are forced into being symbols of resistance.

In so far as there is a message it is sardonic and pessimistic rather than violent and rebellious. 'Youth's a stuff does not endure' is a more frequent theme than 'Burn Baby, Burn'. Parents are sad creatures living in little boxes and not understanding. Authority is stupid if not downright evil. Life must be enjoyed now, before the dread alternatives of the bomb or the system destroy the temporary lotus land. But this is only one strand in a constantly changing pattern. Simple sexual themes remain dominant, while there has lately been an increase in irrational or drug-induced imagism which allows the world to be overlooked altogether.

Pop music has many layers, corresponding to different levels of education, age or musical appreciation. Its importance is that the whole industry is youth controlled and dominated, creating heroes whose every word and action is heeded where those of adult leaders are rejected or simply ignored. A whole generation has been created in the past ten years which is sceptical and hedonistic, critical of the adult world and essentially apart from it. Fortunately this generation has largely been indoctrinated with liberal-radical sentiments on race, morality, personal relationships and authority. Despite the fears of churchmen, 'Lay, lady, lay' is likely to cause less damage than the *Horst Wessel Lied*.

While it remains essentially liberal the youth culture is relatively harmless and even beneficial. Some of its adherents may kill themselves off with heroin, or have their brains smashed in by policemen. But most will come through unscathed, almost ready for the cloying embrace of the affluent society. Where young people threaten liberal institutions as the *easiest* enemy, or play into reactionary hands by destructive attitudes and behaviour, they may be something more than a nuisance. Governor Reagan is becoming more popular by the hour and is already moving against free education in California. Conservatives in Western Europe are gaining strength from parental reaction against youthful extremism. Police forces are being strengthened and armed, while violence enters political life from Ulster to Canberra. As youth becomes better educated and proportionately stronger in most advanced societies, it will demand more influence. It will ask for forms of liberation which cannot be granted. While there is unlikely to be a straightforward battle of generations anywhere, youth will have to be added to the economic and cultural forces in future political equations.

The Nature and Causes of Student Unrest

One of the guitar-slinging prophets of the younger generation, Bob Dylan, sings:

> Come Mothers and Fathers
> Throughout the land
> And don't criticize
> What you don't understand;
> Your sons and your daughters
> Are beyond your command ...

One recurrent theme in the now obsessional attempts to explain student unrest is that the campus sit-in is part of this
wider syndrome of youth rebellion. Student action's own most
vociferous disciples, the collegiate New Left, see themselves
as the vanguard of what Gibbon called 'the brisk intemper-
ance of youth'.

This commonplace analysis of student 'unrest' will not hold
water. However much the growing stridency of the youth
subculture may be one spur to greater student militancy, the
undergraduate New Left are in many ways out of step with
the underlying attitudes of 'youth' in general. Far from being
its vanguard, they are instead a guerrilla brigade so detached
from the main column as almost to be fighting a different
war.

Press coverage of student culture rarely spotlights this difference. The notion of a student revolt has been reinforced
in the public mind by incessant reporting, not only of off-
beam campus ideologists and occasional violent tactics, the
truly *student* revolt, but also of non-political trends among
students to greater, although commonly exaggerated, drug-
taking, promiscuity or rowdyism, which are far more sympto-

*The author was President of the National Union of Students 1968–9.

matic of evolutions in youth culture than in peculiarly student habits.

So much have the specifically political and student become confused through this coverage with the more sociological and youth trends, that any analysis of 'student unrest' must first try to unravel this artificial tapestry. Nothing, it seems, confuses like publicity.

The phenomenon of a socially boisterous student community is far from being an original sin. The 'Love Generation' is hardly more non-conformist than Evelyn Waugh's Oxford 'hearties'! But, whereas the distribution of wealth in former generations provided the financial requirements of youth social rebellion to a limited number, affluence is now the norm for the vast majority of the age-group. The alienation of the young from the conventional wisdom of their elders is, therefore, more widespread and more publicized. John Betjeman portrayed the archetypal Oxford student of the twenties in his Varsity Students' Rag:

And then we smashed up everything and what was the funniest part,
We smashed some rotten old pictures which were priceless works of art.

He began the same poem,

I'm afraid the fellows in Putney rather wished they had
The social ease and manners of a varsity undergrad.

At the level of greater social non-conformity, all that has happened in the sixties is that university expansion has encompassed 'the fellows in Putney'. We are all Socialites nowadays.

Equally, the tendency of students to espouse political causes unpopular with their elders, and to devote an abnormally large amount of time to pursuing peacefully the path of protest, is not a uniquely modern development, even if the Press taking such actions seriously is new. Much that attracts attention as student unrest is therefore either a more raucous version of youth's traditional social divergence, or a more publicized continuation of the idealistic and protest politics of the young.

What are uniquely student, and are original to this generation, are the changed demands that students make, the new tactics of violence they will at times employ and the new ideologies by which some attempt to reconcile these novelties of philosophy. But even here, in the true inner sanctum of student unrest, recent publicity has imported another false over-simplification into the debate – the myth of internationalism. Certain explanations of student revolt may transcend frontiers. Obviously, improved mass communication and travel by students themselves aids trans-national imitations of tactics. But within this world-wide matrix of information, the student body of any nation is still far more likely to take up causes that emerge from their own situation and to pursue them within the political conventions of their national culture. The Sorbonne riots in May 1968 sparked off such acute speculation that Britain's students would follow suit that anyone would think the Communards had been sighted in St James's. These riots were ultimately only possible because of the revolutionary tradition latent in French politics and absent in the British. Similarly, and not to belabour this point, there is surely *some* distinction between the students of Addis Ababa demonstrating, as they did in 1968, against the miniskirt, which they saw as an alien intrusion into Arab conventions, and girls at British Colleges of Education objecting that they *cannot* wear mini-skirts at formal meals!

Although there are international interactions between students, there are still important distinctions in the place of the student body in different societies. In part this is sheer mathematics. In 'developing' nations, massive higher educational programmes are the substitute for the heritage of administrative experience enjoyed by affluent nations. Commonly in this situation, the current undergraduate population outnumbers the pool of past graduates in the country. The student body feels an *ipso facto* political importance, representing the majority of the nation's intelligentsia. In the typical affluent country the reverse applies: past graduates vastly outnumber current undergraduates, and so student opinion is relatively unimportant. In order to impress any views at all on the graduate establishment, students play politics by their conventions. In the expanding affluent nation, which categorizes Britain, the States and much of Western Europe, the student community represents an expanding percentage of the age-group. It is encouraged to be more assertive and tactically non-conformist. Because of numerical strength, it feels it can 'confront the gerontocracy'. But the growing complexity of technological and governmental structures, and widespread public education, make both the student task more involved and their views less significant than they are prompted by their numbers to believe. It may be 'excellent to have a giant's strength', but it is rather disconcerting mistakenly to assume you have it.

To return to those three truly relevant aspects of unrest – the shift in student demands, in tactics and in ideology – the real consequences and nature of each are again often muffled in popular commentary.

There has been a marked introversion of student demands towards problems endemic in their immediate college role and status. Doubts as to the 'justice' of disciplinary systems, as to content of syllabuses and as to college governmental structures have all come 'centre stage' of student discussion. This transition does not necessarily reflect a changed student psychology. Students may be taking these issues up, not because some mass psychosis has driven them to cherish new illusions, but because the problems are 'for real'. In each area of concern there are substantial bodies of teaching staff who also accept the existence of a problem. The quarrel is more over diagnosis and remedy than whether the patient is really sick. At a time when young people are leaving their parental homes earlier and assuming greater responsibilities, and when at home parental domination is diminished, the idea of an *'in loco parentis'* college authority is bound to come under fresh scrutiny. Equally, the trend away from small-scale college communities, where group loyalties were secured by personal relationships, to large academic units, with complex bureaucratic regimes, must necessitate changes in the method of integrating the student into society. There is more truth than slogan in proclaiming for students 'no integration without representation'.

Whatever tensions might stimulate conflict on these issues at present, the real challenge to the university community will come in the debate about course content. Conflicts over method have always proved more easy for institutional resolution than conflicts over aim. The demands of technological society for new manpower prototypes, the mutual uncertainty of teacher and taught as to whether to submit to or resist such pressures, throw this issue into sharp focus. British higher education still has its greatest trauma to come. The Robbins Report calculated the relatively simple equation of matching places with qualified entrants. But it funked the biggest issue. Should 500,000 students in 1980 be studying the same range of subjects and adopting the same academic approach as suited 150,000 in 1960? More may not mean worse, but is not the change more than one of sheer quantity?

This area of conflict threatens the substance of the university tradition rather than its form. The Romantic reaction against the Industrial Revolution stamped British education with its rejection of vocationalism, its belief in the virtue of permanently maintained standards of intellectual excellence. At this threshold of syllabus content and academic approach to learning, the universities are innately preservationist; the students innately reformist, some environmentally revolutionist.

At the level of changed tactics it is remarkable how little outright student revolt there has been in Britain. Leaving aside those instances where students have employed more traditional and peaceful protest techniques, and, concentrating therefore, on those events which have involved personal violence, sit-ins or college occupations, there were between March 1967 (the large-scale British sit-in at L.S.E.) and the end of 1968 serious incidents of direct student action at some seventeen different universities and some six colleges under Local Education Authority control. Of those twenty-three instances, the nature of the issue which sparked off the trouble varied widely. Five centred around student demands for representation on college governing bodies – Aston, Leicester, Keele and Birmingham Universities and Regent Street Polytechnic. Another eight were concerned with a

variety of essentially campus issues, ranging from the suita-
bility of the Director and subsequent disciplinary action
(L.S.E.), examination reform (Hull), the use of student buildings
(Bristol), the activities of campus police (Leeds), academic
dissatisfaction and strained communications (Hornsey and
Guildford Schools of Art), library facilities (Manchester College of Commerce) to inadequate transport facilities between
annexes (Birmingham College of Education). The other ten
were universities where visiting speakers were subjected to
violence or stimulated violent demonstrations (Oxford, Sussex, Cambridge, Essex, Leeds, East Anglia, Kent and Brad-
ford). Of the thirteen instances involving campus issues, ten
led to sit-ins and three to physical occupation of college
property.

Whilst it may be tempting to postulate that the discovery of
such tactics is a symptom of students adopting the lessons of
industrial militancy, an explanation the New Left themselves advance, it is more reasonable to comment that, for
reasons discussed earlier, students are now more willing to
break with accepted conventions of political behaviour, and,
given their inability to inflict economic damage, have resorted
to tactics calculated to cause inconvenience and nuisance to
the college authorities they see as their enemies in the particular dispute.

At the level of ideological shift, once again popular interpretations of student affairs place far too much emphasis on
the impact of new ideas on the student community. Only a
small minority possess any detailed knowledge, or acceptance of New Left thinking – as represented by Marcuse or by
the *New Left Review*. Whilst Guevarist writings and posters
may seem a commonplace among students, we do not yet fully
understand the distinction that must be drawn in our modern
mass-media ridden society between a genuine 'cult' and a
passing 'fashion'. It may be true that, within that small percentage of students with the predilection for extreme left-
wing views, Cuban or Maoist Marxism is currently more
popular than Leninist, but there is little evidence that the
basic percentage is growing. In those incidents of student unrest cited above there were small but vocal groups attempting

to portray the passing issue as symptomatic of a wider class war. But they had little or no impact on the vast majority of participants, who were stirred up far more by the issue itself and who remained determinedly concerned with its educational, not political, significances. The basic feelings which spark off unrest are normally a sense of outrage when the college authorities offend not Marxist tenets but what students see as fundamental and humanitarian liberties. Vice-Chancellors still have more to fear from Mill than Marcuse. When the 'ideologists' apply their attention to the issues which interest the mass of their activist colleagues, such as representation or discipline, they can lead them to be slightly more demanding. Large bodies of students have adopted the idea that students should comprise a large section of governing bodies rather than just having a token presence, but seldom have they swallowed the whole New Left plea for government by a Soviet of 'students, teachers and workers'. It remains surrealism, not reality, to expect staff–student discussion to reach the level of that between the Athenians and Melians, as Thucydides relates:

ATHENIANS: We would fain exercise that empire over you without trouble.

MELIANS: And how, pray, could it turn out as good for us to serve as you to rule?

ATHENIANS: Because you would have the advantage of submitting before suffering the worst, and we should gain by not destroying you.

Student unrest is not, except to its more extreme practitioners, about dominion and destruction. It is far more about transition and reform. In the long run the far more profound shifts in youth culture are likely to be of greater political importance than the transient incidence of violent tactics or revolutionary ideology among some students. In other words, the really vital aspects of student unrest are more likely to be those that are broadly reflective of those greater trends than those which are tangential to them. Student demands for changes in college life and educational content; for a keener identification of justice in discipline; student nonconformity in social standards; student disquiet at the increasing complexity of modern democracy, bureaucracy and technology; these are of more importance than the minority advocacy of political violence and admiration of Mao, Che or Marx.

History will attach much more weight to the words of Lennon and McCartney than to those of Blackburn and Cohn-Bendit. It will not do so because either is very likely to influence the minds of youth, but because the former, at least, echo what the young already think.

In 'Getting Better', the Beatles sing:

> I used to get mad at my school
> The teachers that taught me weren't cool
> You're holding me down, turning me round,
> Filling me up with your rules.

But, like the majority of the young, they continue optimistically:

> I've got to admit it's getting better
> A little better all the time.

And, as for tactics, in 'Revolution Number One':

> You say you'll change the constitution ...
> You tell me it's the institution ...
> But if you go carrying pictures of Chairman Mao,
> You ain't going to make it with anyone anyhow.

Student unrest matters not by virtue of its more heretical advocates, but because it is one manifestation of a strident, very worried, but essentially humanitarian and democratic generation doing its own Thing.

Protest among the Immigrants

The Dilemma of Minority Culture

Gordon K. Lewis*

Few things illustrate more acutely the anomalies of the English political culture than the position of the black Asian and Afro-Caribbean minority communities as a now recognizably permanent feature of the English landscape. It is true, of course, that the political theory that is gradually growing up out of those immigrant communities possesses neither the territorial imperative nor the distinctive linguistic differentiation, the Asiatic groups excepted, of the new Celtic nationalisms. And it is also worth emphasizing, within a climate of Powellite opinion in which the coloured immigrant has increasingly become the scapegoat of English national problems, that it is the Welsh extremists and not the 'black power' ideologues who have reintroduced the strategy of the private bomb into domestic politics. But the coloured immigrant has brought into question at once the ethnic unity and the cultural homogeneity which the English political debate, throughout the full spectrum of its colours, has always been able to take for granted.

Colour has become a new issue, a new frame of reference; and, like imperialism or women's suffrage before it, has cut across the traditional lines of party faith in the responses generated by its presence. Norman St John-Stevas and Lord Soper have more in common with each other on this issue than they have with many of their respective party co-religionists, and the same is true, towards the other edge of the spectrum of prejudice, of Conservatives like Duncan Sandys and Labour Members like Robert Mellish. A 'left-

*The author is Professor of Political Science in the University of Puerto Rico, and author of the recently published *The Growth of the Modern West Indies*, MacGibbon & Kee, 1968, London, 1969. He returned to Britain this last year to study the politics of West Indian communities in England.

wing racialism' is to be found which is no less evil than Powellite Toryism, and has made its own contribution to the escalation of white attitudes since Notting Hill.[1]

Immigrant protest has to be seen within this framework of growing hostility on the part of the host-metropolitan society over the last decade. In part, of course, it is a purely negative protest on the part of groups put unexpectedly on the defensive, constituted of a series of disconnected battles over particular issues, the 1969 Haringey school issue, for example, rather than forming an organized campaign of war with overriding general ends in view. At one point, it will be protest against the police, at another point a defence of the latest immigrant group – the immigrant doctor, the coloured school-leaver in the employment market, the illegal Pakistani entrant – that has been singled out for hostile comment in the latest newspaper attack. Or there is protest, by the more radical elements, at the cultural bias in what has become a distinctive academic growth industry, the new field of 'Race Relations' – a protest that goes as far back as 1948 when the Cardiff Coloured Defence Association questioned Dr Little's strictures on the coloured inhabitants of Bute Town, and then to Neville Maxwell's later critique of Sheila Patterson's *Dark Strangers*. Now *Dark Strangers* was in some ways genuinely pioneer work, but the protest is against the assumption that ultimate assimilation can only be brought about by black and white meeting each other halfway, as if both elements in the total equation are born free and equal; and this illustrates how deeply felt is the resentment of the educated immigrant person against at once the cultural arrogance and the genial optimism of much of the liberal commentary.[2] It would, of course, be misleading to impose a false generality upon the myriad of

1. See generally Paul Foot, *Immigration and Race in British Politics* (Penguin Books, Harmondsworth, 1968), and for a particular case-study Robert C. Reinders, 'Racialism on the Left: E. D. Morel and the Black Horror on the Rhine', *International Review of Social History*, vol. XIII (1968), part I.

2. Sheila Patterson, *Dark Strangers* (Tavistock Publications, London, 1963), and Neville Maxwell, *The Power of Negro Action* (the *Author*, London, 1965).

associations proliferating over a period of two decades or more. So, at times, protest is genuinely collective, albeit short-lived, as the history of organizations like the Campaign Against Racial Discrimination (C.A.R.D.) show; while at other times it bears the stamp of a single flamboyant personality, like Michael Malik, for instance, whose autobiographical memoir uses the image of the Trinidadian *homme moyen sensuel* to frighten English respectability. Looked at from that angle, indeed, the immigrant influx can be seen as nothing so much as an assault by the picaresque sexual mores of the Southern Caribbean upon English puritanism.

This essentially unformed, even inchoate, character of the immigrant organization scene is understandable, of course, once it is remembered that it is the product of a tiny time-period in the history of British race relations. As recently as the 1950s, it was a cardinal article of faith among the new-comers that they were coming 'home' to the 'mother country', and particularly so for the West Indian, so much more culturally English than his Asian counterparts. The lit-erature of disillusionment, correspondingly, following the literature of acclamation, is of recent growth, and to read it is to be made poignantly aware of the general figure of the West Indian, immeasurably saddened by the unexpected hu-miliations of his daily experience, yet responding withal with a characteristic West Indian lack of spite, a capacity, even, to joke about it all, perhaps even ambivalently affectionate for what he so trenchantly derides. There can be little doubt that, as that reservoir of goodwill slowly evaporates, he be-comes increasingly radicalized in his attitude to the total problem. No one who has attended any representative number of meetings of his associations over the two years since the Powell speeches have helped make racialism respectable, or talked at length with any number of migrants, from Brixton to Moss Side, from Tiger Bay to Handsworth, will have failed to note that change of general temper. There is a new atmo-sphere of truculence.

The militant leader more and more supplants the moderate. The thoughtful immigrant is more likely to respond to things

like Marina Maxwell's *Violence in the Toilets*, a literally terri-
fying account of the experience of a black teacher in the Brent
schools, than to the earlier novels, for instance, of E. R.
Braithwaite, *To Sir, With Love* and *Paid Servant*, the central
message of which was that through the possession of immacu-
late manners and sartorial decency the West Indian could
easily work his passage to the graduation ceremonies of British
citizenship. The figures of the hero-worship change: for if
yesterday they were Learie Constantine and Martin Luther
King, today they are Malcolm X, 'our black shining prince',
and the many Anglo-West Indian young militants who model
themselves on his style. More and more, to put it succinctly,
the immigrant sees himself less as a West Indian or a Sikh in
English society, and more as a black man in a white society.
There are times, indeed, as one reads the more apocalyptic
items of the literature, much of it underground and ephemeral,
that one is made to realize that the migrant sees himself as the
victim of a hated and oppressive system, much as the unknown mystic and author of the *Book of Revelation* saw the
Roman imperialism of the first century. The analogy, indeed,
is apposite, for there is a keenly felt personal religious quality
about the West Indian, in particular, evident enough in the
profound contempt in which he holds what, to him, is the
scandalous irreligiosity of the English people.

Faced with this general situation in which, like the Jew, he
feels himself living in desperate exile, the black minority person confronts, essentially, two problems. One is the problem
of strategy; the other is the problem of ideology. As far as
the first problem is concerned, the history of the leading
bodies, the West Indian Standing Conference (W.I.S.C.) and
C.A.R.D., testify to the tremendous difficulties involved in
building up organizations with the special raw material of the
immigrant peoples, who were neither the middle-class radicals
of the Aldermaston marches nor the entrenched producer-
group of the English trade-union movement. The failure of
W.I.S.C. to organize nationally demonstrates, in turn, the
weakness of the federal form of organizational effort and, at
the same time, the danger of seeking to organize everything

from a national centre: the differences between the London
and the Birmingham groups, in fact, nicely illustrate how the
provincial leaderships may resent the superiority-complex of
the people in the national capital, a resentment naturally ex-
acerbated by the emergence of the West Midlands region as
at once the heartland of Powellism and the major citadel of
the urban black worker. The history of C.A.R.D. demonstrated even more complex issues to be resolved. There was, of
course, the confrontation between black militant and white
liberal. But this has been grossly exaggerated by the popular
Press, and even today (1969) West Indian amiability manages
to break through the armour of all black leaders except the
most intractably negrophile. More important, assuredly, was
the problem of discovering the best methods of agitation appropriate to a minority problem which was at one and the
same time a moral cause and an occupational interest. The
issue was never satisfactorily resolved between those, like Dr
David Pitt, who wanted to work in traditional English style
through the channels of the Labour Party, and those who
feared, like his critics, that this would merely make C.A.R.D.
the English equivalent, as it were, of the old coloured legal-
istic black bourgeoisie of the N.A.A.C.P. in the American
struggle. And there was the further division between those
Caribbean leaders like Johnny James, who saw the British
domestic struggle as simply one element in the general movement of the Caribbean revolution (the influence of the political thought of C. L. R. James, the old West Indian Trotskyist
intellectual, has been fundamental here), and those others (of
whom Jeff Crawford in W.I.S.C. is a good example) who saw,
and still see, the problem in terms of the priority of the domestic interests of two million immigrants who, on any showing, are here to stay and must, first and foremost, organize
the terms of their sojourn with the host society. The age-old
conflict between the local and the homeland loyalties, so endemic in the history of American immigrant life, is obvious
enough; and in Britain there is the history of the various
Indian Workers' Associations of the 1950s to show how tempting it is for the immigrant bodies to simply reproduce in a

foreign context the atmosphere of the village politics back home.[3]

The immigrant voices in Britain who seek political expression confront the centralist pressures of a unitary state organization. It is not then surprising that many of them readily follow the Fabian strategy of power at the top, a tactic traditionally rich in the rewards it has given to its English practitioners. That is why many of them will believe that it is worth working with a semi-official body if its chairman is the Archbishop of Canterbury; that explains, too, the still widely held belief of many immigrant public figures that the problem could easily be resolved if only the Queen would appoint a coloured equerry to the Royal Household or, even more, if only a younger member of the Royal Family could be persuaded to marry a coloured partner. The most obvious example of this aspect of the total problem is the history of the immigrant and interracial organizations of the last fifteen years or so in their relations with the civil service structure of the 'Race Relations' scene. Not to collaborate is to lose financial aid, even more, is to abjure the English conviction that the way to get things done is to know the 'important people' at both the national and local governmental levels. To collaborate, on the other hand, is to run the risk of absorption, of being killed by official patronage, of seeming to betray the immigrant interests to a career of comfortable opportunism. It is not too much to say that most of the organizations in the field have decided by now in favour of complete independence, after a long experience of disillusionment. 'The Government', writes a knowledgeable English observer of the scene, summing up the three years between the passage of the Race Relations Bills of 1965 and 1968, 'is no ally to black people; it never meant to get into the position of appearing

3. B. W. Heineman, Jr, 'The Politics of Race: a Study of the Campaign Against Racial Discrimination' (unpublished B.Litt. thesis, Oxford, 1967). For the Asiatic political groups, see R. Desai, *Indian Immigrants in Britain* (O.U.P. for the Institute of Race Relations, London, 1963), and John DeWitt, *Indian Workers' Associations in Britain* (O.U.P. for the Institute of Race Relations, London, 1969).

to be one, but has merely, in its clumsiness, allowed itself to be jockeyed into that position; and it will take all the care it can to see that that never happens again. Three and a half years of treating the Government as in some sort on our side has brought us to the present straits; it would be folly indeed to make the same mistake again.'[4] It is worth adding to that statement, reflecting so accurately as it does the attitude of most self-respecting immigrant leaderships, that the report of the Institute of Race Relations, *Colour and Citizenship* (1969) implicitly repeats the bias in favour of action by the Fabian *état administratif*, so much so indeed that its massive pagination throughout manages to see the immigrant communities still as passive clients of the welfare state instead of independent culture forces making their own positive contribution to the problem, as they see their task, of their own emancipation.[5]

This is the problem, in essence, of strategy. But it obviously relates to the problem of ideology. To will a means is to will an end. The tragedy in one way is that whereas the liberal Establishment has accepted the ideal of the multi-racial society as the desired end, the black intellectual leadership has so far failed to state in any logical fullness its own ideal, has failed, that is to say, to work out what it conceives its status ought to be in the long run. So far it has been satisfied with the 'black power' concept. Yet that concept is an illogical amalgam, so far, of eloquent rhetoric, Garveyite *négritude,* pressure-group political theory and black separatism. As an American imported slogan, it has not so far been adjusted in any analytical sense to the different setting of British society. Its English statements oscillate unsatisfactorily between the call for 'black revolution' and demands, in the best reform group fashion, for changes in housing, educational and immigration policies on the part of the state machinery.[6] Certainly, there is nothing

4. Michael Dummett, 'The Future of Race Relations in Britain, mimeographed, prepared for the West Indian Standing Conference (London, no date), p. 20.

5. *Colour and Citizenship: A Report on British Race Relations* (O.U.P. for the Institute of Race Relations, London, 1969).

6. For examples, see *Black Power in Britain* (Universal Coloured People's Association, London, no date), and *Black People's Alliance, Memorandum* (mimeographed, London, 1969).

to compare with the American literature, Paul Boutelle's *Case for a Black Party*, for example, or the fascinating reprint of the conversations with Trotsky in his Mexican exile in 1939 edited by Paul Breitman.[7] This, of course, is not surprising, granted the antiquity of the American Negro struggle as compared with its novelty in the English case. The fertilization of the English debate by the American will, of course, continue and must be welcome – for the 'problem' in Britain can no longer be regarded as a self-enclosed domestic issue. Yet it is regrettable that, so far, too many of the immigrant efforts in London have been too much the *ad hoc* response to the flying visit of an *éminence grise* of the American vanguard.

What is required, clearly enough, is a restatement of traditional pluralist theory in cultural terms, moving forward from its old obsession with institutional terms. In part, it must be a statement of cultural cosmopolitanism, although in a form more sophisticated than the sort of liberal romantic image of the West Indian picaresque 'spade' adding zest to the English puritan-repressive psyche, based as that image is upon the limited lower order picture of the West Indian in the novels of Selvon and MacInnes. In part, it will be an examination of the possible evolution of separate institutions, so much a part of the life of the Guyana–Trinidad sector of Caribbean society. Nothing could demonstrate more the astonishing parochialism of English academic discussion than the fact that this sort of analysis has hardly yet begun. As its English discussants enter into it they could do no better, perhaps, than to begin their own education by a reading of the definitive statement of the West Indian anthropologist M. G. Smith in his *The Plural Society in the British West Indies* (1955) and the ensuing discussion among the West Indian intelligentsia. The growth of a cultural diversity in which, to employ Furnivall's well-known phrase, the constituent segments mix but do not combine, may well be the new direction that the discussion requires.

Yet one caveat must be entered. The terms of the final

7. Paul Boutelle, *The Case for a Black Party* (Merit Publishers, New York, 1968), and Paul Breitman (ed.), *Leon Trotsky on Black Nationalism and Self-Determination* (Merit Publishers, New York, 1967).

solution, with a black minority so minuscule, will be set overwhelmingly by the white majority. That being so, it is immeasurably urgent that the character of English race attitudes should be correctly analysed. The *Colour and Citizenship* volume correctly dismisses both the colour–class theory, which is the official stance of the British Communist Party, and the theory of the 'archetypal stranger' identified with the writings of Professor Banton.[8] Nor is it enough to suggest, as Bernard Crick's various articles suggest, that the problem offers a new opportunity for the display of English tolerance: to become, after the Jew and the Catholic, the next visible example of national magnanimity may not be a very satisfying role to perform and, in any case, takes immigrant role-theory for granted.[9] Yet in advancing optimistic conclusions from an opinion poll measurement of English attitudes, the *Colour and Citizenship* volume itself may be guilty of adding its own quota of confusion to the debate. The truth is, perhaps, that the technique of quantitative measurement overlooks the tremendous influence, out of all proportion to its numbers, that a militant minority can have on the social climate. And that influence, in its turn, is not simply the myopia of cultural intolerance, but is a racialist antipathy *per se* which has its historical roots – as V. G. Kiernan's book, *The Lords of Human Kind*, shows – in the European conquest of the non-European worlds during the last four centuries. Whether English society can overthrow the inherited debris of that legacy remains yet to be seen. It is worth noting, in that respect, that the *Colour and Citizenship* volume, as its editors have stated, had its genesis, in part, in the inspiration of Gunner Myrdal's classic inquiry into the American race problem. But the original optimism of that inquiry's findings, its liberal assumption, that is to say, that a moral appeal to the conscience of the American Creed would suffice to provoke liberal

8. Michael Banton, *White and Coloured* (Cape, London, 1959), and Harry Bourne, *Racialism, Cause and Cure* (British Communist Party, London, 1965).

9. Bernard Crick, 'The New Meaning of Tolerance', the *Observer*, 13 July 1969.

America to a New Deal for the American Negro, has not in fact been justified by the post-war record; for it is above all the independent militancy of the Negro civil rights movement, more than any white liberal movement, that has been responsible for the gains made over the last fifteen years or so. The assumption, that is to say, that the English inquiry will do for Britain what the Myrdal inquiry allegedly did for the United States looks pretty much like proving to be an empty one.

In the meantime, the character of immigrant protest continues to suffer from the indeterminate status of the immigrant in the society at large. The West Indian, in particular, suffers from his crisis of identity, child of the colonial experience: 'We don't know if we are bloody Jamaicans or bloody British. Blacks here have no stability. We don't have a chance as in Cleveland to elect a Negro mayor.'[10] Thus crippled, it becomes only too easy for black militancy to be corrupted by the careerist who seeks his own advancement. 'It is incredibly easy', in the words of a friendly publication, 'to become a black leader. All that is needed is a letterhead, and a foolscap sheet of paper, that is, the manifesto, not forgetting for a moment the telephone call to Fleet Street and a nice photograph, and by the next day a new Black Power leader is born. Another voice crying out in the wilderness, giving interviews which are meaningless, because the man he is condemning happens to be the man who is interviewing him.'[11] The inevitable consequence is, only too often, apathy on the part of the immigrant masses. They turn inwards into their sports and social welfare organizations, of which the Jamaica Overseas Families' and Friends' Association (J.O.F.F.A.) in South London is as good an example as any. They resist seeing themselves as resistance fighters in the *diaspora*, so that there is a paucity of successful militant papers, with the odd exception like the *West Indian Gazette* edited by the remarkable Claudia Jones in the 1950s. Their leaders will increasingly invoke in their public utterances the remarkable speech in which Winston Churchill, in his long-

10. Quoted by B. W. Heineman, Jr, op. cit., p. 97.
11. *IT*, 14 August 1968.

forgotten Liberal period, reminded the British public that British industrial supremacy owed its genesis to the capital accumulation movements made possible by the exploitation of the West Indian colonial plantations in the eighteenth and nineteenth centuries;[12] but increasingly, too, each new invocation will be accompanied by the suspicion that the British public of the 1960s and 1970s are far too anxious to forget their post-imperial responsibilities to rise to that level of imperial trusteeship.

One final point deserves to be made. 'Every people', said Burke, 'must have some compensation for its slavery.' It is a remarkable testimony to the processes of colonial anglicization that both of the immigrant groups, West Indian and continental Indian, have too much of an ingrained constitutionalist habit to resort, as yet in any case, to strategies of violence. West Indians have been dubbed the 'black Irish'; but so far there has been no West Indian movement seeking, like the Irish Nationalist Party before it, to plan the violent disruption of the parliamentary process. The compensation appears in other, more civilized forms. There are the novels of Andrew Salkey that document the idiocies of English social snobbery. There are the musical forms – the Jamaican 'sound-beat', Trinidad calypso, the Indian ceremonial dirges – that sustain the separate immigrant life-styles. There is the ghetto life, more psychological than physical in character, that builds up defence-mechanisms against the alien English influence; indeed, it is only in the last few years that the West Indian–Somali–Cypriot life of Tiger Bay, cut off from the Cardiff white citizenry by its railway barrier, has given way to assimilative processes precipitated by slum-clearance measures. There is, finally, the intimate tie with the homeland, marked even in the most pro-English group, the West Indians, as the continuing open sale of the Jamaican paper, the *Daily Gleaner,* in the West Indian areas shows. This capacity of the migrant culture to survive has been richly documented, in the

12. See, for example, the quotation from this speech by Rev. Wilfred Woods, in *Dates for Your Diary April*, Camden Committee for Community Relations, April 1969, p. 10.

case of the Puerto Rican exodus to New York Harlem, by Oscar Lewis in his remarkable documentary style, *La Vida*. It only remains, perhaps, for the new Centre for Multi-Racial Studies, set up jointly by the University of Sussex and the University of the West Indies, to undertake a similar service for the new immigrant micro-cultures of English society.

A Protest at Urban Environment

John Page*

The technology of city development is clearly facing a world-wide crisis in the light of its environmental shortcomings. Interestingly, the technologists seem less worried than the citizens who make an important distinction between change and progress. The technologists at least achieve the satisfaction of seeing their ideas turn into urban hardware, even when it is environmentally misconceived. The owners and the occupiers of existing urban property, however, know only too well how easily the dreams of the planners, architects and organizers of urban progress turn into nightmares for individual citizens, who, more often than not have to suffer severe environmental deprivation to make that urban change possible. The present urban technological system does not respect the environmental needs of the individual, whose protest is submerged to the point of ineffectiveness by the power of officialdom so easily the dreams of the planners, architects and organizers of society, and yet not accepting society as a statistical assembly of individuals, each with their individual point of view. Basically, the urban system is out of environmental control as far as the individual is concerned.

It is hardly surprising that we find ourselves in a society where urban change is actively resisted by the majority of citizens close to the places of change, if they can find out soon enough. Naturally there is very great difficulty in finding out soon enough what is going on, for there are plenty of people with a vested interest in not letting others affected know what is happening. The conspiracy of silence is the best way of avoiding protest.

The well-based resistance to change which is usually for the worse, explains the obvious reticence of officialdom to release

*The author is Professor of Building Science at the University of Sheffield and is a member of the Yorkshire--Humberside Planning Council.

information, because the silent secret approach offers the greatest prospect of getting the obviously unacceptable accepted, if at all possible. Protest is stifled by providing no information on which to base an effective protest, or providing it too late; the Skeffington Report on 'People and Planning' exhorts a change, but does not demand it, in a situation where it is the vested interest of officialdom to keep the *status quo* of minimum public involvement. This leaves one doubtful as to whether the Skeffington proposals are workable on a voluntary basis. Even if an individual citizen manages to find out about adverse developments in time, the complications of the administrative machine baffle him, and he is faced with the choice of the escalation of personal costs involved in using lawyers or keeping quiet. For the most part, he grumbles on his way, keeping quiet, so joining that great band of citizens disaffected with the present planning machinery, which claims to represent his social interests, but so obviously in many ways does not. By organizing himself into a wider protest group, he gains some strength, but there are few developments other than airports that affect all citizens simultaneously at one time. Numerically, therefore, a particular protest is usually weakly supported, and officialdom is consequently confirmed in its belief it is serving the wider society. We each, however, tend to have our turn. So piecemeal, year by year, the environmental deterioration steadily proceeds. Many of those that can choose, opt out of the urban environment leaving the city socially deprived. This, in its turn, reduces the level of effective and informed protest, and so the standard deteriorates even more. The acceleration towards down-town status begins.

Any reappraisal of the political problem of environmental deterioration must start with a discussion of the physical and social causes of such deterioration. Basically there are two main aspects of physical environmental deterioration to consider. One aspect is concerned with the physical operation of actually achieving a change of existing urban form, and the appreciable environmental deterioration so often encountered during the planning and construction phases, which may extend over a period of so many years as to become in effect a permanent deterioration for people living near by.

The other aspect is concerned with the permanent environmental changes introduced once the new urban hardware is operational: increased noise, pollution and so on. The official machinery for handling environmental protest essentially gives some but limited weight to the second problem. The deterioration arising while waiting for reconstruction and during the actual construction, which may have a far more destructive environmental influence, is considered transitory and therefore of little importance, though it may sometimes last for ten years or more. The argument that it is going to be hell actually doing it is seldom accepted.

In fact a kind of utopian fallacy hangs over much of official planning practice and there still remains a vague belief that the city will one day be complete and all these transitory redevelopment problems will suddenly disappear. Given time, the well-planned city will be complete. In fact any policy of environmental control needs to be related to the dynamic of urban change which involves continuous reconstruction. This implies that we need not only to control what is done, in the interests of society, but also how it is done. Unfortunately, our laws on how it is done remain for the most part weak and ineffective, if they exist at all.

The deterioration of the physical environment of our cities is primarily the consequence of changing patterns of the use of energy. In some ways, this changing pattern of energy is favourable: for example, the reduction of smoke from domestic premises which has resulted from vastly increased use of gas, electricity and oil. In other ways it is unfavourable: for example, the rising problem of pollution due to motor-vehicle exhausts which has already become a major menace in the U.S.A. and threatens to become an increasingly serious menace in the U.K. I have recently[1] made estimates which

1. See my 'Possible developments in the physical environments of cities in industrialized countries with special reference to the United Kingdom', Conference on the City in the year A.D. 2000, 26–28 September 1969, organized by the Institute of Mechanical Engineers, in *Futures*, June 1970.

showed that urban pollution due to traffic fumes was likely to have increased (using existing technology) by a factor of at least 15 by the year A.D. 2000, compared to A.D. 1950, unless some effective steps are taken to lower pollution levels for individual vehicles. Furthermore, as urban density increases with increasing population pressure, the new urban forms generated will make it more difficult to disperse this pollution effectively to the atmosphere, as effective wind circulation is needed at street level to dilute the pollution with less contaminated air.

The amount of energy used per head is likely to increase by a factor of at least 10 by the year A.D. 2000 and a significant proportion of this energy will be used for transportation purposes. The aircraft transportation system has been growing at a rate of 15 per cent per annum on scheduled services, and 25 per cent or so on charter services, and aircraft are clearly going to become a much more important atmospheric pollution menace in future, especially around airports.

Construction is being revolutionized by the application of vastly increased amounts of energy in equipment, like earthmoving equipment, graders, bulldozers, tower cranes, and so on. Familiar established menaces like pneumatic drills increase in number and are used with greater frequency.

Coming developments in the use of natural gas and electricity imply a total overhaul of our urban energy distribution systems, traditionally buried in our roads. Extrapolating forward on the data given in the Green Paper, 'The Task Ahead',[2] it is easy to show the rate of digging up roads for energy services must increase by a factor of 3 or 4 by 1972, no doubt accompanied by vast amounts of noise from unmuffled pneumatic drills, and extreme traffic congestion with its fume problem.

At the same time, lowered energy costs combined with advances in chemical technology will throw up vast new chemical complexes involving huge problems of environmental pollution and its effective control.

2. Department of Economic Affairs, *The Task Ahead, Economic Assessment to 1972,* Her Majesty's Stationery Office, London, 1969.

On every hand there is mounting evidence that increased rates of deterioration of urban environment must come about if nothing is done. Any extrapolation of environmental factors into the future must therefore engender severe depression to all who are aware of our present *laissez-faire* attitude towards the physical environment, especially if one recognizes the low political prestige that seems to be attached to doing anything about it. Many local politicians seem to be aligned with their technical officers in a conspiracy of silence. It is so much easier that way.

Unfortunately one of the worst by-products of energy utilization is the associated noise-energy problem. Table 1 shows typical noise output in energy units for various sources of urban noise. It shows how adverse some of the recent developments are and, in particular, the magnitude of the noise

Table 1 : *Approximate equivalent sound power radiated in watts emitted by various urban noise hazards.*

Noise source	Approximate sound power radiated in watts	
Human being—soft whisper	0·000000001	
Human being—conversing	0·00005	
Human being—shouting	0·0007	
Luxury limousine at 30 m.p.h.	0·10	
4-tool diesel compressor	0·3	
Miniature passenger car at 30 m.p.h.	0·5	
180 h.p. angle dozer	3·0	
Sports car at 30 m.p.h.	3·0	
Miniature passenger car at 60 m.p.h.	4·0	
Motor-cycle 2-cylinder 4-stroke at 30 m.p.h.	5·0	
Unmuffled concrete breaker	7·0	
Diesel lorry at 30 m.p.h.	7·0	
75-piece orchestra	10·0	(Peak R M S levels over $\frac{1}{8}$ second)
Rubber-tyred tractor scraper	300·0	
S.R.N. 2 Hovercraft	630·0	
V C10 landing	1,600·0	(Under approach path $2\frac{1}{2}$ miles from airport)
Propeller aircraft take-off	10,000·0	
VC10 take-off	100,000·0	(Equivalent power in worst direction)
Supersonic aircraft take-off	500,000·0— 1,000,000·0 ?	(Equivalent power in worst direction)

sources thrown up by modern technology. The mobile society is the noisy society.

How much protection has the ordinary citizen got against noise and pollution? The answer is, in terms of accepted and legally enforceable standards, very little. Transportation technology has clearly failed to set acceptable social standards, and planned developments like the London Motorway Box are going to produce severe environmental deprivation for large numbers of people and consequent financial loss. I remember recently driving in a bus along a residential area of Brussels threatened with a raised motorway down the centre of the road, where at least half the properties on either side were up for sale in a hopeless market. The principle of compensation for substantial environmental deterioration and loss of value has been strongly resisted by government and local authorities, because once acceded, it could open the door to an avalanche of claims in a society with no tradition of environmental standards. There has been some departure from this principle at London Heathrow, but otherwise the picture for any citizen affected is bleak. We have become, in fact, a nation of environmental gamblers, hoping that development goes the other way rather than our way.

The fundamental political question to be answered is what more effective action can be taken to bring our urban systems under environmental control. I am certain any voluntary action will prove quite ineffective in the face of the pressures that exist. There are several good reasons why exhortations directed towards social change cannot be really effective. First, environmental control involves spending more money – for example, on improved silencers, better dust-removing equipment, more land, and so on. Secondly, many individuals are psychologically disposed to enjoy any source of environmental pollution that gives them a sense of individual power. The problem of the adolescent and the motor-cycle or the sports car illustrates this principle too well. Many sports cars and motor-cycles are made deliberately noisier to sell better and afterwards silencers are further doctored to make them even noisier. It is a psychological fact that the noise one makes oneself is more acceptable than the noise others make. Making noise makes the insecure feel more secure.

The problem of resistance to environmental control is not confined to individual resistance. The resistance may be from a whole organization, even from a total local authority. This is particularly common where questions of livelihood are concerned. A good example has been provided by the resistance of the local mining communities to clean-air legislation. This resistance is understandable but not always wise. The effects of pollution on health are well established: bronchitis in many parts of Europe is named 'the English Disease' in colloquial medical terms. The health records of the mining communities are bad, but many still resist strong pressure from central government for effective clean-air programmes. Air from one place moves to another, and parochial policies followed in one place may prejudice the more progressive policies followed in adjacent areas. Can we afford therefore to leave the establishment of environmental standards and policies to individual local authorities, or, acting in our mutual self-interest, do we not have to seek stronger powers at the centre?

As we have had such low standards in the past, many people have come to accept as inevitable the present state of affairs. A common criterion often used in official assessment is whether the new line of action is going to produce a further deterioration beyond the present level, regardless of the fact that the existing situation may be well below any acceptable standard based on consideration of health, well-being and amenity.

The recent political technique for attempting to deal with physical environmental problems seems to have been the establishment of a Royal Commission[3], Committee, or similar body to review the field on a wide basis and to make recommendations to the Government for further action. The report is then left on the shelf and no significant action results. The environment deteriorates further. Its recommendations are

3. This article was written before the recent reorganization of local government structure, and takes no account of the new environmental structure of central government. The new Standing Royal Commission may prove more effective (1970).

considered inappropriate as a consequence of the subsequent changes, and the report is condemned to oblivion as being out of date, and everybody concerned rightly feels they have wasted their time. So the decline goes on.

It would perhaps be appropriate to trace the fate of some of the official environmental reports that have emerged over recent years. In my opinion by far the most successful report, as far as action is concerned, has been the Beaver Committee Report on Clean Air, because a number of the recommendations of the report have been actually adopted and real progress has been made, especially in places where there has been the will to take effective political action. The progress has essentially been towards smokeless rather than clean air, and the problem of control of sulphur dioxide pollution is still far from effective solution. Important gaps in legislation remain.

A number of necessary conditions have had to be fulfilled to make such progress. The first and most basic requirement has been the drafting of the new legislation needed for effective support of the proposed action. The second requirement has been a national financial policy that has helped towards the conversion costs of individual householders so reducing the risk of serious opposition on grounds of individual financial hardship. The third requirement has been the existence of socially acceptable alternative methods of domestic heating that are economically viable, for example, smokeless fuels. As prosperity has increased, fuels of convenience like gas and electricity have replaced more and more traditional fuels, especially in more prosperous areas. Further, the relative price of fuels of convenience has fallen in relation to the cost of traditional fuels like coal and coke. The problem of change has thus been very much eased by advances in technology.

It is interesting to note that in all cases where dramatic progress has been made, real political drive has had to be applied at the local authority level. The existence of the law in itself is not enough; it must be accompanied by the drive and determination to make full use of the new powers offered by the law, and of the administrative and financial aid offered by central government.

As environmental progress costs money, it is not surprising to note that, in general, most progress has been made in the more prosperous regions of the country which, in this respect at least, have had the least severe environmental problems, and slower progress has been made in the less prosperous, highly polluted regions, especially in areas linked with coal production. Many of these areas are desperately depressed environmentally, and need to improve their setting to attract new industry. Unfortunately they are the least well able to afford the extra investment, and the most likely to oppose such change on considerations of existing rather than future livelihood. They are also the areas most conditioned to accept low standards. Places like Sheffield form vigorous exceptions to this kind of statement, and in all such places the quality of the political leadership in environmental fields has been paramount to success.

Serious concern must be expressed about the exemption of statutory undertakings from so much of the legislation concerned with environmental control. The exempted statutory undertakings are bodies of substantial economic power in the wider community, often responsible directly to a Minister in Whitehall. Their actions can have a devasting effect on a local community. One might have hoped that nationalized industries, like the Coal Board, would have shown an exceptional degree of awareness of their general social responsibilities in the environmental field. Four years' experience on the Yorkshire and Humberside Planning Council has convinced me that just the opposite is true, and that the statutory undertakings have for the most part failed to accept their environmental responsibilities. Their record in this area of action demands reconsideration of their privileged status in relation to problems of environmental control at local level. It seems absurd that a Hospital Board can belch black smoke out of its hospital chimneys in defiance of a local authority's clean-air legislation.

If one turns now to the numerous other official reports, the outlook seems bleak for environmental progress in the United Kingdom, for government has ignored the reports, or, at least, the need to face up to the consequent legislation imperative for progress.

The problem of noise, for instance, was discussed in a clear and cogent way in the Report of the Wilson Committee on Noise, which covered the whole field of noise. Little effective action has so far followed despite an accelerating deterioration of the noise environment.[4] In particular, little progress has so far been made towards establishing urban environmental noise standards, and the environment on and around roads, airports and building sites continues to deteriorate. The Wilson Committee, for example, recommended changes in the law relating to statutory undertakings which would remove altogether the present exemption of railway authorities from proceedings for noise nuisance. Suppose the environmental impact of the new proposed high-speed trains was unacceptable to particular local authorities. They are powerless to take any legislative action. As the noise energy produced by transport systems typically varies between the fourth and eighth power of the velocity of travel, how does society intend to deal with this kind of problem within the present law?

Failure to tackle the problem of airport noise is impeding the economic development of the aircraft industry, as the trials and tribulations of the Roskill Commission on the Third London Airport illustrate too well. The Edwards Committee treated the problem of aircraft noise as a trivial feature of their report, and the Roskill Committee in their report have made assumptions about a long-term fall in aircraft noise, but, unsupported by effective international legislation[5], what hope is there of achieving any reduction within the present international climate of aircraft development? Are sonic booms to be symbols of our economic prosperity and export potential, or is the need for environmental standards to be accepted and legislated for politically?

When is some effective action going to be taken about control of noise on building sites, before we are finally bush-hammered and bulldozed into a permanent acoustical daze?

4. A new Committee on Noise has now been set up as part of the environmental reorganization of central government (1970).

5. International agreement has been reached on the long-term reduction of noise from subsonic aircraft. Supersonic aircraft are not included.

Are we to stay with concepts like 'the best means practicable' as a way of justifying the environmental *status quo*?

The Buchanan Report on Traffic in Towns covered another aspect of the environmental problem, but so far little progress has been made towards effectively implementing any of the recommendations. A few scattered pedestrian precincts have emerged, but for the most part the traffic continues in its un-regulated growth, eating cancerously into the structure of our towns destroying unchecked our environment. What effective means of protest has the individual against the traffic problem, for as a community we have never established any standards?

Health and the physical environment, too, are linked. En-vironmental deprivation promotes other problems of the kind discussed in the Seebohm Report. Ill-health of the heads of families and mothers particularly leads on to other social problems. Are we to continue to accept environments that promote the ill-health of their occupants?

Basically, at least, politicians and local government officials seem to think the environmental problems of our technology are too difficult to grapple with, and that it is better to shelve them in the hope that something better will come along, thrown up by some technological benefactor who invents the noiseless plane or the pollution-free car. Effective legislation, in context, would force technological change in a more ac-ceptable social direction.

All projective studies of the future point towards a rapidly accelerating decline of the urban environment, if we continue our present *laissez-faire* approach. There is a real need to take effective anticipatory measures now. This implies that great effort must be directed towards the problem of establishing the necessary standards for urban living, and that these stan-dards must be based on concepts related to demographic and technological growth. There is an inherent danger in attempt-ing to control the future on the standards of the past. Without action, the future is clearly going to be worse than the past. The necessary legislation needs to be drafted with urgency, followed by the adoption of new urban policies directed to-wards positive environmental improvement of cities. This will demand a determined attempt to upgrade the environmental education of architects, town planners, engineers and other officials in town halls. It will imply measures unpopular with pressure groups with vested interests in resisting progress in the control of noxious activities. Above all, it will require political vision to set up goals for the future, goals that are realistic and capable of economic achievement, but goals that are based on human standards and human needs, and not standards that emerge as the accidental by-products of the technology of a particular time.

My protest is therefore against our present political indifference to the future of our urban physical environment, the lack of political drive and foresight, the low priority allocated to environmental legislation, the exception of statutory undertakings for so many of the provisions of the law concerned with environment. I add to my protest my deep concern about the secrecy of officialdom and lack of public discussion of the environmental consequences of planning decisions. Finally, I seek the creation of organizations to represent formally the environmental interests of the citizens, and to provide an effective channel of protest, compulsorily consulted. I reject the voluntary nature of the Skeffington proposals, and demand that the public have the right to be consulted on all planning decisions with serious environmental consequences. I object strongly to the lack of environmental control during the construction process and seek more effective laws to deal with disturbance during construction.

When planners decide what to do, it is often easier for them to forget the subtler consequences of their actions. Towns should be fine places in which to live. Our technology has made too many of them into places from which we try to escape. Rustication unfortunately has become easier for the individual than effective environmental protest, and men no longer live in cities in order that they may be civilized. This is not a necessary state of affairs, but a state we have come to accept through our environmental complacency.

Protest and Disturbance in the Trade-Union Movement

Lawrence Daly*

If there is anything I like better than an unofficial job it's an unofficial strike. And if there's anything I like better than an unofficial strike it's an unofficial lightning strike.
— Brendan Behan, *Confessions of an Irish Rebel*.

Every four or five years in Britain we register our approval or otherwise of the way things are going. When the situation seems really desperate the Labour Party is elected to power with a mandate for change. Simultaneously, a peculiar mental *volte-face* occurs inside the leadership of the trade union movement. Hitherto outside the intimate ring of power-holders, the unions find themselves being cultivated by the politicians, they find their views being carefully listened to, if not acted upon, and they may even experience the difficulties of government by being asked by the Government to take part in some decisions themselves.

This can be a most unnerving situation. The trade union movement is by origin and definition one of protest, a reaction to political and industrial exploitation. Its foundations are the aspirations of workers who want security and freedom and who do not care, and have not cared, a fig about the 'immutable laws' of *laissez-faire*, of diminishing returns, of marginal product or the balance of payments. With a government of indisputable anti-socialists, the trade union movement can unashamedly adopt an idealistic stance. It can rail against the Establishment; it can proclaim lofty ideals; it can resist and struggle. The barricades to be stormed are clear. What to do when they have been won does not seem of prime importance. But when the political wing of the movement achieves power, what a difference! The 'practical' obstacles to change

*The author is Secretary of the National Union of Mineworkers.

are suddenly discovered, the views of those who want radical change are felt to be rash and, though to be sympathized with, impracticable. The injustices of society are no longer intolerable but must be further studied. Before long, criticism is 'destructive' and protest and resistance is undermining the political strength of a decidedly 'pro-working-class government'.

This is a recurrent problem faced by trade unions in Britain when a 'sympathetic' government is in power. Should they squeeze it dry of 'concessions' or should they sacrifice the short- to the long-term advantage? It is a question which has been implicitly at the centre of debate since 1964. And the debate has been the more bitter because of the wide differences in the political views of those in the movement. Thus there is controversy in the movement at the moment and there is more controversy than if a Conservative government were in office. But of late the disputes inside the movement have become more fundamental in character. The reason for this is that the changes in society are becoming more fundamental. There have always been a number of dimensions to conflict inside the trade union movement. There has been conflict between industrial interests, between different political interests and between personalities jockeying for power. These conflicts have, however, taken place in the context of an economic structure based mainly on private enterprise, and on the assumption that national sovereignty was a reality. The fact that the situation is changing has created a general social malaise of which the debate in the trade union movement is one of the most obvious manifestations – it is, after all, the only forum of more or less continuous political discussion outside the political parties.

The nature of the changes causing the malaise are basically twofold though there are many side-effects. Probably the chief spur to internal argument in the trade union movement is the growing centralization of economic decision-making. This is not due to the advance of a new ideology but to the development of production techniques and the improvement of communications and transport. Whilst markets were local and production could be confined to relatively small units, the pattern of ownership could be such that many people could make individually effective investment decisions. The growth of markets and the cost of mass production in factory complexes employing enormous amounts of capital has meant that owners of capital have had to band together to take investment decisions: bigger and bigger investment decisions are taken by fewer and fewer people. Economic power is being concentrated in direct proportion to the increase in size of business organization, both public and private. In the private sphere the number of mergers is indicative of this. In 1968, for example, spending on mergers reached a level unequalled in any other year since the introduction of limited liability. The T.U.C. *Economic Review,* 1969, pointed out that annual expenditure on mergers rose from about £100 million a year in the mid-fifties to £750 million per year between 1964 and 1968. In the latter year, the twenty-eight largest companies in Britain had half the country's total manufacturing assets – 11 per cent more than in 1958. Nor is this process confined within the artificial economic limits of national boundaries. The large international corporation and the principles that determine its attitudes and activities have been the subject of several important studies recently. The real purpose of these studies has been to show the extent to which 'indigenous' industry is falling into the hands of Americans and to show how key decisions affecting investment in Britain and Europe are being taken in the United States. In 1966, about 10 per cent of the output of British manufacturing industry was in the hands of the U.S.-controlled firms and if the trend continues the proportion will rise to 20–25 per cent in 1981.[1] In political terms, the situation is more serious than even these figures indicate because it is not merely a question of economic decisions affecting workers in Britain being taken in the United States, but rather of large corporations struggling to free themselves from the jurisdiction of any national government.

1. J. H. Dunning, *The Role of American Investment in the British Economy,* Political and Economic Planning, 1969.

It is partly this which has led to the drive to cut down national economic barriers as, for example, in the Common Market. On the other hand, the Common Market has also received support because some have felt that only a wider political grouping could exercise any control over the European companies which have already been formed.

In the public sphere there is a similar centralization of economic decision-making. The *overall* level of consumption and production are largely determined by central government decision and a big proportion of national investment is made by the Exchequer. And, of course, there are the nationalized industries. Nationalization has been both the result of, and the signal for, an increasing centralization of decision-making in the industries concerned. It was hoped by many that public ownership would be a socialist foot in a capitalist door but, generally speaking, its effect has been to enable capitalism to work better. Moreover, the public enterprises have themselves been operated according to the tenets of private enterprise.

So, the growing size of economic enterprise and the centralization of decision-making is one of the main developments in economic structure. The other which is relevant here is increasing specialization. This goes hand in hand with more massive business organization. These two trends are beginning to have a profound effect on trade unions. The ideal union organization is one which focuses its resources and takes its decisions opposite those points at which the employer takes economic decisions. To take a contemporary example, it would not be an ideal situation or even a practicable proposition for a union to concentrate its resources at national level to conduct industry-wide bargaining if in fact the distribution of economic power was such that the real bargaining was done at factory level. The evolution of the economy has seemed to call for a stronger central trade union authority to counter the centralization of long-term economic power and a rearrangement of internal union organization to take account of short-term economic power exercised locally by shop stewards due to specialization. It is this first requirement which has given rise to so much heart-burn inside the movement and it cannot be denied that, however necessary – even inevitable – the process may be, there are considerable dangers.

Perhaps the main danger concerns what the relationship of the T.U.C. should be to the State and to trade unionists. As long ago as 1946 Walter Citrine told the T.U.C. that trade unions had passed '. . . from an era of propaganda to one of responsibility'. One wonders if he would feel the same today with the changing structure of the work force and with trade union membership still looking unhealthy. But the sentiment he expressed in 1946 represents the view of a large number of contemporary leaders in the movement. How far should the movement, or any part of it, become part of the apparatus of the State? How far should the trade unions and the T.U.C. participate in decisions of government? What is the effect on the membership of the centralization of authority, let alone the effect of the spectacle of trade union leaders involving themselves as members of the General Council in government decisions? One view – the predominant one at the moment – is that if economic decisions are centralized the trade union movement should jump at the chance of being involved in them on behalf of the working class. The opposite view is that the movement must basically remain one of protest, a potential instrument of social revolution, and that the assumption of 're-sponsibility' in a social system based on private greed can only destroy the hope of more fundamental change.

If the trade unions aim to be 'respected and respectful' – an aspiration of the nineteenth-century craft unions – they could erode their own strength in several ways: they could assume the pragmatic values of rulers and forget or postpone indefinitely idealistic objectives; they could become tightly bound by establishment forces, and, so doing, could lose the confidence of their members. It is classic Marxist theory (according to one school at any rate) that trade unions cannot '. . . in themselves be vehicles of an advance towards socialism. Trade unionism, in whatever form, . . . is an incomplete and deformed variant of class consciousness, which must at any cost be transcended by a growth of *political* consciousness, created and sustained in a *party*.'[2] Trade unions, it would appear, according to this theory, are the passive instrument and the party is the active developer of new theories of social organization. Moreover, the party includes middle-class and intellectual elements as all such movements have shown. Experience tends to justify this view. Trade unions *have* made limited demands on governments and employers; they have never used industrial power to achieve fundamental political ends. The General Strike demonstrated just how dependent the movement was on the political party and its leadership. In Britain, of course, the party in question has not been revolutionary but has evolved a comprehensive set of ideas based on the concept of the 'mixed economy'. When in power, it has itself concentrated on a limited set of reforms; so, on the face of it, there is no reason why the trade unions could not continue to co-operate and participate in the reforms which it believes desirable. But the relationship between the trade union movement and its political arm has changed and will change even more in the future. The centralization of economic power has caused the movement to evolve a coherent set of interrelated policies rather than a series of individual, and sometimes contradictory, reactions to specific proposals. The T.U.C. *Economic Reviews* are by far the best example of this. The movement has never before had such clearly defined collective views on the balance of payments, productive potential, incomes policy, taxation, industrial reorganization, the distribution of wealth and a whole range of economic issues. Neither will collective thinking be limited to the economic problem. George Woodcock, at the 1968 Conference of Executives, said that the 1968 *Review* was concentrating on economic matters because '... they are *the* problems of today. But in future years, if this first year's experiment succeeds, there may be other problems we can deal with collectively as we are trying to deal with these things today.'

In developing such collective views and in supplying the evidence to support them the movement has imported a force

2. Perry Anderson, 'The Limits and Possibilities of Trade Union Action', *The Incompatibles*, Penguin Special.

of intellectuals, and as more white-collar workers are recruited into trade union ranks, their combined influence increases. Alongside this there is a growing rank-and-file movement on basic demands such as equal pay and industrial democracy. The trade union movement is thus becoming an important rival in the development of social organization theory to the Labour Party itself and since the latter is heavily dependent on the former for funds, and since there are many senior members of the Labour Party both in and outside Parliament with close links with the trade union movement, the coherently set out collective views of trade unionists are likely to have more and more impact on the Labour Party's programme. In this way, the trade union movement, especially when a Labour government is in power, will seem to be almost an organ of government.

The uneasiness in the contemporary trade union movement is largely the result of this dilemma – how to be at one and the same time an organization of protest and of social change and yet a participator in pragmatic central government decisions. In recent years the movement has been torn apart by rows on particular policies – incomes policy, industrial relations policy – and these illustrate the underlying issue. Should the T.U.C. attempt to control the movement of wages and salaries, and should it practically replace the D.E.P. by acting as an industrial conciliator? As it is, the role it has been forced to take on has increased rank-and-file sense of bewilderment. Crucially important decisions and policies are all taken and evolved at a level utterly remote from the individual. The same process in society at large has resulted in the feeling that parliamentary parties are powerless to change society. The individual wanders in a Kafka-esque nightmare in which a mindless, fathomless social machine manipulates his destiny. This bewilderment has powerful implications for the trade union movement.

If the individual feels that it is too remote, if he identifies it with the organs of government, he *can* desert it. He cannot desert society, but *can* give vent to his feelings by terminating either his membership of, or his interest in, the unions. If, at the same time, the capitalist forces in society can maintain reasonably full employment and a rise in living standards, the whole union movement could become swallowed up in a corporate state. For me, the lesson is that the movement should formulate ideas about the society it would like ultimately to see and be less satisfied with minimal short-term objectives: more demands and less compromise. The continual acceptance of less than the ideal and the justification of acceptance to members wear the edge off the idealistic spirit of those concerned. Preoccupation with short-term problems and with 'what is possible in the existing situation' breeds the attitude that it is *not* possible to change things very much; that 'it is all more complicated than that'; that theory is all very well but it is not 'practical'. It is interesting to recall the words of Keynes that '... the ideas of economists and philosophers are more powerful than is commonly understood. Indeed, the world is ruled by little else. Practical men who believe themselves to be quite exempt from any intellectual influence are usually the slaves of some defunct economist.'

Dissatisfaction with employer attitudes and trade union timidity often takes the form of unofficial strikes – the impact of which on the economy has been wildly exaggerated by the media, for political reasons. The penal sanctions proposed by the Government in *In Place of Strife* would not have solved the problem. It will remain with us as long as people have to work for low wages, in uncongenial conditions, and are subject to managerial authoritarianism. Perhaps the heart of the matter was best summarized by William Straker (speaking for the Miners' Federation) when, in 1919, he said to the Sankey Commission: 'Many good people have come to the conclusion that working people are so unreasonable that it is useless trying to satisfy them. The fact is that the unrest is deeper than pounds, shillings and pence, necessary as they are. The root of the matter is the straining of the spirit of man to be free.'

When men (or women) decide to withdraw their labour it is usually because experience has taught them that silent pain evokes no response. It may well be that protest and disturbance will remain always with us. But to the extent that it expresses the striving of working people for economic and social justice it is to be welcomed. More so, if, at the same time it impels us in the direction of a more genuinely democratic society than we know today.

The Labour Back-Bencher

Rt Hon. Douglas Houghton, C.H., M.P.*

So much is said and written about Parliament and all its works that those of us in the thick of it scarcely know what to believe. My particular study for the past two and a half years has been the Government back-bencher. I preside over him and try to keep him in good humour, and calm fears that his licence may be withdrawn by an angry master. Ian Gilmour, M.P. (in *The Body Politic*) says that 'Government back-benchers, like Parliament itself, are not a body, they are an artificial entity'. Nothing in Parliament is, I suppose, a body. Certainly not the Opposition, and not even the Government.

In the Labour Party back-benchers are, let us say, a natural entity. They are supposed to subscribe to the same policies; all sign the same pledges; all are endorsed by the same party executive; and all are elected to support the same party caucus or government. When they do so they are scorned as lobby-fodder; when they don't they are branded as rebels and get their names in the papers. There is a whole library about Parliament in which tame, docile, subservient Members come in for criticism. 'The usual estimate of back-benchers', says Ian Gilmour, 'is that they are powerless and contemptible, careless of conscience and punctilious in discipline, hungry for patronage, bullied by the Whips and their local parties alike. Back-benchers never have had a good press.'

This legend is hallowed by antiquity. Coleridge, Meredith and Kipling all embroidered it. Gilbert and Sullivan composed a ditty on this theme in *Iolanthe*. The Sentry's song reported of M.P.s that

*The author is chairman of the Parliamentary Labour Party. Some paragraphs in this essay originally formed part of his 'Giving Backbench M.P.s a Role in Decision Making' in *The Times*, 28 August 1969 – by permission of whose editor they are reprinted.

> if they've brain and cerebellum too:
> They have to leave both outside
> And vote as their leaders tell 'em to.

Almost all M.P.s who write about their trade go out of their way to put the record straight – Mr Ian Gilmour himself, and Mr Angus Maude also (*The Common Problem*): 'The independence of the back-bench M.P., currently so thoughtlessly dismissed as non-existent, still survives and is jealously guarded.' By contrast a layman's account of the matter is that 'Through his control of his party the Prime Minister can be certain that the Commons will support his Government and accept his measures. His will becomes an Act of Parliament ...' (G. W. Jones in *Crisis in British Government*, edited by W. J. Stankiewiez).

There are some doubts about this. In 1969, two major Government Bills were dropped: Lords reform, after nine days of obstruction in Committee Stage on the floor of the House of Commons; and the Bill dealing with unconstitutional strikes, which was bartered with the T.U.C. for their 'solemn and binding undertaking'. In fact two major proposals in the Government's economic strategy were abandoned under strong back-bench pressure (the second one was the substantial saving to be made on sickness benefit by changes in the 'first three days' rule). The present (1966) Parliament has, therefore, provided ample evidence of the stubborn independence of the back-bencher with its displays of indiscipline, disobedience and rebellion.

The traditional sequel to this is expected to be 'a tighter rein' as the Whips crack down. Heads may fall. Yet 'when an M.P. decides that he cannot support his party there is not much the Whips can do. They can if they wish have the whip withdrawn ...' (Ian Gilmour). Can they? Not from a Labour back-bencher without a decision of a party meeting on a recommendation from the Shadow Cabinet (when in opposition), or the back-bench Liaison Committee when in government.

Experience proves that disciplinary action is no remedy for serious discontent, still less for disunity. Discipline in parliamentary parties is really part of the mythology of politics. There are few and slender sanctions behind it. The Tories are believed to have used the hope of patronage as a carrot, and the threat of trouble in the constituency party as a stick to secure good behaviour. A Labour Chief Whip can use neither. A Prime Minister who, quite rightly, will make no political honours either for M.P.s or for party workers in the constituencies, and who rules out hereditary titles of any kind, has little consolation to offer to disappointed or disaffected supporters. That is why a Labour Prime Minister must rely upon a different kind of cement to keep his party together. There can be nothing subtle or secret about it. No Labour rebel can be punished behind the scenes. What is done has to be seen to be done. Labour's disciplines are imposed in public.

The firm principle behind disciplinary powers is that no Member may have his membership of the Parliamentary Party, or his full freedom of action within it, curtailed or taken away except by meeting of the Parliamentary Party. The meeting must be properly convened for that purpose, held only after due notice, and the right of self-defence given to the accused. The sole disciplinary action a Labour Chief Whip can take off his own bat is a reprimand. The role of the Chief Whip in the whole judicial system of the party is to make his recommendation to the Shadow Cabinet when in opposition, or the Liaision Committee when in government. That recommendation may be endorsed, modified, or even totally rejected by the committee. The Liaison Committee comprises four elected back-bench members, and the leader of the House and Chief Whip *ex-officio*. This Committee has the same authority as the Shadow Cabinet in matters of discipline.

It follows that if these elaborate safeguards against the use of arbitrary power, hidden or overt, against a delinquent back-bencher are judged to be essential, there has to be a code of law. Punishment can be meted out only for a breach of an accepted code of conduct.

The basis of all crime and punishment in the Parliamentary Labour Party from the earliest days was either intolerable behaviour, like attacking one's friends or being consistently out of step on policy, or voting in the House of Commons contrary to a decision of a Party Meeting. These have stood since the inception of the Parliamentary Party in 1906. The first is usually interpreted with tolerance and even indulgence. The second causes most of the trouble, and for four reasons. First, there is a conscience clause which permits abstention (only) on grounds of deeply held personal conviction (put there originally for the benefit of pacifists and temperance reformers). Secondly, it is not always possible to stop some particular mischief and bring offenders within reach of the Code of Conduct by getting a decision of the Parliamentary Labour Party in time and in the terms to do it. Thirdly, the undue influence on Party decisions which 70 ministerial votes may throw into the scales lessens the respect which some members may feel towards Party decisions. And, fourthly, when it comes to rebellion there is safety in numbers.

The emotional and political difficulties, not to mention damage to personal relationships, of the trial and punishment of platoons of rebels need no elaboration. Twenty speeches from the dock, in self-defence, one after another, hour after hour, can do a great deal more harm than good.

Early in 1969 it was found necessary to add to the crime book deliberate abstention on a vote of confidence in a Labour Government. This followed an incident where 20 Labour Members stayed out of the Lobby on a Government motion which the Chief Whip had forewarned all concerned would be a vote of confidence. This had never happened before and no provision had been made for it in the Code of Conduct. Abstention from a vote of confidence is now a serious offence with no excuses or concessions to conscience. The lesson to be drawn from this unusual occurrence is that the Government should beware of making a formal challenge to the Opposition when in reality it is a challenge to discontent *within* the Government party itself.

A common misconception about discipline is that when the Labour Party is in government, the Prime Minister or the Chief Whip, or both, have greater authority over the back-benchers than in periods of opposition. That is not so. The

Liaison Committee of elected back-benchers, with the Leader of the House and the Chief Whip *ex-officio*, have precisely the same powers (and restraints) over crime and punishment as the Shadow Cabinet. That is not to deny that other influences towards party unity and individual behaviour are stronger when the party is in government. Of course they are, and for obvious reasons. But experience has shown that on some issues of policy Labour Members can be obdurate to the point of defiance, no matter what the consequences.

If disciplinary measures may fail in their purpose, what is the alternative? Can underlying causes of disaffection be removed or reduced to the absolute minimum?

One way is for Government to avoid straining the loyalty of its supporters too far. The root cause of these troubles in the Parliamentary Labour Party has been politically repugnant measures which they have been pressed to support. It has been claimed that some of these measures (for example, prices and incomes legislation, and health charges) were not only contrary to Party policy but in breach of pledges given by party leaders. No changes in the machinery for consultation and of party management will overcome objections of great strength and determination on the Government back-benches. The Government must either compromise, in which case they will be accused of weakness and surrender to back-bench pressure, or 'force' unpopular measures through the House in face of open revolt within the Party if they feel strong enough to do so. (On an increase in health charges, the Government withstood a determined attack by 50 back-benchers because it was known that the Conservative Opposition would not for doctrinal reasons vote against charges which they are pledged in principle to introduce themselves.)

In general, however, the more consultation between Ministers and the back-benchers, the greater the harmony between them. This is the particular difficulty of being in the Government party. When in Opposition, the Leader, Deputy Leader, Chief Whip and the 'Shadow Cabinet' of twelve members, were elected by ballot at the beginning of each session. Policy decisions of the 'Shadow Cabinet' were reported to weekly

Party meetings for approval. Specialist groups of back-benchers and 'Shadow Ministers' were busy with studies and discussions to enable them to become a well-informed and constructive Opposition. These groups were constantly feeding the Shadow Cabinet with facts and opinions upon which decisions on policy could be made. The Parliamentary Party was a hive of industry and was happy in its work.

This activity and participation of back-benchers was cut off when the Party became the Government. Their role changed. It was not to mount opposition and formulate alternative policies, but to support the Government. The Parliamentary Party ceased to have the same close relationship with its leaders. A new and less intimate form of contact with them was secured through an elected Liaison Committee composed of an elected Chairman, three Vice-Chairmen, the Leader of the House and the Chief Whip.

The change from participation in formulating Opposition policies to non-participation in government creates a gap which it has been difficult to bridge. It becomes dangerous to Party unity when the Government has to embark on unpopular policies which have not carried conviction with a large section of the Party. This gap can be narrowed only by closer liaison, a coming together if not in joint responsibility, at least in mutual understanding. The initiative and responsibility for achieving this rests with Ministers, and it needs conscious effort and perseverance to do it. Otherwise, the Party and the Government drift apart and lead separate lives.

No remedy for this state of affairs is possible without a close and confidential relationship between Ministers and their back-bench supporters, which may startle traditionalists in parliamentary practice. It is, however, important for a Government to keep the goodwill and support of its own back-benchers, and this is the only way. Otherwise, Government back-benchers will complain (as they have) that they are the last to be consulted. Once Government intentions and actions are announced, it takes a serious revolt in the Party to change them. This is bad for the morale of the back-benchers and is disheartening for supporters in the country. Charges of disloyalty may be made and the question of penal sanctions may be raised. This can become both tiresome and futile.

The truth is that the back-bencher today is not mere lobby-fodder, dozing in the library waiting for the division bells to ring. He is as restive as many of his constituents, especially the younger ones. Votes at 18 will by no means satisfy their demands for a share in the use of power, any more than a young M.P. is satisfied to be merely a check on the use of power by someone else. If he is a Government supporter he aims at being able to influence decisions and policies before finality is reached. His support must not be taken for granted in controversial matters. He wants to be 'in' on things.

To meet this new and thrusting demand, a significant recasting of the role of back-bencher has been undertaken in recent months. Party meetings are held more frequently; Ministers are requested to be present to speak, or answer questions; and at the close of every meeting a full account of the proceedings is given by the Chairman to Lobby Correspondents. The specialist work is undertaken by closer study and discussion in numerous 'Subject Groups' broadly related to the work of individual Ministers. Regional interests and problems are taken care of by 'Regional Groups'. The Subject Groups are the point of the most sensitive and confidential contact between back-benchers and Ministers. For greater co-ordination and better understanding of overall policy, the Special Group Chairmen have meetings of their own and a monthly meeting with the Prime Minister.

The nature of the relationship between the Subject Group Chairmen and their respective departmental Ministers largely depends upon events, but above all on trust. The aim of the new arrangements is to enable Ministers to have constant help and advice from a Party viewpoint. Nothing angers the back-benchers more than to be taken completely by surprise by Ministerial announcements of, for example, increased charges for health services and school meals. Every possible safeguard will be taken against this happening in future.

The form and timing of this consultation with the Subject Group Chairman is left to the discretion of the Minister, though the Subject Groups will want to see Ministers to put their own ideas and proposals on matters of current interest.

The test of the success of this closer liaison will be the avoidance both of causes of friction and misunderstanding, and 'failure of communications'. Within reason the Subject Group Chairman should know what his Minister is doing; the members of the Group should have a feeling of being associated with the work of the Government in their particular field of interest. Ministers can talk to the Groups, brief them and generally try to keep in step with them. Otherwise, the danger is that Government back-benchers may feel they have little influence on decisions and policies which they find objectionable and therefore feel free to oppose. This is the rift which all this network of 'liaison', contact and consultation is designed to avoid.

And then, to make sure that there is overall contact and consultation with back-benchers, weekly meetings take place between the Prime Minister and the Chairman of the Parliamentary Party. These are without precedent in any previous Labour Government. They provide an opportunity for a weekly look at what is going on, and what is coming forward in Government action, policies and parliamentary business. Anything relevant to the unity and morale of the Parliamentary Party is within the scope of these informal talks begun in 1969 on the initiative of the Prime Minister.

These arrangements are the culmination of a long but steady process of strengthening liaison between the back-benchers and the Government. This is more important in a Labour administration because the traditional democratic processes in our Party lead to firmer expectations about consultation and involvement in policy-making decisions.

All this, of course, is the machinery of the matter. The need for it arises because Government thinking can be so out of touch with a substantial body of opinion in the Party, both in Parliament and in the country. When this occurs on economic and financial policies, or on foreign affairs, back-benchers are usually prepared to accept ministerial judgement on complex matters upon which government has fuller information and advice. But on some things – industrial relations particularly – at least a hundred Labour back-benchers claim to know better than ministerial academics. What puzzled and angered many of the 'trade union M.P.s' was how the Government came to reach the conclusions they did. Where did the inspiration and advice to fly in the face of Donovan come from? The plainest warnings from back-benchers (not to mention the T.U.C.) appeared to make little impression. During many hours in seven meetings of the Parliamentary Labour Party not half a dozen voices were raised to support the Government's so-called penal clauses. And on health charges, the Government must have known what they were doing to the Labour Party, even if the clumsiness of announcing these controversial increases for teeth and spectacles was largely accidental.

These and other traumatic experiences have built up the demand for closer liaison between back-benchers and the Government. This back-bench unrest has brought about a new dimension and added strength to the Liaison Committee. Its terms of reference now go far beyond the relatively narrow issues of Party management and a forward look at parliamentary business. It is now more than a sounding-board from which the Chief Whip reports to the Prime Minister and the Cabinet. The Liaison Committee, and in particular the Party Chairman, claims the right to do this directly. The root of this worrying problem is that too many Labour Ministers are removed by education and life's experience from the great mass of the Movement outside, and from a substantial section of Labour M.P.s in Parliament. They appear at times to be alienated from working-class thinking.

This is 'the failure of communications' we hear so much about. This is a greater danger within the Labour Party because of the ascendancy of an intellectual élite within the power structure of the Parliamentary Party and the Government so widely separated from the 'grass roots' of the rank and file. That is what made the resignations of Gunter and George Brown such a misfortune.

This goes far more deeply into questions of Party leadership and Cabinet policy-making than the simple mechanism of consultation and liaison will overcome. Only plain warnings may do it, but these weaken government and cause divisions within the Party.

The function of the back-bencher, as an essential part of our system of parliamentary government, is changing and needs constant reassessment. While the discontents and heart-searchings continue in Parliament, government by strikes, marches, demonstrations, protests and actual revolt gains momentum and success. These methods cannot, however, change the law, though they can influence reforms and may even make them possible. All forms of articulate opinion are relevant and important today.

There are two directions in which the back-bencher has put himself at the head of some contemporary demands. One is for more facilities for dealing with moral questions and other matters upon which deep personal convictions cut across Party lines and inhibit official Party policies and government action (for example: divorce, homosexuality, abortion, Sunday entertainment and even capital punishment). The other is in the right of scrutiny and investigation into administration and development in areas of government aid, participation or control (for example, nationalized industries, scientific research and experiment, and agriculture).

The first has persuaded the Labour Government to end the hypocrisies and frustrations of the traditional procedure on Private Members' Bills. Whereas in the past organized minority obstruction could kill any controversial Bill for want of time, the Labour Government has given facilities for Parliament to come to conclusions upon Bills which reflect a substantial body of opinion in the House and outside in favour of change. This has enabled Parliament to function in a field in which parties and governments fear to tread. Repeated attempts to bring about reforms in laws relating to sexual and marital life have been defeated in previous Parliaments simply by minority obstruction which governments have not had the will to stop. In these matters the back-benchers on both sides of the House have had their greatest triumphs. Not since A.

P. Herbert's Divorce Bill over thirty years ago has this been possible. Governments have not previously raised a finger to end the filibuster on Private Members' Bills. They have cynically regarded them as the appropriate means of parliamentary action in some contentious non-party matters, knowing full well that it requires only half a dozen resolute opponents to wreck any such Bill.

On Select Committees, the struggle of the back-bencher to require government departments to reveal themselves and their activities still continues. Discontent has been aroused by the Government's objection to prolonging the life of specialist Select Committees (for example, Agriculture) beyond the point at which the Government feels the Committee has fulfilled its purpose. In other cases (for example, Bank of England) the Government has limited the scope of the Select Committee and has banned excursions into sensitive fields of policy. It is clear that the Sessional Committee in our Parliament will not be copied from the Congressional Committee in the U.S.A. Nonetheless, the area of back-bench study of administration has been widened considerably in the past four years. Limitations of parliamentary staff and accommodation are stressed by the Leader of the House whenever this subject is raised.

That, however, is only part of the wider alliance within the Establishment to discourage back-benchers from being over-zealous in their ambitions to usurp the functions and responsibilities of the Executive. Inadequacies in pay, accommodation, secretarial and other help in doing their job curb a Member of Parliament's potentiality for mischief. The devil, it is said, finds work for idle hands to do – but not without a shorthand typist, or a place to put one's papers, or a desk of one's own; and not when the more work, the greater the expense and the less the take-home pay. There are a few institutions in Britain still operating in the last century but none, as far as I am aware, is screeching about modernization and efficiency and new ideas from a Victorian slum like the Palace of Westminster, which has not even enough lavatories.

But the great awakening has begun. What junior clerks

have been given to do their work for half a century, including a desk to work at, and stamps and all that, are now to be given to Members of Parliament without compelling them to cut down on food and to spend nights on the train because it is cheaper than an hotel bedroom. I believe that the back-bencher is now mobilizing for an advance on the concentration of ministerial and executive power. The broad institutional framework of Parliament itself will, I hope, be preserved against the possibility of a far different and sinister assault, but discontents within it could propel Parliament towards a truer democracy within the next decade.

Some Literature on Student Revolt

A. H. Hanson*

The title of this essay is intended to be precise. I have not read
– nor do I intend to read – *all* the literature with which it is
concerned, but I have read enough to form some judgement
of its quality and importance. This literature is not primarily
devoted to the ideas that students have produced about reforming university institutions, but to the idea that some
students – usually called 'radicals' – have conceived of *captur-
ing* these institutions and of using them for purposes entirely
different from those that they at present serve: as bases for
the transformation of the whole social and political order. It
is both to this idea and to the activities through which it finds
expression that the books and articles I shall be mentioning
are mainly devoted. A possible objection to this self-imposed
limitation of scope is that, in practice, distinction between
'radicals' and 'reformers' is difficult to make, since radicals
take up the cause of reform for tactical purposes, while reformers, when feeling frustrated, are liable to come under the
influence of the radicals and to adopt their characteristic
methods. The relationship between the two is indeed a fluctuat-
ing one, and differs from university to university and from
country to country. Nevertheless, the distinction, although
very fuzzy at the edges, is real; for among the large number
of students who feel specific dissatisfactions for which they

*The author is Professor of Politics at Leeds University and has written
Public Enterprise and Economic Development (Routledge, 1959) and *Planning and the Politicians*(Routledge, 1969) among other books. Passages from
this essay have already appeared in reviews he contributed to the *Times
Literary Supplement*, to the editor of which journal the author is grateful
for permission to reproduce them here; and his thanks are also due to Mr
Peter Sawyer, the editor of the *University of Leeds Review*, in which this
essay was originally published, for his permission to reprint it here – in a
slightly expanded form.

demand specific remedies, there are a few who regard the
universities of which they are members as essentially evil
institutions of an essentially evil society, and who work to cap-
ture the former with a view to overthrowing the latter. In pursuit of these aims, they try to enlist the support of those of
more moderate persuasions, and sometimes succeed in doing
so.

'Student power' is the slogan that they use, and *Student
Power* provides the title of at least two of their books, one
edited by Alexander Cockburn and Robin Blackburn[1] the
other by Julian Nagel.[2] The analogy with Black Power is obvious, and sometimes made explicit by complimentary gestures towards Stokely Carmichael and Rapp Brown. Both of
these symposia, however, are in effect[3] commentaries on the
main text from which most student revolutionaries seem to
derive their basic ideas and – even more – their characteristic
language: Daniel Cohn-Bendit's *Obsolete Communism: the
Left-Wing Alternative*.[4] This poorly-organized series of re-
flections on the Days of May, when the Sorbonne was in
student hands and the Student–Worker Alliance seemed about
to materialize, will be found tedious reading by any non-
revolutionary, and one doubts whether it would have had a
very marked impact on the student revolutionaries themselves
if its young author, through an extraordinary conjunction of
circumstances, had not been the initiator of a movement
which could have led – if Charles de Gaulle had been less
skilful and the P.C.F. less constitutionally-minded – to another
French revolution. Cohn-Bendit undoubtedly has *charisma*,
but his ideas about the reorganization of society seem to be
inspired by a strange mixture of Trotskyism and anarcho-
syndicalism, and his revolutionary strategy – to the extent
that he has one – reflects a belief in the virtues of 'spon-

1. Penguin, 1969.
2. Merlin Press, 1969.
3. I say 'in effect' because, although Cohn-Bendit's ideas have been
available for consideration for some time, his book did not appear until the
two 'Student Power' symposia must have been virtually completed.
4. André Deutsch, 1968; Penguin, 1969.

taneity' which few *serious* revolutionaries have been able to entertain since Lenin wrote his *What is to be Done?* in 1903. Moreover, as a piece of sociological theory, which it claims to be, the essay is extremely naïve, and one can hardly understand why several of its reviewers who are competent sociologists should have treated it with such solemn deference.

Indeed, if we take the three books here selected as expressive of the basic *ideology* of student power, as I think we are entitled to do, we find that it is not outstandingly original. Essentially, the student radical is a libertarian whose ideals have a strong anarchistic flavour. In a sense, the whole student power movement might well be regarded as a latter-day manifestation of the anarchist tradition in political thought, even though its leaders quote more frequently and approvingly from Marx, Gramsci, Mao Tse-tung and Fidel Castro than they do from Bakunin, Kropotkin and Malatesta. The Marx that provides their inspiration is almost exclusively the young Marx of the *Paris Manuscripts*, where the stress is on the alienation of the producer from his product and on the need to end it as a condition for the achievement of the good life and the realization of man's great historical potentialities. In their view, all present-day societies, with the possible exceptions of Mao's China, Ho Chi Minh's Vietnam and Castro's Cuba, are both exploitative and manipulative. Russian communism is almost as guilty in this respect as western capitalism – but not *quite* equally guilty, since, through nationalizing the means of production, it has at least laid the basis for the libertarian social order of the future, whereas western capitalism has exploitative and manipulative characteristics built into its very substance. The object of the revolutionary overthrow of both systems is to replace the present domination of man by technology with the domination of technology by man, so that life, to use a favourite expression of Marx and Engels, will become more 'truly human' and the grim prospect of the '1984' upon which both systems appear to be rapidly converging may be averted. The need for such a revolution has now become extremely urgent; for, under capitalist and bureaucratic control, the new technology is being increasingly used for utterly destructive purposes, such as the manufacture of H-bombs, poisonous gases and deadly microbiological organisms, which threaten the extinction of human life itself; or for purposes totally irrelevant to human needs, such as the conquest of outer space. After the revolution, the rule of capitalists and bureaucrats will be replaced by the rule of the people, not in the bogus form of the 'dictatorship of the proletariat', Soviet-style, but in the true form of mass participation in the making of political and all other decisions at all levels – through the establishment of a great variety of communal and co-operative institutions whereby the ordinary man, freed from the constraints which have frustrated him throughout history, will be enabled to express his real will. Immediately, the task is not only to mobilize the people for the final struggle, but to do so by methods which will lay the foundations of the participatory democracy of the future. Participation *now*, moreover, means the driving of revolutionary, democratic wedges into the capitalist and bureaucratic social order, which can be extended as consciousness of its evils increases and as the process of participation itself dispels apathy and develops self-confidence.

So far, so good. Utopian as this vision of the future may be, and vague as the strategy for realizing it may seem, there is nothing here which does not have a perfectly reputable ancestry in the history of radical political thought. What is new, or partly new, is the role cast for the student as such in this revolutionary process. The student is seen both as a particularly sensitive victim of capitalist and bureaucratic institutions and as an unusually favourably-placed agent for their overthrow. He is a victim both because he is a member of an institution which is itself, as an inseparable part of the existing social order, bureaucratically-organized, and because the basic purpose of this institution is both to condition him ideologically and to equip him technically for his future absorption into the system in some responsible but subordinate capacity. He is particularly sensitive because, by one of the contradictions inherent in the whole system, part of the conditioning process itself is a training in the art of *thought*;

and, as one who has received the 'privilege', if only for a few years, of greater personal freedom and greater leisure than the vast majority of the population, he has opportunities for independent activity denied to most others. If, to the 'intellectualism' which enables him – if he should choose so to employ it – to 'grasp the historical process as a whole', is added the leisure and independence which give him temporary exemption from a 'nose to the grindstone' kind of existence, it becomes obvious that he is peculiarly well-placed as a revolutionary agent. Moreover, the institution of which he is a subordinate member happens to be particularly susceptible to attack: it is run by people who are reluctant to use violence and who, in their queer way, have a genuine if ill-formulated belief in a 'community of scholars' and also are themselves divided, as a result of the resentment felt by junior members of the staff at the hierarchical way in which the universities are organized. Students, therefore, have a special and vital revolutionary role which they can well discharge if they have the courage to wage a determined no-holds-barred type of campaign, centred on the Student Power slogan. Although they themselves cannot bring about a revolution, they can inspire others and provide them with an example, and thus forge a student-and-worker alliance which, in the long run, will be all-powerful.

As I have said, this view of the student role is only partly new. Much of its ideological ancestry can be traced back, as Lewis Feuer has traced it in his *Conflict of Generations*,[5] to the early-nineteenth-century *Burschenschaft* in Germany; and in the 'back-to-the-people' movement of the late-nineteenth-century Russian Narodniks it became much more explicit and specifically associated with socialism of a libertarian variety with marked similarities to that advocated by our modern student revolutionaries, except in respect of the former's strongly agrarian bias. Its present formulation, however, possesses a degree of sophistication which has hitherto been absent, largely because it can draw on a great body of

5. New York and London, Basic Books and Heinemann, 1969. See also his 'Patterns of Irrationality' in *Survey*, no. 69, October 1968, p. 43 passim.

Marxist and anarchist theory and on the rich revolutionary experience of the last hundred years. Although its expression by the students themselves is usually rhetorical and repetitive, it has among a handful of junior members of university staffs some very much more able exponents, represented in the books here under consideration by Robin Blackburn. It has also enlisted the services of a few intellectually distinguished marginal sympathizers, such as Norman Birnbaum and Stuart Hall, whose articles in the Nagel symposium, entitled 'The Staggering Colossus' and 'The Hippies – An American "Movement"', deserve careful reading.

Although I would wish to challenge some of these views about the condition of our society and – far more strongly – the remedies for it that are proposed, it is not my purpose here to present a critique of either, but rather to examine what other people have said about why such views and proposals should have become so suddenly prominent in the 1960s, in so many different countries, and about the attitudes that should be adopted towards them by university teachers and administrators who are not revolutionaries – or at least not revolutionaries of that particular kind.

From what has already been written, it is clear enough that there is no *single* explanation of the phenomenon, but a number of different explanations, varying in their relevance from country to country. In many countries, it comes as no surprise at all that students should be revolutionary-minded or susceptible to revolutionary influence. A 'progressive' student in South Africa, for instance, has no alternative but to struggle, to the best of his ability, both against his government and – to the extent that the institution of which he is a member gives its support to that government's policies – against the university administration; although he does not, as a result, necessarily come to accept the *corpus* of ideas outlined above. Students in the communist countries, who are subjected to ideological conditioning and institutional discipline far fiercer than those prevailing even in capitalist countries that have authoritarian governments, are even more justified in becoming disaffected. Moreover, accepting as they usually do the *general* superiority of communism over capitalism, it is natural that they should express their disaffection in terms of a libertarian type of communism, similar to that which provides the basic ideology for student revolutionaries in our own country.

It is equally obvious that, partly but not entirely as a result of the increase in the size of universities, students in many countries are acutely unhappy about the conditions in which they live and work. Some of them, particularly in the under-developed countries, where the supply of graduates is quite out of relation with demand, are justifiably despondent about their prospects. Both of these reasons for bloody-mindedness may be observed, for instance, in almost every Indian university.[6] On the continent of Europe, too, students have cause to complain of the way their universities treat them – of the formalized instruction, the large classes, the lack of any real staff–student dialogue, the remoteness of professors, as well as, in many cases; of poor accommodation and facilities. Such grievances, which have been amply documented, but no-where better than in John Gretton's account of the Days of May, entitled *Students and Workers*[7], can all too easily be absorbed into a generalized grievance against society at large, rendering its possessor extremely susceptible to the appeal of revolutionary ideologies. And although conditions in Britain and the United States are obviously far better in every way, students in these countries have similar if milder causes of dis-content: the increasing impersonality of university adminis-tration and the preoccupation of their seniors not only with research but with the great variety of public duties into which competent professors, professing 'relevant' subjects, so easily and willingly become drawn. Such grievances have certainly

6. See P. H. Reddy, 'Indian Student Rebellion: Some Neglected Factors', in *Economic and Political Weekly*, Bombay, Vol. IV, No. 7, 15 February 1969. A full treatment of the Indian student movement is provided by Aileen D. Ross, *Student Unrest in India. A Comparative Approach* (Montreal, McGill-Queen's University Press, 1969). Among the more 'positive' func-tions of the frequent, and often violent, Indian student demonstrations, Professor Ross emphasizes the attention that they draw 'to inadequacy or corruption within educational systems' (p. 263).

7. Macdonald, London, 1969.

had some share of responsibility for the 'troubles' both at Berkeley and at the L.S.E. The student who has been brought up permissively by Spockian parents and watched over solicitously while at school does not like to feel undervalued and neglected when he reaches the university.

Over and beyond all this is the element of inter-generational conflict, a form of tension, always present in any society, that has of recent years reached a very high level. Student revolutionaries themselves occasionally choose to stress this phenomenon by alleging that their elders have 'failed' or 'betrayed' them, and it provides the main theme of Lewis Feuer's massive work. According to him, the conflict of generations is liable to become particularly acute in circumstances when, for one reason or another, the sons have ceased to place any confidence in the wisdom and integrity of their fathers.[8] He illustrates this thesis with abundant historical examples, placing particular emphasis on the Narodnik experience in late-nineteenth-century Russia, which he tends to treat almost as an Ideal Type. Unfortunately, this great effort of synthesis fails to carry complete conviction, since the historical evidence on which it is based, besides being highly selective, tends to be self-validating. (In other words, student revolt is a symptom of inter-generation conflict, which is evidence that fathers have failed their sons). The thesis is also tricked out with a monstrous deal of rather elementary Freudian psychology,[9] which leans far too exclusively on one of the weakest and least

8. Or as Feuer puts it, when there is an 'interrelation of generational conflict with the special historical circumstances making for the de-authorization of the older generation'.

9. Just how elementary may be judged from the following 'explanation' of right-wing student activism during the Third Republic: '... the bifurcation of Joan and Marianne in the students' minds was the most significant expression of their deepest conflict. Sons who are in revolt against their fathers are horrified by the thought of the sexual relations to which their m thers have had perforce to submit. Marianne, the "slut" of the Republic, was indeed their mother prostituted to their bourgeois fathers: she had been rendered impure, a creature for sale to the series of monetary bidders. The Maid of Orleans, on the other hand, virgin, untainted by bourgeois fathers – here the mother was rendered fine and noble. The intensity of devotion to

convincing of the master's works, *Totem and Taboo,* in which he displays more of his ignorance of anthropology than of his mastery of psychology. For these reasons, it fails adequately to explain why the inter-generational conflict of which student revolt is a manifestation should have broken out so suddenly, with such unusual vigour and in so many countries with such dissimilar cultures, precisely in the seventh decade of the twentieth century. Nevertheless, it makes fascinating reading, and there can be little doubt that Feuer has at least *part* of the total explanation. In particular, it seems to be clear that the sense of intra-generational solidarity that is the *alter ego* of inter-generational conflict explains the readiness shown by so many moderate-minded students to line up behind the banners raised aloft by the radicals. A very interesting expression of this solidarity is provided by Harriet Crawley, whose discursive *Degree of Defiance*[10] records the progress of the somewhat privileged European university-crawl with which she occupied the time before settling down to read history at King's College, London. Although Miss Crawley mixes a good deal of percipience with her naïveté, although she entirely lacks what a student revolutionary would call ideological stamina, and although she obviously dislikes both the manners and customs of the radicals and finds delight in the strange mixture of decorum and eccentricity characteristic of undergraduate culture in our two ancient universities, she chooses to end her work with the following extraordinary declaration:

Joan was proportionate to the intensity of rejection of bourgeois fathers. If the French working class had not already achieved its independence, and regarded the intellectual askance, the student activists might have assumed a more proletarian identity; if the French peasantry had not rested secure in the ownership of their parcels of land the students might have sought them out as allies. But in the France of the Bourgeois Republic where fathers were engulfed in the pursuit of gain, the law of generational conflict produced strange vectors – a generation of right-wing activists who sought a restoration of Virginity to their Mothers from the Rape by their fathers.' (op. cit. p. 276). The Oedipus complex is here made to carry a heavy historical load!

10. Weidenfeld and Nicolson, London, 1969.

I don't suppose we are as unusual as we like to think. Violence has classified us as a renegade generation, and the general public throughout Western Europe is our hostile enemy: neither a worrying nor a surprising development. It seems to me that any age has its drop-ins and drop-outs. If anything is new it is the growing sense of community in this technological world. But for myself and for many others, the strongest feeling is also the least original. We revel in being young, and despite the great British, Italian, French and German publics, we are going to have a riot.

Silly? Yes, of course; but as an expression of crude intra-generational solidarity it could hardly be bettered. One suspects that there are enough young people who feel this way to give the radicals considerable encouragement.

A simpler 'psychologistic' explanation of student radicalism is that it is a product of the general permissiveness that has invaded our society and penetrated our educational system. Young people, used to getting their own way at home and in school, resent the comparatively mild behavioural restraints and rather harder intellectual disciplines that the university tries to impose on them, and with the generalizing facility for which the young are so distinguished, present themselves to themselves as pure-souled libertarians doing battle against a reactionary and restrictive social order. This is the theme of the much-publicized 'Black Paper',[11] one of the most vigorous and indiscriminate attacks on 'progressivism' in education to have been published for a long time. With its general thesis I am in entire disagreement; nevertheless one must reluctantly admit that *some* student behaviour would appear, *prima facie*, to validate some of the claims that it makes. The radicals' insistence that university education should be a perpetual 'dialogue', that the 'mere' learning of facts is a waste of time, and that examinations are an inhuman imposition suggests, at least to me, that they are not particularly enamoured of hard work and disciplined study. Moreover, their habit of presenting *demands* (never requests) in the most offensive language they dare use and of sitting down and shouting if these de-

11. C. B. Cox and A. E. Dyson (eds.), *Fight for Education: A Black Paper* (*Critical Quarterly*, 1969).

mands are rejected reminds me most forcibly – as it has reminded David Martin – of the screaming tantrums of the
pampered nursery child.

Academics today, he writes in the symposium that he has
edited, *Anarchy and Culture*,[12]

> now barely experience any awareness of change when they pass from
> home to work or from week to weekend. Previously a weekend with the
> children was very different from a week at the school. At home the
> children were fascinating creatures, exposed to every irrational whim,
> quite amoral and charmingly spontaneous. One moment they would
> bury their heads in your bosom, the next beat you unmercifully between
> the eyes. Students on the other hand appeared as responsible adults,
> apparently well able to look after themselves without detailed super-
> vision, and content with reasonable fulfilments of academic duty. At
> home the children wanted to be loved; at university the students wanted
> to be taught. The transition from one to the other seemed clear.
> Then quite suddenly all was changed. The façade of disciplined
> student endeavour was rolled away revealing an entirely new scenario
> in the making: the Houghton Street Day Nursery of Revolution. . . .
> The life of the academic became all of a piece: he just moved from one
> nursery to another.

The impression that many of the radicals are suffering from
emotional immaturity will be strengthened by a reading of Mr
Ronald Goldman's excellent book, *Angry Adolescents*,[13]
which offers a sensitive analysis of the deviant behaviour of a
group of underprivileged working-class youngsters. This re-
veals, rather strikingly, the behavioural similarities between
'the gang' and students who express their 'revolutionary' fer-
vour by smashing gates, stealing documents, throwing paint
and disrupting the meetings of parliamentary committees of
inquiry. Even the language used is not so very different. The
only real difference lies in the degree of sophistication and the
level of articulateness – and even here it is less wide than one
might expect. According to Stephen Spender[14] the American

12. Routledge and Kegan Paul, London, 1969.
13. Routledge and Kegan Paul, 1969.
14. *The Year of the Young Rebels*, Weidenfeld and Nicolson, London,
1969.

student leader Mark Rudd addressed his university president as follows:

> There is only one thing left to say. It may sound nihilistic to you, since it is the opening shot in a war of liberation. I'll use the words of Leroi Jones, whom I'm sure you don't like a whole lot: 'Up against the wall, motherfucker, this is a stick-up', Yours for freedom, Mark.

There is a clear complementarity between the language of the gutter and the behaviour of the guttersnipe.[15]

However, there is a danger of making too much of a meal of all this. The 'L.S.E. Day Nursery' is not typical, nor, fortunately, is Mark Rudd's distinctive style of political utterance. As for the deleterious influence of slack parental control and permissive schooling, this remains to be proved, and I would suspect that, were an attempt made to discover a correlation between these and student radicalism, it might well turn out to be a negative one. Nevertheless, it would seem to me that at least *some* of the current radical manifestations in our universities are the product of *some* form of emotional immaturity, whatever its source may be.

When all this has been said one must face the fact that young people today are confronted with a world which does *really* hover on the brink of disaster. Are not we all? it may be asked. Of course we are, but for the young the situation is particularly poignant – and most of all for the young intellectual, who has more to fear precisely because he knows more. Consider what it is like to be young, educated and idealistic at the beginning of the last third of the twentieth century. With most of one's life still to live, one sees mankind, having recently failed, but only by a hair's-breadth, in two deter-

15. Since writing the above I have had an opportunity to read the excellent account of the Columbia fracas in Jerry L. Avorn and others: *University in Revolt* (Macdonald, London, 1969). Rudd's slogan, apparently, is the standard threat employed by the New York police when engaged in 'cleaning up' operations in Harlem. His attempt to justify it, in the appendix he contributes to this book, does nothing to reconcile me to the use of such an expression, which gained considerable currency even among the young ladies of Barnard College. It is surely the most remarkable crudity ever to be uttered by people claiming membership of an intellectual élite.

mined efforts to destroy its civilization, poised for take-off into nuclear annihilation, while doing its damnedest to ensure that, should it by some miracle escape this fate, it will collectively perish as a result of excessive multiplication or the progressive poisoning of the environment or both. The image of the Gadarene Swine is inadequate, since the wretched animals are not rushing down a steep slope but being carried down it in vehicles they have proudly paid for, while enjoying the solace of an equally expensive programme of canned entertainment designed to make them forget the direction in which they are going. Even if they never reach their ultimate destination, their potential for swinishness, in the sense of dehumanization, seems to increase alarmingly at every stage in what they amusingly call their 'progress'. For the threat of the earth's becoming like the moon is complemented by that of a computer-dominated '1984'. Can one wonder, therefore, that it is precisely the young, educated and idealistic who have taken to expressing themselves with such 'shocking' violence and even, on occasion, to using actual physical violence? Acutely conscious of the transitoriness of their own unique situation, they feel that they must 'do something' while the going is still comparatively good, without paying undue respect to due process through the usual – and usually clogged – channels. Their positive beliefs are in social justice and social salvation rather than in the 'order' favoured by so many of their elders. As Spender puts it, they reject the idea that 'man is made for the society of a Witches' Sabbath' and believe in 'a human Sabbath made for man'. This is the positive side of the students' revolt, which over-emphasis on the antics of paint-throwing and gate-breaking yahoos is liable to obscure. With a poet's insight into human motives, together with a natural sympathy for young rebels springing from his own unrepudiated activities of the 1930s, Spender is well-equipped to understand it. It is this that makes his *Year of the Young Rebels* probably the best book on student revolt yet to be published. The main conclusion that one may draw from it is that the revolt is not something that can be treated as a specific disease, for which an appropriate cure may be prescribed, but a symptom of a much more generalized and much more dangerous complaint that demands social surgery of a pretty drastic kind. A secondary conclusion – but one of equal importance in the context of the present essay – is that the student revolutionaries mistake their own symptomatic behaviour for the operative activity of the surgeon himself. For, to the extent that they direct their energies against the university which, with all its faults, is one of the most liberal of all institutions in 'bourgeois' society, they are engaged in no more than the self-defeating operation of sawing off the branch on which they are sitting. The question is how they may be made to recognize this mistake.

What, indeed, can be done by those who, like myself, profoundly believe not only that the university can be improved but that, in a relatively free society, it embodies, however imperfectly, traditions of scholarship, both humane and utilitarian, whose preservation and extension are of the utmost importance? There is no lack of prescribers. Feuer, for instance, seems to think that if only today's revolutionary students can be persuaded to study the historical record left by their predecessors, they will find in it conclusive proof that student revolt has consequences that negate the intentions of the protagonists. The historical evidence, he holds, indicates that student movements

have probably been the most irrational force in modern history. We can show this briefly by reference to the three most consequential student movements in European history. The German student movement of 1815–1819 was largely responsible for the defeat of German liberalism for the next generation. The Russian student movement of the 1870s and 1880s was largely responsible for the destruction of the fragile beginnings of a Russian constitutionalism. The Bosnian student movement did more than any other group of individuals to bring about the First World War.[16]

Of the contemporary situation in the United States, he writes:

If the United States were to fail to meet its problems of racial relations in a liberal, rational spirit, that failure would be largely the outcome of the actions of its student movement. If the United States were to fail

16. 'Patterns of Irrationality' in *Survey*, no. 69, October 1968.

as the world's centre of liberal democracy, and thereby make possible a resurgence of neo-Stalinism among both European communist and democratic countries, and among the Asian nations as well, then the responsibility for that failure would lie in much part with the tactics of the student movement.

Feuer evidently belongs to the 'scare-the-pants-off-them'[17] school. Although he has discovered, or at least illuminated, some partial truths, I cannot believe that his obvious exaggerations, based as they are on an extremely naïve and unilinear view of the historical process, are likely to make much impact on young men and women who have studied their Marxism, however superficially.

Nor can I place my confidence in the 'read-'em-a-good lecture' school, as represented by George Kennan.[18] Kennan delivers a rather solemn and ponderous discourse about democratic values and the idea of a university, designed to show the student rebels that their aims are mostly wrong and their tactics entirely misconceived. With a great deal of what he says I entirely agree, but he leaves out so much, and makes so many assumptions which cannot possibly be accepted by young men in a hurry, or even by older men in not so much of a hurry, that I fear he will be treated as a fuddy-duddy with very little of contemporary relevance to offer. Certainly, he seems to be on an entirely different wave-length from his critics, a selection of whose letters, in reply to the 'Swarthmore' address which forms the first section of this book, he reproduces, with the openness and honesty typical of a really distinguished scholar. Some of these are just silly; others, such

17. Although I believe this to be essentially true, justice to Feuer demands that his purpose should be expressed in his own words. He hopes that 'by bringing to consciousness the irrationalities and self-destruction components in the history of student movements, it will be possible to overcome them at least in part'; and adds: 'Student movements are the product of selfless, altruistic idealism combined with resentment and aggression of one generation against another. It is the latter component which imparts a demonic quality to the students' emotions and actions. If social understanding can isolate and study that component, perhaps the hatreds, projections and guilts of generational conflict may be rendered less dominant, and a higher idealism emerge' (op. cit. pp. viii–ix).

18. *Democracy and the Student Left*, Hutchinson, London, 1968.

as the letter from W. H. Auden, make telling points to which his answers are less than convincing.

I think, too, that a vote of something less than confidence has to be given to the 'bash 'em' school of prescribers, whose most distinguished representatives in this country are John Sparrow and Max Beloff, both of All Souls.[19] With their determination to maintain good order in the universities there can be no quarrel: the universities, like the Queen's Government, must be carried on. The question is whether the rather simplistic methods they prescribe for dealing with a very complex situation are likely to be effective in achieving this end, even temporarily. Sparrow believes that the university authorities should first do everything they can 'to maintain a channel for understanding between teachers and taught' and then, if still faced with force, 'should not hesitate, after due warning, to hit back hard, calling in the police when necessary, and in appropriate cases, expelling rather than rusticating serious offenders'. Good strong stuff, this, and much after the style of Governor Reagan; but can John Sparrow be *absolutely* certain that his remedy may not aggravate rather than cure the disease? And does Max Beloff *really* feel that it is of any help to describe the behaviour of student rebels as 'fascist barbarism', and to demand that it be 'put down'?[20] That there is a potentially fascist element in student rebellion is true. I have made the point myself in a review of Cohn-Bendit's book and it is disturbingly underscored by an article by P. Vita-Finzi contributed to S. S. Woolf's symposium on *The Nature of Fascism*.[21] But the 'fascism' is potential only, and not all violence, ugly as it may be, is necessarily fascist in character. It seems to me that both writers give insufficient credit to the genuine idealism that inspires their young opponents, and

19. Harry Kidd, formerly Secretary of L.S.E., is sometimes put down as a member of this school, in so far as, in his *The Trouble at L.S.E.* (O.U.P. London, 1969), he advocates that, in certain circumstances, the police should be called in; but a careful reading of his two excellent chapters entitled 'Rejections' and 'Discipline' should dispel the impression that he is a straightforward 'basher'.

20. 'Universities and Violence' in *Survey*, no. 69, October 1968.

21. Weidenfeld and Nicolson, 1968.

place too much confidence on the ability of a university institution to use strong-arm methods without undermining its very *raison d'etre*. Indeed, so long as university teachers run the universities – which one hopes they will continue to do – 'the administration' suffers from built-in inhibitions about using counter-violence beyond a certain point. For, as Peter Wiles says in the 'Martin' symposium which includes Sparrow's own contribution, the don is

a specialized person, too modest to indulge in bold general visions. He has learned disillusion and self-control, usually at the cost of emotional richness; whereas the quintessence of the New Left is the principled rejection of self-control. Again, he is not a politician; almost by definition he has renounced wider power and mostly he is too busy and too interested in his job to care even about power in the university.

This, of course, is a source of weakness; but it cannot easily be overcome. Perhaps the student rebels, if they persist long enough, will persuade even dons to gird up their loins. But this exercise is so un-donlike that it could hardly be more than a last, desperate expedient.

However, the 'bash 'em' school at least has a clear and intelligible policy, which can hardly be said of the members of the 'Belinda' fraternity. (For the benefit of those who have forgotten their Pope, I should perhaps explain that Belinda was the young lady who, 'saying she would ne'er consent, consented'.) Belindism has, for obvious reasons, received little overt expression in the literature of student revolt and therefore will have to be briefly dismissed, despite its importance. Its exponents, like so many worried parents, constantly deplore the behaviour of their noisy and disobedient charges, but almost invariably give in to them, 'just for this once,' accompanying their surrender by 'thus-far-and-no-further' types of admonition. By doing so, they of course play into the hands of those extreme revolutionaries, usually of the Trotskyist persuasion, whose policy is one of continuous escalation of demands.

The line between Belindism and genuine reformism, unfortunately, is so fine as to be difficult to distinguish, particularly as the Belindists invariably present themselves as reformers and repeatedly deny that they are being pushed around by anyone. And there is a real case for reform, in so far as, for better or worse, we are now in a social situation where even non-revolutionary students are less than enamoured of the *in statu pupillari* position that the revolutionary students themselves of former years (for example in the 1930s, when I was one of them) seemed content enough to occupy. It is often a moot question, therefore, whether the reformers are saying and doing the things they say and do because they think them right or because they are having their arms twisted. Take, for instance, the 'Hart' Report.[22] This makes proposals for the reform of disciplinary procedures and for the association of students with the process of academic decision-taking which seem to me both well-conceived and overdue. These it smoothly presents as inherently 'desirable as a contribution to the quality of the life and to the liveliness of the University', and, for greater certainty, it adds that 'in no case' were they recommended 'as mere defensive measures to damp down or contain unrest'. Yet one wonders whether this is a full and complete account of the Committee's motivation, particularly when one finds it admitting that 'the main body of Junior Members do not think about and are not concerned to criticize the present university structure or to demand arrangements which would involve Junior Members in the University's government even in a consultative capacity.' If this is factually true, can it be seriously doubted that threats of disruption by a small minority of radicals were the real *fons et origo* of the proposed reforms, and indeed the main reason for the appointment of the Committee itself?

Belindism, however, is a charge that one would be reluctant to level at the members of the Hart Committee. The 'school' in which they find their most natural location is that of the Dividers, the most popular school of all. The Divider makes a contrast, which usually corresponds with reality, between the great mass of moderate reformist-minded students and the small minority of revolutionaries. The problem is to prevent the latter from acquiring leadership of the former. Its

22. *Report of the Committee on Relations with Junior Members*, Oxford University Press, 1969.

solution demands that the moderates shall be provided with representative institutions and that care shall be taken not to give the revolutionaries any opportunity or excuse effectively to present the quarrels they pick with the university authorities as involving civil liberties issues around which they can mobilize widespread student support. The Divider's view of the situation, being so common in university circles, hardly requires documentation. Although perfectly sensible, it does not always work in practice, for reasons which are becoming generally understood. The most important of these is that the radical minority, although it obviously welcomes wide student support and hopes eventually to win it, does not *need* it to effect a considerable disruption of university life. Its tactics, based on those of the Che Guevara-type guerrilla band, are flexible enough to accommodate varying degrees of support and hostility from the 'peasantry'.

Finally, there are the Diversionists, of whom Stephen Spender is the most distinguished. Spender does not look with much favour on increased student 'participation' in university government either as an attempt to satisfy the radicals or as a means of dividing them from their potential followers – although he regards *some* new forms of participation as in-inevitable. Indeed, he fears that 'too much involvement of this kind may divert the students from the concern with politics which was the starting point of their movement' – a concern of which he approves. What he hopes to be able to do is to direct student energy outwards, towards the real problems of 'war and armaments, of racial inequality, of the deterioration of the cities, of the pollution of the atmosphere and of the destruction of the countryside'. If the energy of the rebels can be channelled into an attack on these recognized evils, instead of wasting itself on assaulting the university, there is no reason in Spender's view why the university should not be able to 'accommodate both scholars and revolutionaries: for it to become, as it were, an agora beside a citadel (or even an ivory tower).' The essential requirements for success of this live-and-let-live policy, he considers, are 'that the militants should allow the non-political scholars to get on with their work, and that the academics should not regard as unacceptable the presence on the campus of students who want to change the society in which they live and who agitate in order to achieve this end.'

This kind of advocacy takes us back to the university of the 1930s. As a relic of that period, I find it sensible and acceptable. Indeed, were I required to nail my own colours to the mast, I should be inclined to describe myself as a Spenderian Diversionist, particularly as Spender qualifies his main thesis in a manner of which I approve. On the whole, I should evince just a little more enthusiasm for 'participation' than he displays, although subjecting it to rather more severe limitations than might be acceptable to my leftward-moving colleagues. To me it seems essential, for instance, that, whatever degree of self-government may be granted to students, all vital decisions about academic policy should remain in the hands of the people whom the Hart Report describes as 'senior' members of the university. But I agree entirely with Spender in his belief that 'the first task of universities is to safeguard the rights of scholars and academics, of those who are making the most effective use of the machinery which the university provides', and on this issue I must declare myself, albeit reluctantly and with many qualifications, on the side of the Sparrovians and Beloffians when it comes to the crunch. Such expressions of faith, however, solve no problems, although they may well provide a framework of discourse within which a solution may be sought. The essential thing is that a genuine dialogue should continue, and not be replaced by a confrontation. For if the universities cease to be places in which national discussion is the norm, the struggle for rationality in the conduct of human affairs must be regarded as lost.

Student Unrest in India

Shanti Swarup*

India today is seething with discontent and protest and they have been growing very rapidly for almost a decade. They exist today at almost all levels of society. Strikes, processions, *gheraoes* and a series of new forms of protest have been gaining in respectability. *Bandhs*, for example, have quite often paralysed normal life in a far more effective manner than any general strike conceptualized in the West.

Strange though it may seem, this large-scale discontent has led neither to a strong movement of intellectual dissent, nor to the type of protest movements which have shaken the affluent western societies over the past few years. We look in vain for a Cohn-Bendit, or a Tariq Ali, nor do we come across a Marcuse to articulate the discontent which seems so obvious. There are, no doubt, such men as Jaya Prakash Narain, but neither do their writings show any awareness of the new situation and the new tensions of our society nor, indeed, do they excite the imagination of the younger generation. At best they touch the fringes.

If there is no genuine articulation of this new movement of enormous dimensions, neither is there any first-class sociological or socio-political analysis of it. Reasons for this lack, both of articulation and of analysis, are not far to seek. For, unlike the movement in the West, the discontent and therefore protest in India has many facets. The protest movement in India is far more complex and difficult to comprehend and since its nature and form vary at different levels of the social spectrum, it is far more difficult, unlike in the case of Marcuse in the United States, to synthesize all these in one single framework.

*The author is Professor of Political Science at the University of Dibrugarh (Assam India) and is author of *A Study of the Chinese Communist Movement* (Oxford University Press, 1966).

And since one of the most fashionable techniques is the questionnaire, it has failed to produce the required answer because a uni-directional questionnaire is unsuitable for multi-dimensional data.

Not that no explanations have been given or prescriptions offered. Some argue that it is due to the 'revolt of the youth against the adult world', others that it is due to the 'difference between generations', still others that it is due to 'sex starvation' and 'obsession', or 'change from tradition to modernity', or 'idealism of the youth' or a 'protest against urban environment'.

Such explanations, however, suffer from a number of difficulties. In the first place, it has not occurred to those who talk of the revolt of the youth against the adult world to pose to themselves some very simple questions: if what we are witnessing is a revolt against the adult world, how do we account for the fact that the Indian youth, perhaps not the only one in the world, still looks to the adults – perhaps worse adults – for leadership? How else could we explain that it is some politicians who are not only the source of inspiration to the various student agitations, but are also messing up the universities due precisely to the fact that they can utilize or misuse the student community? A similar kind of question will show the inadequacy of each one of these explanations.

Nor, secondly, are single answers adequate to explain any complex reality. Socio-political movements are always complex phenomena. This is not to suggest that none of these answers has any validity whatsoever. But in so far as the Indian movement of protest is complex, it is important to identify the diverse elements which are involved in the movement and to examine what precisely are the motivations of each of these groups within the movement. Only then would it be possible to determine for what reasons, at what levels and in what form do all or some of these disconnected and disjointed elements get united in a moment of crisis.

And, thirdly, it seems clear to anyone acquainted with the literature of the protest movement in the West that the explanations referred to above are by and large taken from the

West and applied ready-made, as it were, to the Indian situation.

This is by no means intended to imply that there are no similarities between the western and Indian protest movements. To be sure, there are. And given the present-day communication system and information media, it would be most surprising if there was no interaction between them. After all India is modernizing – and many do not draw any distinction between modernization and westernization. In a volume devoted largely to protest in the affluent western societies, it would be a good idea to begin with that element of the protest in India which has some resemblance to the western situation. For instance, both the movements are of a mass character, are aggressive and in a sense violent, both are unconventional and above all both are anti-*status quo*.

Even here, however, the comparisons should not be pushed too far. For instance, the rejection of the *status quo* in the West involves a rejection of those very symbols which go with status: in language, in dress, in behaviour pattern. Unlike men of status, those who reject status tend to employ violence in language and behaviour. And to slightly change the well-known sentence of Rousseau, since men and women of status, though born naked, are everywhere punctilious about full dress, those who reject the *status quo* could legitimately go about nude or as near nude as possible. Hence the jeans, the whiskers, rudeness and crudeness, public display of love-making and nudism – that is a rejection of all those values which till recently were deemed to be the *sine qua non* of a respectable man. Since more and more people are accepting middle-class values and developing middle-class consciousness, there is simultaneously a more violent rejection of those values. And in so far as symbols have meanings beyond symbols, a rejection of the old symbols in the West (and the adoption of the new ones) is tantamount to a rejection of the old value systems in the western societies.

Now it is of course true that some of the old western symbols have existed in India for some time and still exist, while some of the new symbols are becoming fashionable,

The problem, therefore, is to find out whether they convey the same meaning. For the same symbols may sometimes convey totally different meanings in two distinct socio-political situations.

A careful look at the Indian protest movement can be highly rewarding. Almost the very first thing we notice is that the adoption of these new western symbols is largely confined to a very small group in the Indian social situation, namely the children of the educated upper-middle-class parents. This group constitutes only one of the four major currents and is perhaps not the most important of these.

We do come across in the streets of big cities – or shall we say, the more westernized areas within those cities – the stripes, the whiskers, pop music, the unshaven boys and the loosely dressed girls. But to see in these a rejection of the value system and the status symbols of the adults would be superficial in the extreme. It has to be remembered that in the developing societies such as India 'westernism' has itself acquired a status symbol. And the mere fact that certain things are being done in the West acquires a prestige value. The accepance of such status symptoms as whiskers and jeans or taking Coca-cola and ice-cream in winter is essentially an adoption of the *latest* brand of 'westernism'. In a nutshell, the absorption of the latest western fads not only does not constitute a rejection of status *qua* status, it is in fact an element in status which puts a man above his fellows in the competitive scale of 'westernism'. Not surprisingly, therefore, while putting on jeans and keeping uncombed hair, many of them are most at ease when talking of their father's big cars or of refrigerators, lipsticks and their parents' servants. No less interesting is the fact that unconventional though their dresses are, these girls should want to have dozens of them.

Unlike the western youth, however, this particular category of the Indian youth does not have to face the same moral dilemma. Completely alienated from the rest of Indian society already, and in fact having very little sympathy with it, it stands at the fringe of the Indian movement of protest.

No less imitative is the revolt of the so-called progressives. They are shocked at the manner in which the Indian Communist movement has been tamed and converted into one of the various 'instruments' of parliamentary democracy. The thought that the Communist Party and the Communist Party (Marxist) should join forces with a religious communal party such as the Muslim League in Kerala, or with the Bangla Congress drawing its support from the richer peasantry in West Bengal, seems to them to be a 'betrayal' of Communist revolutionary faith. It is understandable that Castro's beard has not caught the imagination of these people, nor for that matter has Ho Chi Minh's beard. But the proscribed Red Book containing the 'Thoughts of Mao' is eagerly read: this in a way is the acceptance of what they believe to be the latest brand of 'progressive' idea applicable to 'all' 'colonial' and 'neo-colonial' societies. Just as their Communist predecessors of fifty years ago – and even through the purges, Stalin's terror and then Khrushchev's 'revisionism' – believed Russia to be the most 'progressive' form of social system, they see in Mao's theory of 'armed uprising' the latest model of this same 'progressivism'.

The youngsters in this category, called the Naxalites, are already feeling disturbed at the fact that they cannot get the sort of following they had anticipated. The failure of the Naxalite movement – and the Telengana movement before that – and the relative success of those Marxists who have committed themselves to the democratic process has already led to questionings among the Naxalites of the validity of 'armed uprising' in the Indian situation. It is true, of course, that they hit the news headlines from time to time, but this coverage is arranged by the conservative Press and the Government largely to embarrass the Communists. The actual strength of the movement remains insignificant and on the periphery of the main stream of Indian youth attitudes.

There are, however, two major currents in the protest movements which are rapidly becoming important. In the first place, there is a small, highly intelligent and very sensitive group among the Indian youth who question our ancient and present-day values. Brought up in apparently 'western' environment, they are shocked at two things. In the first place, they have a deep sense of concern at the self-centred and even selfish attitude of the westernized educated upper class which tends to be oblivious of the needs of the vast masses of the Indian people. Secondly they are disturbed by the pretensions of their upper-class society and values. As Edward Shils has noticed – and this point has often been dealt with so very tellingly in Indian novels – an Indian intellectual is a dual personality, a curious amalgam of old and new, who is able somehow to permit within his own personality the co-existence of otherwise irreconcilable ideas and modes of behaviour. The fact that very often an apparently sophisticated and 'modernized' exterior hides deep-seated prejudices, cannot but cause considerable agony. Brought up in this atmosphere, the more sensitive of the young boys and girls cannot but question the formless and inchoate values of the upper middle class of Indian society. Only these people appear, like their western counterparts, to reject all the values of their own society. It is not surprising that they should grow whiskers, go about unshaven, remain dirty or in general reject the idea of an external polish superimposed on a medieval personality. To revert to the idea of the symbols, the same symbols which in the first group imply status, in this case involve its rejection.

Balanced, rational, scientific and modern (as distinct from western), this group nevertheless has limited influence. The reasons for this are not far to seek. Although most people in this group have an enormous sympathy for the under-dog, they are also impatient with his prejudices. Influential because of their intellectual power, genuinely respected because of their sympathy for the poorer segments of the society and the youth, this group nevertheless remains alienated from the latter. For this reason, this form of protest, however annoying it may be for the parents, does not have much influence on the youth movement as such, for it cannot establish an emotional rapport with the bulk of the youth.

In one sense, however, the involvement of this group in the movement of protest makes the socio-political system more responsive to their urges. Often being the sons and daughters of some important figures in public life, they constitute a powerful if informal pressure group, exerting an influence out of all proportion to their numerical strength.

Numerically the most powerful group in the upper-class strata is still traditional, albeit with some modifications. Some members of this group have completely changed their dress, their eating habits and even some of their values as a result of the inevitable impact of the modern world. Most of the people in this category are the sons and daughters of the traditional élite, the political leadership or the senior bureaucrats (generally state-level bureaucrats). Very often, though not always, their fathers have combined two or three of these roles. They are conscious of their status – or rather their parents' status, of which they partake – and are anxious to retain it.

But before discussing the impact of this status consciousness on contemporary politics, let us for a moment have a look at the implications of status in Indian society. Unlike, for example, the Chinese Confucian literati, the Japanese Samurai and the European feudal aristocracy, India never developed an aristocracy at a national level. There is a sense in which all aristocracies had a basic power based in a locality. But in China, Japan, and Europe, the aristocracy or at least some significant part of it gained both a national influence and a national consciousness, which transcended in many ways their local ties. For various reasons, which would be irrelevant here, this did not happen in India. The only real continuum was caste and, after the Muslim period, the religious communities; but these groups were too large to be effective as groups at the national level. Status consciousness based on caste or community was therefore largely local, and at best regional. So neither has the consciousness of this traditional élite transcended the local or at best regional level, nor has its leadership reached the national level. And now their position and status is threatened by the impact of modernization which, whatever its other implications, leads to what sociologists characterize as an 'achievement-oriented society'. Such a society involves mobility of capital leading to the emergence of a new élite, occupational mobility and regional mobility. Of these three factors, occupational mobility is the least threatening, for very few of the people from the lower stratum of society are able to compete with them in the very first generation.

Accepting the value of their tradition, the discontented young from this group also accept adult leadership. The fact that their parents develop anxiety about their agitational approach is not the crucial point. What is crucial is that their thinking does bear some relationship to the thinking and discussions which take place in their parents' drawing rooms. The parents are, however, inhibited from action because they are government servants, employees in big firms or politicians who have all accepted, at least on paper, the supraregional national loyalty. For this reason, the young listen with rapt attention to those politicians whose ideas bear some resemblance to the discussions in the drawing rooms of their parents.

But in accepting this peculiar sectarian type of adult leadership, they are in a sense doing almost exactly what their parents would themselves have liked to do, had they been freer agents. It is probably because of this factor that agitations, violence, threats of violence by the student community largely go unpunished. Law and order being within the state sphere of jurisdiction and the children of state politicians and bureaucrats being among the agitating students, the former cannot allow their own children to be beaten up and shot for an objective for which they themselves have full sympathy. That explains why student agitations gain momentum and 'achieve results' in a manner denied to a far more powerful trade union movement. Narrower in outlook than any of the first three categories discussed above, accepting at least partly the ascriptive rather than the achievement-oriented conception of status, basing themselves sometimes on *sentiments* of caste, at other times of community and at still other times of regions and religion, their politics are by and large sectional and often irrational.

Despite the narrowness of its outlook, the political power of this group is considerable. Their power arises out of the fact that they are, in some manner, linked to another group: the large number of first-generation student youth coming from the urban lower middle class and the peasant families. It has to be remembered that there has been an enormous change in the socio-economic composition of our university students over the last twenty years. And in order to comprehend the link of which we are talking, it is necessary to examine the changing attitude of this large majority of young Indian students.

The attitude of this group, it is important to realize, was originally different from its present attitude. In the early stages after independence, the success of state institutions had created a general spirit of hope and confidence. Times, it was believed, were changing and in this climate of change, the poorer segments would benefit. It was in this atmosphere that the Government of India decided upon a policy of rapid industrialization. But in order to stimulate a rapid growth of the economy, it was necessary to achieve an infrastructure of development which included among other things quick expansion of educational facilities. The atmosphere of change at that time gave people considerable hope about the future. Many people from the ranks of the urban lower middle class, the skilled labourers and the poor peasantry sent the brightest son of the family to the university or college at great sacrifice. Sometimes whole families including the husband, the wife, and young brothers and tiny sisters had to work hard to pay for the education of one boy of the family. This they did in the hope that the boy would not only give to the family financial assistance, but above all give to it prestige and status in society. So much indeed hinges on a job in India: the status of an individual and his family and even the nature of marriage relations for the sisters. The realization that the sacrifice made by the whole family may come to nothing can be deeply humiliating and frustrating.

These were no simple exceptional cases; they constituted quite a large percentage of the total student population. From a tiny percentage among the student population in the colleges and universities, the rural element alone rose to approximately 36 per cent even by 1961.

In the beginning, however, the economy was by and large expanding, and a number of new opportunities for engineers and others opened up. By the early sixties stagnation had set in and the economy showed no signs of recovery. This economic factor, coupled with India's defeat in the Sino-Indian Border War, led to a decline in the authority of the Central Government. In the language of political sociology, the Central Government was rapidly losing its political legitimacy. And this less sophisticated vast mass of students and other people was looking in other directions for substitutes of leadership. Even during the latter period of Nehru's life, the new type of situation was already apparent.

Amid this vacuum of leadership at national level, the local and regional leadership was the only visible alternative. As a result, this leadership provided a link between this category of young students and the children of the traditional élite groups – to whom they had much the same appeal. Whereas the one group was threatened by loss of status, the other was shocked by the dashing of its hopes of acquiring a status. Facing by and large a similar (not the identical) problem, they needed the same sort of leadership.

Other similarities of attitude exist between the two groups: neither of them, for instance, are anti-adult. The reasons for this in the case of the children of the élite groups have already been discussed. In the case of the children of the peasantry, there is a feeling of gratitude for the parents who have educated them at enormous personal sacrifice. Nor is it possible that in the very first generation of entry in the university, they should be able to shake off all their prejudices *as a group* and become totally modern. Some bright individual students are able to achieve this, but they are the exception rather than the rule. In a sense, both these groups had a similarity of approach. The conditions had thus emerged for a number of strong sectional movements.

The so-called movement of student protest in India is not a single movement but a series of unconnected sectional, regional and local movements. Had the main strength of this movement come from any one of the first three categories, it would have led to a strong nation-wide protest movement. As things are, however, it is their techniques which have become common, not their objectives. The meaning of Bengal Bandh is not the same as that of Assam Bandh. While the aim of the organizers of the Panjab Bandh was to secure the city of Chandigarh for Panjab, that of Haryana Bandh was intended to secure the place for Haryana. These movements are not complementary; they are at least mutually exclusive and sometimes in contradiction to each other. The only thing they have in common is that they are anti-centre and, whether intentionally or not, reduce the legitimacy of central authority and thus, in some sense, confuse national identity.

Hard to believe though it may seem, the first shot in this direction was fired by the enthusiasts for Hindi – inspired by the local leadership of the Hindi heartland – that is, precisely the group in whose ultimate interests it was to discourage regional loyalties. At once the students were on the streets after wrecking the property of the universities themselves, raising the slogan 'Angrezi hatao, Hindi chalao' (get rid of English and introduce Hindi). This slogan at first seemed to the unsophisticated to be purely nationalistic (being directed against the English language). But perhaps at the back of the mind of the protagonists of Hindi was the idea that if the Tamilians, the Bengalis, the Assamese and the Kerala-ites were sent packing home, they would have a superabundance of jobs. Perhaps I am being too cynical. But I have heard students talking seriously about it. In any case, life in the universities of Bihar, Uttar Pradesh, Rajasthan and at Delhi University in the heart of the capital city, was completely paralysed. Kerala-ite teachers in Bihar universities began looking for other jobs and some scholars of international repute in Delhi University began thinking of going abroad. Some young 'progressive' professors who had no objection to terror per se, immediately noticed that it was a different kind of terror and protested.

In such situations, men are known to hit back. Once the Hindi agitation, aided and abetted by the local politicians and bureaucracy, got off to a start, others were not slow to follow. The cry of 'Maharashtra for Maharashtrians', 'Save Panjabi language and culture', 'Assam for Assamese' and 'Harvana for Haryanvi Jats' soon went up. In a sense, the supra-regional national loyalties were superseded by local and regional loyalties. And any anti-centre movement – or any stick to beat the centre with – caught the imagination of the student community. The worst, of course, happened in Madras (now Tamil Nadu) where a known secessionist party, the DMK, which has since given up its openly secessionist policies, got power – perhaps the reward for guiding a student agitation of enormous dimensions. The support of the Shiv Sena among the students in Maharashtra is very great indeed. And although in Assam nobody will accept the idea that the Lachit Sena has any influence on them, or the society in general, this is perhaps true only in so far as they do not have organizational links with it. The arguments used in discussion among the students bear a close resemblance to its principles.

So dominant have these local regional loyalties become in the states on the periphery of India, that even such parties as the Communists, which, whatever their other faults cannot be accused of localism, have had to use regional arguments to keep this vast educated mass in good humour. Thus the West Bengal Government, which until recently was Marxist-dominated, had to give informal advice to the administration not to employ the 'outsiders'.

It would therefore be an error to think that the protest movement among the Indian students is merely political. This is an over-simplification, for besides being political it has fundamental socio-economic causes. There is no doubt, of course, that both in its impact and in its outward manifestation, it may seem essentially political. But basically speaking it is multi-dimensional and very complex indeed. It is hardly surprising that it has political implications, far more surprising that it has caste, communal and regional political implicatons. These developments did not take place, however, until after the time of confidence and hope when the students generally tended to ignore regional and local loyalties. Once began, however, recession and the economy stagnated, local communal and regional leadership was able to make a strong bid for loyalty.

A short bibliography may be useful to the reader:

Philip G. Altbach, 'The Transformation of the Indian Student Movement', *Asian Survey*, vol. VI, no. 8 (August 1966), pp. 448–60.

Chitta Ranjan, 'Thoughts on Student Unrest', *Mainstream*, vol. V, no. 7 (15 October 1966), pp. 8–12.

Commentator (pseudonym), 'The Price of Alienation', *Economic and Political Weekly*, 22 October 1966, pp. 393–5.

'Crisis on the Campus: a symposium', *Seminar*, no. 44 (April 1963), pp. 10–41.

P. C. Joshi, 'Social Background of Social Unrest', *Mainstream*, vol V, no. 8 (22 October 1966), pp. 18–20.

'Students in Turmoil', *Seminar*, no. 88, pp. 10–48.

'Violence', *Seminar*, no. 116 (April 1969), pp. 10–41.

Japan in Transition

Fukuji Taguchi*

When foreigners think of protest and discontent in present-day Japan, many of them will imagine a group of radical students wearing helmets and throwing petrol bombs. These are only one superficial caricature, however, of the discontents which underlie contemporary Japanese social and economic conditons. It is difficult in present-day Japan to find any social group which has no discontents.

Workers complain that their wages and salaries are low when compared with the high accumulation of capital in the companies in which they work. They also complain of the growing specialization and monotony of their jobs. Peasants suffer as their children leave for the cities to work in big companies, for this loss of labour creates many problems for small farmers. Intellectuals, particularly of the left, are dissatisfied with the Government's domestic and foreign policies and express hostility to the Government's attitudes towards the Vietnam War and the Okinawa problem. Students are discontented not only with Government policies but also with their poor living conditions, inadequate academic facilities, and the insensitive administration of many universities. City dwellers are continuously harassed by problems of high rents, overcrowding, traffic, and air pollution. Housewives complain of rising prices and inflation.

What are the causes of these complaints and discontents? Setting aside international conditions, the social and economic discontents of the Japanese people are principally the inevitable results of the so-called 'High Economic Growth' of Japan which began in 1955–6. At the same time the pheno-

*The author is a Professor of Politics in Meiji University at Tokyo and was a Visiting Fellow from 1969–70 at the Centre for Japanese Studies, Sheffield University.

menon of 'High Economic Growth' has had a very important impact on the established political structure which has been called the 'Régime of 1955'. Economic growth has partly strengthened the established political scheme, but fundamentally it is contributing to its long-term decline. The extremist and violent student movements of the present are merely one symptom of the gradual collapse of the 'Régime of 1955'.

In the following paragraphs I intend to explain the true significance of the 'Régime of 1955' and the social, economic, and political consequences of 'High Economic Growth'.

What is the 'Régime of 1955'? After the end of the American Occupation, there followed a remarkable process of organization and realignment among many social, political and economic groupings.

In the social and economic field, various kinds of occupational and interest groups began to organize and consolidate so as to influence the Government. Typical examples are the Federation of Economic Organizations (Keidanren), the Japanese Federation of Employers' Associations (Nikkeiren) and the Japanese Management Association (Dōyūkai) which represent financial groups and big business; the Political Federation of Japanese Small Businesses (Chuseiren) which represents small enterprises; the General Council of Trade Unions ((Sōhyō) and the Trade Union Congress (Zenrō) representing labour; the Agricultural Co-operative Associations (Nōkyō) representing peasants, and the Japan Medical Association representing doctors. The condition of 'organizational democracy' in Japan was clearly apparent by 1955.

In the political sphere, two conservative parties, the Liberal Party and the Democratic Party, responded to demands from Japanese financial circles for 'conservative solidarity' and joined together to form the Liberal Democratic Party in November 1955. A little earlier in the same month, two socialist parties, the so-called Left Socialist and Right Socialists (which had split in 1951 over the Peace Treaty and the Japan–U.S. Security Pact), united and again formed the Japan Socialist Party. In view of the rising percentage of Socialist votes in previous elections (in 1955 Socialists had about one-third of the seats in the Japanese Lower House), the Socialists hoped that they would soon gain office. As a result the two-party system first came into existence in post-war Japanese politics. At that time, the third party, the Japanese Communist Party, was almost negligible. It had been weakened by the anti-Communist policies of the Occupation Army and the unpopularity which it had incurred through its tactics of violent revolution during the period 1951–3.[1]

This was not, of course, a true two-party system, and it is better to refer to it as 'a one-and-one-half party system'. The Government party, the Liberal Democratic Party, has in fact held about two-thirds of the seats in the National Diet since 1955, while the Japan Socialist Party has remained a one-third minority.

What were the characteristics of the 'Régime of 1955'? Especially what were the particular relations which existed between the two main political parties and various types of organized groups? Firstly, as the term 'one-and-one-half party system' suggests, it was a conservative régime whose rule seemed to be absolutely invulnerable. In contrast, left-wing groups remained a one-third minority, which was represented, at least in the Diet, by the Socialist Party. It is true that there were acute tensions between the conservative and progressive camps, but after 1960, the year of the struggle against the revision of the Security Treaty, there arose a tendency for the parliamentary Socialist Party to become a mere complement to conservative rule. There developed on the one hand intimate and exclusive connexions between the conservative party and various organizations representing financial and industrial interests, as well as other conservative pressure groups, and on the other between the Socialist Party and the trade unions, mainly those affiliated with Sōhyō.[2]

If we consider the permanence of conservative rule and

1. It is suggested that both Chinese and Soviet influences helped to produce these violent tactics.

2. See my article, 'Pressure Groups in Japanese Politics', in *The Developing Economies* V, 1–4 (December 1968), pp. 468–86.

the new links between parties and pressure groups, we can draw some political conclusions. (i) The political structure of conservative rule means in fact the quasi-monopolistic usurpation of the decision-making function by the 'Triangular League'. This consists of leaders of the ruling party, senior government officials and big business circles which lead a host of conservative-inclined pressure groups. (ii) The JSP-Sōhyō bloc, alienated from political power, developed its own relationship of mutual dependence. The Sōhyō-affiliated unions, by officially deciding to support JSP, provide the JSP with candidates, votes and funds for elections; and the JSP, in return, offers party-tickets to trade-union leaders who have ascended to the top of the 'status escalator' and engage in tactful manoeuvring inside the Diet, to promote the interests of the Sōhyō unions and to protect them from Government attacks. (iii) The 'Régime of 1955' was one of minority politics, not only because political power had long been monopolized by the conservative camp, the nucleus of which was composed of the 'Triangular League', but also because pressure group politics might be equated with minority group politics in three senses. First, among the countless interests in Japanese society which deserve representation, only those of a few groups, including organized labour, are protected in this system. For example, the interests of the mass of urban consumers are barely represented. Again, in the case of industrial workers, the interests of the unorganized employees of small and medium-sized companies, who make up two-thirds of the total industrial labour force, are left undefended. Second, among those groups which actually articulate their own interests, there are considerable differences between the degrees of influence which they can exercise on Government. Third, as oligarchic control is well developed within the pressure groups themselves, the fruits of the activities undertaken in the name of groups are more often than not enjoyed almost exclusively by group officials and a few others. If the 'Régime of 1955' is nothing but minority politics, where and how will the demands and the interests which aspire for realization and representation find their outlets? But before answering this question, we must proceed to discuss the consequences of 'High Economic Growth'.

Japanese high economic growth is a fact which is widely acknowledged, sometimes with envy, sometimes with admiration. I do not want to discuss in detail the causes which produced this growth, but merely to mention the consequences which it has produced. Economically high economic growth meant for Japanese big business not only the rapid growth and development of its huge productive power, but also a high rate of capital accumulation, which prepared the material and economic base for what Socialists call the 'imperialistic and militaristic' revival of Japanese capitalism. It is perhaps unnecessary to say that this in fact strengthened the controlling power of big business and financial circles over small and medium enterprises, and over the conservative Government which was in turn reinforced by the increasing economic and social power of big business.

The chief political landmark of this trend can be seen in the appearance of the present Satō Government, which is one of the most reactionary cabinets in post-war Japanese politics. In 1965, this Government signed the Japan–South Korea Treaty, which aimed at the consolidation of the anti-Communist camp in the Far East, and at economic penetration into South Korea. Economic expansion into South East Asia has also been an important political tendency. The co-operation and support given to the American war against the Vietnamese people is another important aspect of recent Government policy. The Satō Government's moves towards extreme conservatism at home and imperialistic and anti-Communist expansion and aggressiveness abroad have produced fierce hostility among many people, not only among those who are left-wing. Even those who are conservative-inclined, but who are imbued with the spirit of the so-called 'Peace Constitution', oppose many aspects of Government policy.

Since high economic growth has taken place with the aim of the unlimited pursuit of profit on capital, and has been achieved through an anarchic and plundering exploitation of the country's land and resources, there has been a rapid and haphazard process of urbanization. For example, there has been a large concentration of population into metropolitan areas – such as 11 million people living in Greater Tokyo. It has impaired the living and working environment of the population, especially in the cities, and is gradually damaging their lives and health. In other words, it has produced serious social problems, often termed 'public hazards' or 'problems of environment', as well as worsening of the level of social welfare and aggravating the condition of housing and traffic. Viewed from this standpoint, high economic growth has deepened the contradictions between the conservative Government and the common people and increased serious discontents among the people, especially city-dwellers.

There was another aspect of the consequences of high economic growth: the drastic transformation of the social and industrial structure of Japan. A rapid industrialization accompanied by too rapid urbanization has produced territorial imbalances in population, level of development, and wealth. These trends have created, on the one hand, the over-concentrated metropolitan areas like Greater Tokyo; and, on the other hand, the over-dispersed rural areas where there remain only a few old people and animals. It has also produced a huge transformation in the employment structure. The working men, in the broadest sense, those who earn their livings through wages and salaries, have come to include over 50 per cent of the total population, while the agricultural population has recently fallen to 20 per cent, compared with over 40 per cent in 1955. Among these only one-fifth can earn a living by farming alone and the rest have to pursue other jobs on the side to supplement their income from agriculture.

What are the political effects of these transformations of Japan's social and industrial structure? The economic decline of rural areas and their depopulation will certainly damage conservative strength, because the countryside has so far been the main stronghold of the Liberal Democratic Party and has enabled it to maintain its overwhelming majority in the

National Diet. In addition, tension between the LDP and the Agricultural Co-operative Associations has been increasing. These Co-operative Associations, which contain all farming families (over five million) and have provided the LDP with a very large percentage of peasant votes, are among the biggest pressure groups in Japan. They have come to be more and more in conflict with the Government which has recently rejected their demand for an increase in the price of rice, using 'over-production' as a pretext. Thus one of the main bases on which conservative dominance and the 'Régime of 1955' was built is now being undermined.

In urban areas there are now many newcomers from the countryside as well as the original inhabitants. I have already outlined the increasing problems and difficulties of urban life which have been caused by Japan's high rate of economic growth, and have pointed to some of the growing discontents and dissatisfactions of city dwellers. These discontents and complaints about their deteriorating environment, coupled with their antipathy towards Government policies, are leading to a more rapid decline in LDP support. Recently the voting strength of the Liberal Democratic Party in big cities has ranged from 25 to 40 per cent, and symbolically in April 1967 Tokyo elected as its governor Mr R. Minobe, who was supported by both the Socialist and Communist parties and by a broad grouping of progressive intellectuals and trade unionists. These developments are certainly manifestations of protest against conservative rule.

Does the tendency to decline of the Liberal Democratic Party, particularly in urban areas, benefit the Socialist Party, Japan's biggest opposition party? Alas, it does not. For the strength of the Japan Socialist Party is, in fact, declining as rapidly or even more rapidly than that of the Government party. Many reasons can be given: the Socialist Party's very low membership, its very heavy dependence on Sōhyō-affiliated trade unions, the weakness of its extra-parliamentary organizations, and its lack of independent sources of party funds, all reduce its effectiveness. Furthermore, the party suffers from fierce factional struggles. Certainly the JSP has failed to attract workers who have to come to the cities from rural areas, whether they be young employees of large companies or older men working in small traditional enterprises. In addition the Socialist Party has failed to maintain its traditional support among Sōhyō-affiliated trade-unionists. This has been partly caused by the decline of Sōhyō's relative position, which is the result of Japan's changing industrial structure. At the same time new offensives by Government, management and another big Trade Union Federation (Zenrō, now known as Dōmei) have further weakened the position of Sōhyō. Even within Sōhyō's affiliated unions the cry for freedom to support any political party has been voiced among rank and file members.

In view of these changes, how are people who feel disillusioned with the two main parties able to express their dissatisfactions? A small percentage of them, particularly in Dōmei and what are termed the 'political-neutral independent trade unions' support the Democratic Socialist Party. This right-wing social democratic party broke away from the JSP in 1960. However the majority of new and old urban dwellers who are alienated from the 'prosperity' and 'abundance' of 'High Economic Growth' are now being organized as political supporters of either Kōmei-to (the 'clean-government' Party) or the Japanese Communist Party. These alienated groups are composed of workers in small and medium enterprises, poor craftsmen and owners of very small shops and factories. Of the parties these people support, Kōmei-to is based upon Sōka-gakkai, one of the biggest new religious bodies in contemporary Japan. Kōmei-to and Sōka-gakkai both advocate the integration of politics and 'the' religion which is, in fact, a branch of the medieval Buddhist Nichiren sect, and promise to produce benefits on earth as well as innovations in Japanese politics. They are gathering support and claim a membership of six million households.

The Communist Party, which recovered its strength from 1961 when it adopted its new programme, now has 300,000 party-members and a voting strength of three million. The recovery of its strength was accelerated by its 'independent' attitude towards both Maoism and Moscow in recent years. The JCP probably wants to become both a 'mass' and 'national' party which decides its policies independently, and acts on its own irrespective of the intentions of Peking and Moscow. The JCP competes fiercely with Kōmei-to to attract the same alienated city dwellers. It has also a strong influence on the Japanese student movement and 65 per cent of student unions of Japanese universities are under its leadership.

As a result of these developments, a tendency towards a multi-party system, especially in urban areas, is appearing in contemporary Japan. For example, in the election for the Tokyo Metropolitan Assembly on 13 July 1969, the results were as follows:

	Seats	Percentage of total vote	Comparison with percentage in previous election
LDP (Liberal Democratic Party)	54	33·0	+2·8
JSP (Japan Socialist Party)	24	24·2	−3·8
KMT (religious 'clean government' party)	25	17·3	+4·0
JCP (Japanese Communist Party)	18	14·5	+4·4
DSP (Democratic Socialist Party)	4	4·9	−1·9

As can be seen, the LDP recovered some strength, but its voting strength remains at one third of the total vote. The JSP failed to halt its decline and slipped into third place. In contrast, for the first time, Kōmei-to became the second biggest party, and the JCP increased substantially its seats and voting strength.

It is still too early to say that 'Régime of 1955' has collapsed, mainly because the LDP still manages to preserve its
overall majority in the National Diet. But one cannot doubt
that the 'Régime of 1955' is now declining – ironically enough,
as the result of high economic growth. The tendency towards
a 'multi-party system' in the present-day Japan is certainly
one of the most marked expressions of discontents and protests among ordinary people.

There are some people, particularly some young students,
some young labourers, and some left-wing intellectuals, who
are dissatisfied not only with the conservative and Socialist
parties, but with all existing political parties, including the
Japanese Communist Party. In other words, some people
strongly dislike not only the 'Régime of 1955', but also the
whole present political situation in Japan. They form the so-
called 'New Left'. The main forces of 'New Left' are composed of various factions of the student movements, such as
Trotskyists, Maoists, anarchists and 'militant structural reformists'. These various student factions oppose each other
very fiercely, but try to unite themselves to fight against the
Japanese Communist Party and the Communist-led student
movement.[3]

Generally they act under the slogan of 'Anti-imperialism
and Anti-Stalinism' which means opposition to the Satō
Government and 'Japanese monopolistic capitalism', to
'American imperialism' and to 'World Communism' (particularly in the case of the JCP).

The 'Anti-War Action Committees' of young trade

3. Curiously enough, there are now three '*Zengakuren*' organizations in
the Japanese student movement. One is Communist-led, another is composed of one faction of Trotskyist groups, and the third is a mixed brigade
of factions of some Trotskyists, Maoists, 'structural reformists' and other
groups. The latter two organizations, together with their sympathizers
among teachers and some other intellectuals, formed the 'Federation of All
University Fronts' (*Zenkyōtō-Rengō*) in summer 1969. But there arose
constant internal, and often violent, disputes among its component groups.
See, for example, 'The Japanese Student Movement' in the *Japan Quarterly*,
vol. 15, no. 4 (October–December 1968) and continued in vol. 16, no. 1
(January–March 1969).

unionists and some, though not all, 'citizens movements' (for example, the Confederation for Peace in Vietnam) are also part of this 'New Left' movement. These have generally very strong sympathy towards the extreme student movements and very deep antipathy towards the Communist Party.

Here I should like to explain the attitude of the so-called Japanese progressive forces towards the extreme student movement. The Communist Party defines them as the political 'provocateurs' and 'destroyers of the democratic united front'. The leadership of Sōhyō condemns them on the grounds that they often disturb the unity of anti-Government movements, but Sōhyō's criticism is less fierce than that of the Communists. The attitude of the Socialist Party is rather complex. The left-wing of the party, particularly the Maoists, give more or less open support to the students, but the leadership of the party criticizes their violent behaviour a little and at the same time makes gestures of sympathy towards the students' 'genuine' motives – with the aim of utilizing their energies to fight both the conservatives and the Communists. But so far the leaders of the JSP are failing in this strategy, and in fact there have been many disturbances among Socialist Party organizations which have been infiltrated by extremists.

The rise of 'new' radicalism, typically represented by the extreme student movement of recent years, is of course an international phenomenon, especially in the advanced capitalist countries. One can recognize many common factors internationally in the conditions which produced the Japanese extremist student movement and also in its ideologies and behaviour. These common international conditions include the world monetary crisis, 'poverty in prosperity', and the 'dirty Vietnam War' on the one hand, and the 'crisis and fragmentation of Marxism (Communism)', which began in 1956, on the other.

Ideologically this 'new' radicalism, which is linked to these international factors, denounces all established movements and institutions and advocates 'direct democracy', 'autonomous control' and 'direct action' (frequently 'violent direct action') as their counterparts in other countries do. Don't these slogans recall those of Proudhonism, Bakuninism, Blanquism and Anarcho-Syndicalism of a century or half a century ago?

Psychologically many participants in the radical student movement feel that they cannot communicate with other people, and also feel completely alone. As a result, they confirm their identity by the negation of all the established institutions and by proclaiming the idea of direct action. They also appeal to violence as a means to their endless process of self-affirmation. This psychology represents one of the typical 'true believer' who finds his relief in mass movements. One writer has described this ideology and mentality as 'an amalgam of an existentialist view of life with political nihilism, adorned with empty revolutionary words'.

If the behaviour of Japanese extremist radical movements has any special characteristics, these are merely their use of staves and shields in almost ritualistic violence. This violence is directed not only at the riot police, but also at the students who belong to rival factions or who belong to the same faction but object to some aspects of the faction's policy (people call this sort of violence 'internal violence'). What are the causes and conditions of this ritualistic violence? I think that these consist of curious mixtures of traditional and ultra-modern elements. In speaking of traditional elements I am referring to a similarity between the violent tactics of present-day students and those of radical right-wing movements among the young military in the 1930s. The pre-war rightists did not believe in the strength of reasonable persuasion and advocated a *coup d'état* and carried out political assassinations. In speaking of ultra-modern elements, I am referring to the fear of freedom of the 'shaken up' generation in the conditions of a highly managed society. They can find reassurance only in practising a ritual of violence against the riot police and 'fellow' students. The common factors which these two elements contain are a lack of faith both in reason and in oneself, and a furious resentment against an uncontrollable and repressive régime, and the resort to violence as a compensation for a lack of self-confidence and as part of their resentment at the 'oppressive tolerance' of society.

But aren't the extreme movements, especially violent student movements, at least one expression of discontent and protest in contemporary Japan? Yes, they certainly are. Behind these movements there are many of the discontents and grievances of ordinary students. The expansion and multiplication of Japanese universities began in 1949, and has been accelerated by the impact of Japan's high economic growth. There are now some one and a half million university and college students, one in five of the same age group. They are no longer an élite in any sense, but just the 'student masses'. Many of them have no prospect of a good future career. Furthermore, academic conditions are terrible and the attitudes of university management are completely obsolete. Students also generally feel that the conservative Government is very reactionary and that the Government policies towards Vietnam and Okinawa are immoral. Some of them also suspect that both the Socialist and Communist parties are consciously or unconsciously part of the mechanism of conservative rule, or are merely inert despite the seriousness of the present situation. In this climate it is not surprising, however lamentable, that a small percentage of students are attracted towards extremism and will join violent factions. (Although one must not forget that more students are organized by the Communist Party than by the extremists. Kōmei-to also has a campaign to organize its own student movement. Besides these, there are some very small student groups which have connexions with the Socialist Party, the Democratic Socialist Party, the Liberal Democratic Party and some right-wing organizations.)

I should like, however, to add two further points. Firstly, these movements have so far advanced by utilizing the historical assets and the present accumulation of strength of all progressive forces. These forces include both the Socialist and Communist parties as well as trade unions – which they attack fiercely as the 'Old Left' or the 'Established Left Wing'. They claim to be exploiting these historical assets, but they are in fact 'protected' by them. Is it not a paradox or a self-conceit that they are deeply dependent on 'enemy forces' which they furiously deny? It is rather ridiculous that they over-estimate their 'physical strength' as a result of their own conceit.

Secondly, one can also note the mutual relationship which has emerged between the extreme student movement and the conservative Government. We can recognize such relationships between them in the process of the so-called 'university struggles' which reached their peak in the attacks and counter-attacks around the Yasuda Auditorium at Tokyo University in January 1969. The university struggles are being ended by the Government's 'University Control' legislation which was forced through the Diet in the summer of 1969. In these struggles extremist students demanded the disorganization of universities, barricaded themselves in university buildings, and fought against riot police with petrol bombs, stones and other weapons. The Government exploited these extraordinary situations and utilized the antipathy of ordinary citizens towards extremist students in order to enact the University Control Law which was adopted despite the strong resistance of all opposition parties. In this way, the Government gained the legal right to intervene in university disputes and to control the management of universities. Conversely Japanese universities lost at least some of their rights of self-government. In short, the students behave in an ultra-leftist and adventurist way, pretending to be the only force involved in a fundamental confrontation with the reactionary Government. Government in turn tries to exploit their violent behaviour as a pretext for suppressing the democratic rights and freedoms of all working-class and progressive forces. Thus if we evaluate the political role of the extremist violent student movement, we must conclude that their role is one of a political 'provocateur'.

The extreme student groups were badly hit by the Government during their struggle against Prime Minister Satō's visit to the United States in November 1969. Most of the leading activists were arrested by the riot police. After these widespread arrests it has been difficult for these extreme organizations to revive and regroup. The worst result of these struggles has been the Government's increasingly oppressive attitude not only towards students but towards all progressive forces. I feel very uneasy when I hear that many city-dwellers, particularly small shopkeepers, tradesmen and craftsmen have organized 'self-protection bands' against students' violence. These remind me of the war-time 'neighbourhood associations' ('Tonari-Gumi') and 'street associations' ('Chōnai-Kai's')[4] which were basic units of Japanese fascist social and political organization. I hope that my fear will not be realized, but one cannot deny that the conservative mood of public opinion was strengthened by both the behaviour of the ex-tremist movement and the manoeuvres of the conservative Government.

It is certainly necessary to make fundamental changes in the political and economic régime of contemporary Japan. As I mentioned above, the decline of the 'Régime of 1955' and the appearance of a trend towards a multi-party system are obvious signs that changes are necessary. But the conservative camp tries to halt its decline and to recover and consolidate its strength. In contrast the so-called progressive forces have many difficulties. These include the failure of the Socialists to halt their decline, the stagnation of united action and the poor prospects for a united front. The different attitudes of progressive forces towards extremist student groups and Maoism further aggravate the difficulty of left-wing forces. Kōmei-to is ideologically one of the 'middle of the road' parties. Its programme is very similar to that of the Democratic Socialist Party, but its future behaviour is difficult to predict. And these two 'middle of the road' parties fiercely oppose each other.

As the present political situation of Japan is so complex and chaotic, it is too early and too difficult to predict the next stage of Japanese political development. But one thing is cer-

4. These associations were organized from above by the Government and served as mutual supervising systems as well as war-time administrative units.

tain. Japanese politics is now passing through a transitional phase: from the 'Régime of 1955' and its decline to . . .? It is as yet impossible to predict what Japan's next régime will be.

Generations in America

David C. Rapoport*

*The fathers have eaten sour grapes and the children's teeth
are set on edge.*
Ezekiel.

Many observers compared Europe's discontents in 1968 with
its revolutionary upsurges in 1848. Juxtaposing these two
points in American history yields even more startling parallels.[1] In some respects the issues raised are identical; even the
very scene today looks like a repeat performance.

In 1848 the Mexican War deeply divided America. The opposition, including the young Congressman Abraham Lincoln,
accused the President of deceitfully manipulating Congress
into declaring an unwanted, unjust war. So extraordinary
did the credibility question seem, so powerful were the passions evoked, that one scholar much later, from the vantage
of the more placid Eisenhower administration, characterized
the situation as one beyond the range of the modern American's political imagination.

Today it is almost inconceivable that we should be involved in a foreign
war in which the President could be denounced as the aggressor and a
foreign enemy could be described as the victim by leading members of
the opposition. Lincoln's denunciation of [President] Polk in the
House came very close to what a later and an earlier age would call
treason or at least criminal disloyalty.[2]

*The author teaches political theory at the University of California,
Los Angeles, and has published a variety of articles on corruption and
military conspiracy.

1. I am indebted to my colleague Leo Snowiss for suggesting the possibility of a fruitful comparison of 1848 and 1968.

2. H. V. Jaffa, *Crisis of the House Divided* (New York, 1959), p. 67.
Lincoln himself was denounced in similar terms when he became President.

Then as now the war was inseparable from the nation's racial predicament. The opposition of '48 insisted that the war was undertaken to spread slave territory; today most believe that the unintended consequence of Vietnam is a massive diversion of energies from the prime domestic question – justice for the black man. Earlier, impatience with the existing constitutional procedures stimulated first a doctrine of civil disobedience, vividly expressed by anarchists like Thoreau, and then a fascination with violent direct action as represented by abolitionists like John Brown. Recently the pattern has been repeated again.

In both periods, a President decided not to run for a second term. Earlier, the majority coalition forged by Jackson collapsed; nowadays, the Roosevelt coalition is in shambles. When the Mexican War ended, domestic opponents became *more* rather than *less* inflexible; and there are good reasons to think that the same thing will happen again.

These parallels are not simply striking sets of coincidences. Every system has its own perennial moral questions; in raising one, impulses are generated to raise the others again.[3] Constitutions, moreover, channel outrage in specific directions. In America indignation concerning war immediately involves the President, so comprehensive is his responsibility for foreign policy and for military movements. When the black question is re-examined, the party arrangements are threatened because ever since the Civil War regional and national alliances have been composed in the light of certain assumptions concerning the black man's place in the system.

What then distinguishes 1968 from 1848? Most contemporaries would say that we have a 'generation gap' while they did not. Yet Lincoln's speeches suggest that his period had this problem too. In 1838, he interpreted the growing pro-

Although Lyndon Johnson discomforted critics by comparing himself to Lincoln during the Civil War, neither he nor they seemed to grasp the irony of Lincoln's fate.

3. The movement for 'female emancipation' in America began in the 1840s, and during the present discontents the issue has been revived in the Women's Liberation Front and similar groups.

pensity to mob violence throughout all portions of America to signify that his generation was in spiritual revolt against its fathers, who had established the constitution. The result could be catastrophic:

That our government should have been maintained in its original form from its establishment until now, is not much to be wondered at. It had many props to support its establishment through that period which now are decayed, and crumbled away. Through that period it was felt by all to be an undecided experiment; now it is understood to be a successful one. Then, all that sought celebrity and fame and distinction, expected to find them in the success of that experiment. Their all was staked upon it; their destiny was inseparably linked with it. Their ambition aspired to display before an admiring world, a practical demonstration of the truth of a proposition, which had hitherto been considered, at best no better, than problematical; namely the capability of a people to govern themselves. If they succeeded they were to be immortalized.... If they failed, they were to be called knaves and fools and fanatics.... They succeeded.... [T] he game is caught; and I believe it is true, that with the catching, end the pleasures of the chase. This field of glory is harvested, and the crop is already appropriated. But new reapers will arise and they, too, will seek a field.... The question then is can [their ruling passion] be gratified in supporting and maintaining an edifice erected by others. Most certainly it cannot.... Towering genius disdains a beaten path. It seeks no distinction in adding story to story, upon the monuments of fame erected to the memory of others. It denies that it is glory enough to serve under any chief. It scorns to tread in the footsteps of any predecessor, however illustrious. *It thirsts and burns for distinction; and if possible, it will have it, whether at the expense of emancipating slaves or enslaving freemen* (my emphasis).

I

There are differences between the rivalry of generations in 1848 and 1968. Earlier the conflict involved a 'competition' between the dead and the living who were unable to confront each other directly. There was no recognizable political distinction between young and old men for the young lacked a belief in their own unity. As society's most passionate elements, the young became militants within existing social groupings, and the ensuing violence was largely *between* youths.

'Youth' today is self-conscious and the battle is joined directly with the old. The extraordinary expansion of the universities has given youth a predominant occupation and provided spawning grounds for his political energies. Visualize the difference between 1848 and 1968 in Marxist categories: the young men of the nineteenth-century, like Marx's peasant, were too dispersed to see themselves as members of a class, but the geography of the university, like that of the factory before it, has wrought a fundamental change.

For several decades, the development of youth as a class was becoming visible before that unit was expressed in political terms. After World War II the affluence of suburban life gave young men time and money. They constituted a special *market*, a unique sub-culture, and their needs were stimulated and communicated by mass media and satisfied by mass production. The sense of common identity grew stronger and more definite in time, embracing wider and wider ranges of activities.

Mass luxury markets are created by advertisers, so the New Left would have us believe. If the dogma is true, a delicious neo-Marxist dialectical irony could be in process. For though youth is only an 'artificial' class fashioned by the hated hucksters, still it, like all real dialectical classes, will finally destroy its creator. Marx argued that the virility of new classes, the reason for their victory, lay in their productive capacities. The weaknesses of the old classes, and the cause for their ultimate extinction, derives from their parasitic condition. Modern youth, however, unlike the bourgeoisie, has never produced, has always been simply a consumer or a parasite. And youth *knows* himself to be a parasite!

A sense of his own shame gives fuel to the youth's desperation. It thwarts his search for worthy allies. Workers, especially younger ones, openly flaunt their contempt. The black man, the prime object of the youth's advances, rubs salt into open wounds, asking the student radical how one who has never worked, never suffered, and never will suffer because his parents are middle class, can ever be reliable? The need to demonstrate that he is not a parasite, that he's not playing at a game which involves no permanent personal risks, conditions the youth's tactics. When the Students for a Democratic Society crumbled in June 1969, the principal factions taunted each other with cries of 'comfortable revolutionary' and 'parasite'. All factions felt compelled to leave the university, their natural constituency and sanctuary, to prove themselves in the society at large. The Weathermen, the most belligerent element, openly compared themselves to the middle-class student revolutionaries of late nineteenth-century Russia 'going back to the peasants and terrorism'.

As Lincoln noted, the conflict between generations always has deep unconscious roots, and the frantic behaviour of our youth has, as one might expect, provided American psychiatrists with delightful possibilities. Bruno Bettelheim has written one of the more sensible accounts, 'Obsolete Youth: Towards a Psychograph of Adolescent Rebellion';[4] it has been widely discussed in the universities, although now that Vice-President Agnew has endorsed the argument in a prepared speech on 10 December 1969, one wonders how seriously academics will continue to treat it.

Bettelheim believes that the issues youth addresses itself to are not those which really concern them, and that the solution to present difficulties presupposes that Americans realize that they 'prolong adolescence long beyond that which any other period in history thought desirable.' In adolescence, Bettelheim notes, the search for identity culminates in excruciating agony and stimulates the most violent aggressive impulses which are directed alternatively against society and against oneself. The adolescent cannot wait to become a man, to prove that he has the relevant knowledge and firmness. A century ago most young men assumed a productive role earlier. Society no longer automatically provides means for establishing their worth; for, Bettelheim notes, we have become so wealthy that the time young men must provide for themselves can be postponed. We keep them in school too long and compound natural frustrations by the sense of dependency

4. *Encounter*, September 1969, pp. 29–42.

that an education paid for by someone else always fosters. 'Since they feel themselves to be parasites ... they come to hate a world which gives them such a feeling.'

The youth of today is dominated by hate, not a desire for a better world. His fascination with violence, contempt for reason, craving for destruction and revenge, passionate effort to use political causes to create personal significance – all these things and many more stem from his own suspicion that he lacks real worth. Bettelheim's simple solution, identical to the one the philosopher William James propounded in 'The Moral Equivalent of War' nearly sixty years ago, is a compulsory 'youth service programme for a few years' duration in which young people could work on socially relevant projects while earning pay and getting higher professional training as they do.'

Although much in Bettelheim's discussion is worth commending, the moral and political issues youth raise cannot be explained away by references to *their* psychic disorders and *our* badly-contrived institutions. When Bettelheim uses this formula alone to explain why students object so violently to the Vietnam War, even readers most sympathetic to his diagnosis will wince. The Government, he says, has stupidly allowed students special exemption from the draft thus arousing massive guilt feelings. 'Because if I am exempt from serving in Vietnam while others are not I can only live in peace with myself by believing it an amoral war. (As if there ever was a moral war!)' (Now that Americans have introduced a lottery in the conscription process, Bettelheim's thesis will be put to the test!)

But let us lay the various moral and political questions aside in order to grapple with Bettelheim on his own ground. Profoundly disturbed children usually have uneasy insecure parents; and if a real source of the youth's problems are his parents, can his discontent be properly treated by legislative enactments alone?

Plato argued that the relationship of generations is the key concept in any treatment of political change. The contradictions and ambivalences of the father come to light in the son, who forms a different uneasy equilibrium which subsequently dissolves in the disorders of his progeny. The concept is simple and well-known, pregnant with immense possibilities and subtle elaborations. Yet no American social scientist seems to have grasped the idea, for although enormous energies have been spent studying the psychic disturbances of youth, the parents have remained ignored and are presumably uninteresting subjects.

Bettelheim, it is true, does see the trace of another trail or two, as he hurries after bigger game. As a psychiatrist he finds the enormous change in child-rearing patterns since World War II disturbing. We have been spoiling our children, being 'unwilling to risk displeasure from the child by imposing controls' – a tendency which has been strengthened by a vulgar misinterpretation of Freud's teaching to suggest that repression is wrong. Lacking a true justification for punishment, we coerce and yield erratically, as *our* convenience, not the need of the child, dictates. The child learns that punishment is inconsistent and vindictive, and intuitively senses our guilt and indecision. Unwittingly, we teach him that we can be bullied and he goes through life thinking that everyone else can be pushed around too.

A father who cannot discipline his son is obviously uncertain of his own right to rule. He cannot respect his own standards. A crucial question is what does he really think of himself? Bettelheim, unfortunately, does not treat the question; in fact he makes no effort to demonstrate his belief that insecure permissive parents do produce student revolutionaries. Although laymen have always been quick to relate student discontent to the failure of parents, academics, for reasons interesting to speculate about, have generally ignored the suggestion. The evidence of Samuel Lubell's essay, 'That "Generation Gap"', although collected for different purposes, however, does indicate that those who most resist student radicalism or use of drugs mostly come from strictly run homes.[5]

5. *The Public Interest*, Autumn, 1968, pp. 52–60.

II

Why has the father lost confidence in himself?[6] One important reason, generally overlooked, is that we no longer believe that age gives a man seasoning and perspective. In societies where age was respected, the presumption had to be that as one grew older, one gained more experience, and hence wisdom, to handle the same recurring problems. Now the very word wisdom sticks in our throats, especially and paradoxically, it should be added, in the universities. Even if we understood what it could possibly have meant once, we would be too embarrassed to use it now. What place is there for wisdom when social scientists, journalists, and politicians day after day declare every issue revolutionary, when we are told that the past only teaches us that we are different, when we say that all forms of 'skills' and knowledge will be soon antiquated, when the very term 'modern' suggests something better and something which has never happened before!

Quite obviously there is some truth in the picture Americans paint of themselves, but the monstrous distortions involved are passed over quickly especially in the universities, where the lust for novelty becomes almost unbearable. Whatever their real intention, the parents and the universities have declared themselves irrelevant, suggested that youth experiences something we cannot comprehend, and indicated our envy for their good fortune. Can we blame youth for calling us hypocrites when we will not or cannot yield our official status?

These comments may shed light on the contribution of the 'educated' parents and the universities to the youth's agony; they do not illuminate the relation between the *political* aspirations of the two generations. Every study shows that the overwhelming number of leading student revolutionaries come from liberal or left-wing homes. Bettelheim explains that the 'son has a desperate wish to do better than the

6. I am concentrating on the father but the mother is obviously crucial. The psychiatrist Kenneth Keniston, who generally approves of student radicals, suggests that they come from homes where the female is dominant and the male submissive. (Kenneth Keniston, *The Young Radicals*, Harcourt, Brace and World, New York, 1968).

parents, especially where the parent has become weak in his beliefs.' The young, hence, do accept the values of their parents, but they detect ambivalence and differences between private talk and public behaviour, and they aim to eliminate inconsistencies. The real question, the one everyone ignores, is what happened to the older generation's search for political identity?

Our formative political experiences were depression, war, and post-war recovery. The depression made many hate the community while simultaneously stimulating splendid hopes that they could create a brighter better one to replace it. Contrary to expectation, war revitalized the constitution. Pearl Harbour gave us an indisputably just cause, being the first war in American history to raise no moral doubts, and the victory produced an immense fund of credit which carried us through the post-war period. Unemployment, the most visible evil of the thirties, disappeared. Our recovery seemed miraculous, a product of circumstance rather than conscious effort.

Some critics obviously had a genuine change of heart and recognized that they had been blind to the constitution's virtues and potentialities. But many were stilled because the system's success dazzled them, because there were no alternatives, because they accepted what they *said* they would always despise or reject – money and status – or because they felt too weary or vulnerable to continue the fight. Such men cannot be truly reconciled; the feeling that they have been unworthy gnaws at their souls, distorting their thoughts, language, and deeds.

Note the reaction of one old reformer, now a prominent educator and consultant, to the demands of the young:

My generation accepted the precepts of its parents.... The new generation rejects them. We were wrong and the new generation is right. Our precepts were good but still the new generation is right. They are right because preceptorial is as preceptorial does. We were – and, of course, are – pious frauds. They are impious Abelards ...

It was an unjust America of course. Blacks were Negroes, Negroes were niggers and niggers were ineducable. . . . Jews knew their place and did not take forcible possession of the boardroom. The revolution is long overdue – the revolution which Jeremiah and Jefferson invoked when they said that God's justice would not sleep forever. The evils that were containable under kings are no longer containable under politicians. [Our world] ... is not susceptible of reform. It calls for revolution ...

I am one of the elders of whom I speak. The young terrify me. They terrify me because I have mine, which I got by the exercise of good precepts I learned from my parents plus being white and landing on my feet every time I fell on my face.[7]

What can the young learn from one who declares himself a 'pious fraud', states that the position *he* occupies is unrelated to his merit, and implies that he might be a coward? An answer is contained in Dostoyevsky's *The Possessed*, a novel much in vogue among our youth, for there too the older or liberal generation feels that it has betrayed its dreams and wallows in self-contempt. Creatures of the establishment, they 'relieve' their guilt by spiteful talk about everyone and everything around them, and are haunted by a passage from *Revelations*: 'I know thy works, that thou art neither cold nor hot: I would thou wert cold or hot. So then because thou art lukewarm ... I will spew thee out of my mouth.'

Sour grapes did set the child's teeth on edge. The son became a nihilist whose creed was sincerity. Acting out his father's fantasies he stormed the walls of Jericho with trumpet blasts. A single 'moral' deed would dissolve a corrupt world, or, at least, he reckoned that in the country of the timid the bold always triumph.

The hatred of our youth appals us because it results in senseless destructive acts. But the hatred of our 'enlightened' middle-aged, manifested in constant, cheap, and captious talk, scarcely draws our attention. When egalitarianism was not taken for granted, men did probe the unconscious drives behind the liberal's rhetoric. Nietzsche, Dostoyevsky, and Sorel insisted that the liberal's idealization of the weak really masked a desire to wreak vengeance on the strong for his own inadequacies. They only caught a small portion of our sub-conscious but they did see an essential part, one which in different circumstances, when apprehension of immediate

7. Professor Milton Mayer, 'Children's Crusade: A Search for Light', *Los Angeles Times*, 16 November 1969.

consequences wanes, becomes the dominant passion. The logic of *The Possessed* is that the distance between the desire to inflict or receive pain and an intense delight in doing so is only one generation.

The young really do not know what they want, we complain, but they could easily throw the complaint back in our faces if they weren't so busy exploiting our confusions. So often does the elder generation abandon ordinary standards of *truth* when confronted by moral dilemmas that the 'guilt-ridden liberal' has become a great unanalysed truism of American politics in the past decade.

As one might expect the liberal's shame is most clearly revealed when the black question, American's perennial moral predicament, is discussed. In 1967 justice for the black meant indifference to the colour of a man's skin. Integration or equal rights for *individuals* was the liberal ideal, an ideal consistent with the magnificent traditions of liberal thought. Nowadays, justice for the black means giving him special privileges and rights justified by the fact that he belongs to a separate *community* defined by skin colour. Of course deeper reflection on the meaning of justice may lead one to believe that it was right to alter our basic assumption, but this enormous shift took place in two years without much discussion or soul-searching. It is difficult not to believe that we thought segregation bad when advocated by southern whites and good when it became the policy of the most militant blacks! Ironically, most blacks do not want segregation, and our sentimentalism may in effect make their lot even more cruel, or so Bayard Rustin, whose credentials as a devoted black leader are beyond question, tells us:

The belated and massive rush of the universities, those

It is not the *lumpen-proletariat*, the Negro working classes, the Negro working poor, who are proclaiming: 'We want Negro principals, we want Negro supervisors, we want Negro teachers in our schools.' It is the educated Negroes.... Being blocked from moving up, [they] become not only interested in Negro children, but in getting those teaching jobs, supervisory jobs, and principal jobs for [their] own economic interest.[8]

8. 'Towards Integration as a Goal', *Separatism or Integration: Which*

great well-springs of American liberalism, to deal with the black question demonstrates the same shameful unwillingness to apply ordinary standards of argument and justice. Many have adopted a quota system virtually guaranteeing that the number of black students will be equal to the pro-proportion of black citizens; some academics use double standards of grading; these changes and others as serious are taking place without public consideration of the implications for other minorities, for the nation as a whole, or for the university.

We do not even question the implications for the blacks themselves. Liberals confide that the black man will never have pride and self-confidence until his community has its share of professional men, that this crash programme is a temporary arrangement, and that in time blacks will compete with whites as equals. But currently what happens to the pride of the black who knows he has a second-class degree, what happens to his patient or client, and what happens if the purpose of the programmes are corrupted? Nobody asks, for who can live with the charge of 'racism'?

Does the liberal's guilt prevent him from being truly responsible to the black, from treating him as a man capable of foolish as well as wise actions? In the autumn of 1969 I attended a faculty assembly which vigorously applauded black students who illustrated the meaning of academic freedom to us by quoting extensive passages from the writings of Nkrumah! And yet we continue to lament that our youth is contemptuous.

III

One of the more interesting features of modern youth is his taste for Civil War clothing and hair styles. It is almost as though he is searching for the attire appropriate to relive the most profound emotional upheaval in American history. The wild talk about guerrilla war among the student radicals and the historical parallels to the issues raised give this interpretation superficial plausibility.

Way for America (A. Phillip Randolph Education Fund, 1968), p. 18. The parallel with our attitudes towards the underdeveloped world is striking. The liberal's 'benevolence' made him tolerate dictatorships everywhere as long as dictators used the right slogans.

But the awesome epic of nineteenth-century America will not be repeated. Youth is too parasitic, and his status too transitory for him to create more than a few sporadic and weak terrorist movements. In this respect it would pay us all to look at the experience of nineteenth-century Russia again, where student fury antagonized the peasants and induced the Tsars to halt projected reforms.

In the 1950s when Joseph McCarthy dominated the American scene, apologists used to infuriate liberals by noting that good ends were being accomplished by improper means. Today many liberals use identical arguments to justify student excesses. Youth they say has already improved the moral quality of American politics by compelling a re-examination of one war and calling attention to the black man's plight. Both points are testaments to the liberal's extraordinary indifference to our historical experiences. No student protested at the Korean War but when casualties mounted, the discontent of *voters* unseated a President and his party and forced withdrawal before a peace was concluded. In the more recent case, it is certainly conceivable that student violence over the Vietnam War actually intensified determination to hold on longer.

The young radical and middle-aged liberal fervently believe that the end of the Vietnam War will release sufficient energies to solve finally the black question – a question which, in one form or another, has been present ever since the colonial period. Let us hope they are right. Unfortunately, there are good reasons to think that the end of the war will make the situation worse. The blood shed by the black for his country will no longer be irresistible emotional 'proof' of the justice of his demands, the need to end the war will no longer exist as a compelling reason to yield to domestic pressures, the costly irresponsible sentimentalism of liberal approaches will become more obvious, and, the worst tragedy of all, the black militant may discover that the rhetoric of segregation has made him more vulnerable than he ever thought possible.

Our rancour and irresolution have magnified America's

difficulties immensely, while sapping the strength of our children to cope when they finally inherit our positions. How sour then will the grapes taste! What sort of children can they possibly produce?

Protest in France

Henry Cavanna*

When a Frenchman – a 'continental' – speaks of revolt, revolution or 'events', an Englishman quite simply translates
such words by 'protest and dissatisfaction'. Is the Englishman
too sober or is the Frenchman too grandiloquent? France, no
doubt, is more inclined to have revolutions than Great Britain.
That being said, however, I think one ought to try to find
more accurate terms than 'revolution' or 'protest' to describe the state of mind in France today. The first is too pom-
pous, the second too flat.

France has obviously not had a revolution. The government now in power is, by and large, a faithful continuation of
the government in power in April 1968. The new laws concerning the universities aim to do no more than reform the
university world. French society remains unchanged: parliamentary majority, opposition parties, trade unions, etc. Even
the 'notable' who, one imagined, had disappeared from national political life, reappeared at the time of M. Poher's can-
didature for the Presidency of the Republic. Cohn-Bendit
was, therefore, quite right when he said: 'Those who start
revolutions are always the cuckolds of History.'

And yet, although the establishment (which naturally includes the Communist Party and the C.G.T.) is still in a healthy
condition, the shock caused by the crisis in May 1968 has made
the country aware of a series of factors capable of leading to a
fundamental modification of the structures of traditional
France. France is going through a difficult period; important changes are in the air. In such a context, protest and dis-

*The author is editor of the monthly journal *La Table Ronde*, and was
editor of the recent symposium, *Analyse d'un Vertige*, S.E.P.A.L., Paris,
1969. The article is translated by Mr John Holyoake of the Department of
French, Sheffield University.

satisfaction, whose diversity and multiplicity are the common denominators of any political year, become 'conventional' acts devoid of meaning.

When one analyses the situation in France, however, one must distinguish between what is common to other over-developed countries and what is a specifically French pheno-menon. This second aspect relates especially to the economic, social and political structures of the country. The first, on the other hand, is no more than a particular manifestation of a much wider phenomenon: the crisis of contemporary Western civilization.

Let us first of all examine the specifically French side of the problem. It is really a question of a certain ageing process. In fact, one might say that the organization of administrative structures, indeed of the educational system, is based on the structures inherited from Napoleon Bonaparte. The division of France into *départements* – still governed by prefects appointed by an interfering central authority which finds it difficult to keep its fingers out of departmental affairs – is a good example of this. The work of Napoleon has been only slightly modified in the course of the last one hundred and fifty years. The university system, which Edgar Faure (Minis-ter of Education until the formation of Chaban-Delmas' government) tried to reform, is still l'université imperiale. The École Normale Supérieure, a hot-house for highly qualified university teachers and various other intellectuals, and the École Polytechnique, where top-level industrial and ad-ministrative management receive their training, were founded as early as 1749. The École Nationale d'Administration, foun-ded after the Liberation, is barely an exception to the rule.

The French centralized system, in any case, is a pheno-menon which dates from the *ancien régime*. Inherited from the kings of France, it was adopted and developed by the Revolution, the Empire and the Republics. Moreover, the new political map of France, established by the Emperor and still in force, eliminated the old historical regions but preserved the existing local administrative areas. The result is that to-day France has a total of 38,000 'communes' as compared with 1,354 in Great Britain and 3,475 in Japan. But the population explosion and the boom conditions in urban conurbations demand huge investment programmes: housing and all communal facilities – transport, education, commerce, leisure. French budgetary resources at the local level are insufficient to meet these expenses. To get some idea one need only consider that total expenditure at local level amounts to approximately 22 per cent of expenditure by the central government; that budgets at local level are based on loans – which account for more than 50 per cent of all expenditure on investments – as well as on grants – approximately 30 per cent of expenditure on investments. A scheme worked out by the Club Jean Moulin[1] proposes a reorganization of French local government: 'So far as sizeable administrative areas are concerned, France should consist of 2,000 communes and a dozen regions.'

The countless communes which cover the map of France and the consequent dispersal of financial resources partly explain the gap which exists between the administrative structure, now some two centuries old, and the needs created by the rapid development in the post-war period. Need one add that often the commercial and industrial infrastructures are not adapted to the economic realities of world markets and that, in striving to resolve a social and political problem, the Government has created a further economic problem since it has to face up to extremely large annual deficits? (This is what has happened in the nationalization of many industries.) Nor should one forget the numerous and costly grants made to sectors of the economy which are running down – agriculture, coal-mining, etc. – at a time when these grants are necessary to finance new investments in vital and developing sectors of the economy.

The Government is aware of the gravity of the situation and is trying to remedy it. The flexible '*dirigisme*' of the Plan, the appointment of regional prefects, the desire to decentralize, the plans for regional reorganization are all steps in the right

1. A group of intellectuals and highly placed civil servants of reformist left-wing tendencies.

direction. Time passes quickly, however, and the gap between needs and reality becomes a more and more pressing problem. The fact that the Government is obliged to keep its election promises does not facilitate the implementation of the necessary reforms. This is particularly true in the case of the problem of agricultural workers.

Nevertheless, one must take account of progress which has been made. In spite of the present state of uneasiness, this has been considerable even in the realm of state education; while the school and university population has increased from 8,072,000 in 1956 to 11,534,000 in 1968 – with a 7 per cent increase in the total population of France in the same period – the Ministry of Education's budget has increased from 9.4 per cent to 16.88 per cent of the total budget of the central government.

There is another point which may help one to understand the many reasons for dissatisfaction. De Gaulle, having given France political stability, has unwittingly created a further problem which Professor Duverger, a well-known left-winger, analysed in *Le Monde* (11 June 1969):

Even during the Fourth Republic there were 'parallel' police forces, there were activist groups in the corridors of power, there was tight control over television and radio, there was favouritism in the promotion of civil servants and in the allocation of grants, and there was pressure brought to bear on the judiciary. But at that time power often changed hands so that the group of men seeking preferment also changed. Government instability engendered a sort of equality among the parties, each one being assured of having, in turn, its share of the cake, its share of control (Communists excepted). . . . By conferring power on the same men over a period of years, our new political system has meant the disappearance of this balancing and compensatory mechanism. Now it is a question of establishing different mechanisms. If Great Britain has developed control of the police force, independence of the B.B.C., the Civil Service and the judiciary to a greater extent than any other country, it is because Great Britain has had to deal with a similar problem for many years now.

More deep-seated and much more important is the 'crisis of civilization' which in France, as elsewhere, is a cause of concern to the younger generation. The sense of uneasiness, even of disgust, which the affluent society causes in French students is well known:

'Happiness is not a myth. Adam Smith and Jeremy Bentham rejoice!' cries one of the founders of the '*Internationale Situationiste*'. 'The more we produce, the better we shall live,' writes the humanist Fourastié, whilst another genius, General Eisenhower, echoes this sentiment: 'To save the economy, we must buy, buy no matter what.' 'Production and consumption are the twin breasts at which modern society feeds; being suckled in this way, humanity increases in beauty and strength. . . . Yes, the Golden Age is in sight – it's only spitting distance away.'[2]

In a more sober style, but springing from the same inspiration, one of the revolutionaries of May 1968 scrawled on the stonework of an apartment building, in the rue de Mirbel: 'Consume more, you will live less.'

France would like to be thought, and tries to give the impression of, a very intellectual country. Her cultural tradition, in any case, proves her inclination towards great metaphysical and ideological constructions. We are quite far removed, especially in Paris, from the British or American climate of opinion in which research and the most successful intellectual work are the result of reflection about precise facts and concrete evidence. We French are more interested in the meaning of a civilization, in the future of man, in a word, in the human condition. Fine words once again, more than one victim of Parisian sophistication will remark, snidely. And Heaven knows he will often, but not always, be right. All of this helps to explain the soul-searching which the changes that French society is undergoing provoke in the student world.

Unfortunately, this soul-searching leads to nothing except a rejection of everything as it exists now. But this rejection is based on certain profound reasons, or rather feelings. Cohn-Bendit, the most articulate of the student leaders, explained this on the radio on 4 May 1968:

2. Raoul Vaneigem, *Traité de savoir-vivre à l'usage des jeunes générations*, Gallimard, Paris, 1967.

We are not madmen. Such a term would tend to prove that our motives were simply connected with our passions. Nor are we revolutionaries for we have no well-defined plan of action. Probably the most suitable description would be rebels. Yes, we are in rebellion. Yes, we are fed up with everything.

They are fed up and they are afraid because, for the first time in the history of all utopias, man feels incapable of imagining or even of dreaming of a better world which will *work* and which will *last*. A later commentator on the May events has recognized the fact that there is not the slighest trace of conceptual language in the verbal arsenal of the rebels. 'Money, socialism even, are not so much as mentioned.'[3] Everything is questioned, but no alternatives are offered.

'Society is a carnivorous flower', proclaims one of the graffiti, which finds its logical development in another: 'The economy is sick; so let it die'; or again: 'Your happiness is being paid for, STEAL IT.' There is no escape from the ruined old citadel except by desperate measures: 'Run comrade, the Old World is after you.' Everyone must trust his luck: 'The individual is all-important.' You must act quickly before it is too late: 'Off with your chains and enjoy yourself; live each moment as if it were the last.' If anything tries to block your way, it's up to you to remove it: 'Out of my sight, object', 'For me my ideas are reality since I believe in the reality of my ideas.' After all, perhaps it is the faith I have in my desires which has led me to discover that 'beneath the paving stones lies the sea-shore'.[4]

The revolt of May 1968 was an instinctive and passionate reaction, demonstrating an ancient desire for liberty. It claimed to be a sort of '*fête*', that is to say, an accident interrupting the dull, monotonous, day-to-day tasks of a society

3. Walter Levino, *L'imagination au pouvoir*, Eric Losfeld, Paris, 1968.

4. The force of these graffiti is better appreciated in their original form, reproduced here *seriatim* (translator's note):

'*La société est une fleur carnivore*'; '*L'économie est blessée, qu'elle crève*'; '*On achète ton bonheur, VOLE-LE*'; '*Cours, camarade, le Vieux-Monde est derrière toi*'; '*Seul l'un existe*'; '*Jouissez sans entraves, Vivez sans temps mort*'; '*Cache-toi, objet*'; '*je prends mes désirs pour la réalité, car je crois en la réalité des mes désirs*'; '*dessous les pavés, c'est la plage*'.

which is supremely well and mechanically organized. There are some who assert that this revolt is not simply a protest against a certain order of things 'but also a demand for a different sort of order. Youth is in revolt against restrictions, but also against the nihilism of the affluent society. Youth demands a world which makes sense, which is founded on reason, or, failing that, on a mystique.'[5] Perhaps, in a way, this is true.

Such an impulse is certainly worth something. It is the instinctive reaction of one's being, the vital force asserting its rights; but it would be stupidly wasted unless it were properly channelled in the right direction. For one must not forget that:

The desire which denies all limits, which challenges all restrictions, is not capable of keeping its promise of liberty. Pure passion is ultimately no more than alienation; its tumultuous force soon becomes wearisome and quickly spends itself. . . . The important thing to understand is that liberty cannot escape from the passion which alienates it, seeing that liberty challenges reason in order to overthrow petrified structures. Our language is neither derivative, nor an instrument which the life of desire makes necessary, indeed exalts, but which it also menaces and ruins. Language exists in our lives at a different level – indispensable and irreducible. It exists on the level of good sense, of logic and of universality. We can only make use of it by bending to its need for communication and rationality.[6]

This lucid analysis of the dialectic of revolt is unfortunately not widely known and I fear that our students may not be able to find, in the panoply of contemporary ideas, the materials they need to build the future. Indeed intellectuals today lack the necessary impetus and imagination for the task of reconstructing a new world. They have fallen into a regrettable masochism which leaves them powerless. They have lost faith in reason and in themselves. They believe neither in 'Christian truth', nor in 'atheistic truth', 'conservative truth',

5. Bernard Charbonneau, 'L'émeute et le plan', in *Analyse d'un Vertige*, S.E.P.A.L., Paris, 1969.
6. Claude Bruaire, 'Crise de l'esprit et requête de sa vie', in *Analyse d'un Vertige*, ibid.

or 'socialist truth'. They do not even believe in 'potential truth' or in 'appropriate truth' either.

Nowadays, even the ideas of truth and reason, that is to say, man himself, are questioned. This explains the comment of the mad philosopher: we are oppressed by rationality. But where does this oppression stop? 'Hell is other people', wrote Sartre in 1944, and later, in 1948, 'Ideologies are liberty when they are in the making, oppression when they are made.' This lack of confidence in oneself, this fear of becoming the slave of one's achievements, is not, however, exclusive to Sartre.

All power stems ultimately from the Right.... My view, and I re-affirm it here, is that all power, at least all power which lasts more than a few weeks, has always been, and cannot help being, until nowadays perhaps, a power which comes from the Right.[7]

Man rejects his work because he thinks that his work, in turn, is in the process of repudiating him. The logical out-come of such a dialectic leads the creator to disown himself. But let us begin at the beginning. In the beginning was the father, and this brings us to the source of our misfortunes. So let us revolt against him, for 'there is no such thing as a good father'.[8] It would be better if revolt were not necessary, if the source of trouble were dried up from childhood. This, in fact, was the case. 'Had he lived, my father would have lain on top of me, with his full weight, and crushed me. Fortunately he died young. . . .'[9] 'Having no father, Sartre can set him-self up as the fatherless child who is indeed *causa sui*.[10] 'My good luck was to be born to a dead man.'[11] It is a pity, the wager was almost won. If only it had not been for those 'few drops of sperm which are the normal cost of a child'[12] which the dead father had secreted before he breathed his last . . .

7. Jean-François Revel, *Lettre ouverte à la droite*, Albin Michel, Paris, 1968.

8. Jean-Paul Sartre, *Les mots*, Gallimard, Paris.

9. Ibid.

10. Jean Brun, 'Démythisation de la démythisation', dans *Mythe et Foi*, Aubier, Paris, 1966.

11. Jean-Paul Sartre, *Les mots*, Gallimard, Paris.

12. Ibid.

So we still have to seek for that person we have dreamt of, that person who has no origins: the man whose existence is non-existent. The affluent society, constantly reviled, will however provide us with a most perfect counterpart: a man who grows as he destroys himself, who affirms his existence by self-denial. In fact, we forget that our post-industrial societies are based on a consumer economy which produces a whole vision of the world. Consumption has become a way of life, an adventure and an escape which has turned us into omnivorous beings consuming goods, values, ideas, time, space.

Dialectic itself has for some time been no more than a gigantic method of consumption which assimilates everything: truth, falsehood, lies, base behaviour, *flagrante delicto*.... Dialectic can feed on anything for it recognizes that everything, at one time or another, has contributed to its nourishment; but when the source of nourishment has been consumed, and is of no further use, it is rejected and dubbed 'out of date'.[13]

Authenticity is thus a function of consumption and 'the man of successive states of sincerity' is the one whose self-consumption is performed with lucidity. Jean-Paul Sartre can, with good cause, flatter himself that he plays the part to perfection:

I turned traitor and I stayed a traitor. However wholeheartedly I enter into anything, however much I involve myself in my work, in anger, in friendship, I know that a moment later I shall deliberately deny it all; indeed I betray myself even at the height of passionate commitment by the joyous presentiment of my future betrayal.[14]

Raymond Aron has just written in one of his books: 'After obsession with the quality of goods, comes care for the quality of existence', and he adds, in the same book, 'Protests, renewal of partisan passions, result from a contradiction between aspiration towards the absolute and rejection of the transcendent.'[15] Personally, considering the nature of the con-

13. Jean Brun, 'Christianisme et Consommation', in *Archivio di Filosofia*, Rome, 1968.

14. Jean-Paul Sartre, *Les mots*, Gallimard. Paris,

15. Raymond Aron, *Les désillusions du progrès*, Calmann-Lévy, Paris, 1969.

flict, I find it hard to see what Jean-Paul Sartre's dictum – betrayal as a permanent attitude – could usefully contribute towards a satisfactory solution of the crisis. But one is forced to recognize that if the unconscious calls on the transcendent, the conscious stubbornly remains on this side of the 'beyond'. Could not dialectic, just for once, help to resolve the antithesis of man, which is created 'out of man's dreams, out of the dreams of a creature who, whilst remaining in "intimate communion" with himself, continually longs for the "beyond" which he had hoped to dispense with altogether'?[16]

Let us hope so. There will be a long road to travel before it will be possible to ensure simultaneously the development of the *over*-privileged and the well-being of the *under*-privileged in the full flowering of the individual.

16. Jean Brun, *Le Retour de Dionysos*, Desclée et Cie, Paris, 1969.

Myth, Ideology and Revolution

Ernest Gellner*

The ideology of the protest movement has two marked traits: totality and facility. It stands for 'total commitment'. This it contrasts with the partial, humdrum, moral and intellectual compromises of ordinary society. Compromise is treason. Any structure, intellectual or social, is likewise treason. When, during the first big sit-in at the L.S.E., some of the rebellious students organized a 'free' or counter-university, one of its leading spirits announced that it would distinguish itself from the other place in as far as in it, teachers would be *totally committed* to what they taught, and students *totally committed* to what they learnt.

What could this mean? Presumably, it implies that any tentative exploration of ideas, the entertaining of suppositions for the purpose of exploring their soundness, is *out*. Sexual experimentation is perfectly permissible – but intellectual experimentation, exploration, tentativeness, anything short of 'commitment', are viewed with a neo-Victorian prudery. Propositions at least may only be embraced with total love.

The implications of this view are interesting. In effect it rejects the division of labour, not merely in production, but also, and above all, in cognition: only that which is known by the 'whole being' is sound and healthy. The hypothetical method, whether in its Socratic form or as practised by experimental science, in which the implications of this view or that are explored for the light they throw on the initial assumption, whilst that initial assumption is only entertained tentatively – all that is rejected. The pure intellect does not play with assumptions and inferences any more than it haggles

*The writer is Professor of Philosophy in the Department of Sociology at the London School of Economics and is author of *Words and Things* (1959), *Thought and Change* (1965) and *Saints of the Atlas* (1969),

or bargains. It gives itself wholeheartedly, in careless rapture in which cognition becomes similar to amorous ecstasy. It is ardent rather than lucid.

The origins of this totalist view of knowledge (and social life, of course) are no doubt various. In part, it is the revival of a very old mystical and antinomian tradition, as David Martin has pointed out. More specifically, in America, it is the continuation and inversion of the populist protestant tradition – a protestantism not of the Book but of the heart, of the view that the hearts of pure and simple men are the safe repositories and oracles of truth. Justification by Commitment seems clearly descended from Justification by Faith. They carry a similar epistemology and ethic. One is bearing witness, not exploring the world. An exemption from rational criticism is not merely permissible, but mandatory. The son of the mid-western preacher (spiritually and perhaps sometimes literally speaking), secularized and transported to the more luscious climate of the campuses, articulates a luxuriant variant of the paternal creed. The totalism of the dissident creed is, and is meant to be, in opposition to the sordid horse-dealing, half-measures and compromises of the established order.

But the *facility* of the creed, and of the stance of its holders, is somehow continuous with the doctrine-less, pragmatic, non-ideological posture of the official society, as indeed it conceives itself to be. The rebels reach their faith and its articulation, such as it is, without any struggles or labour. Truth, whatever it be, appears to be obvious and easily accessible.

No one fully understands the present protest movement. Perhaps we have here a foretaste of the general problem of social control in affluent and liberal society. The emergence of man from the realm of necessity, and the first shy steps into the realm of freedom, are accompanied by none of the features which optimistic social philosophers had forecast. The removal of the stick, the carrot, and the faith – the relative absence of sanctions, of effective rewards, or of a legitimating set of beliefs, have led not to spontaneous harmony, but to chaotic rebellion amongst those upon whom the greatest

amount of physical, social and intellectual freedom is thrust –
the students.

The general features of the protest movement are familiar
enough, though they are not really self-explanatory. This
jeunesse dorée of the affluent and welfare society takes the
institutional and economic framework within which they rebel
– and which make the rebellion possible, painless and riskless
– totally and utterly for granted: their superficial and verbal
radicalism is accompanied by a curious absence of social imagination. They reserve their social imagination for nebulous,
carte blanche alternatives, which are only identified through
abstract nouns purporting to name a condition known to be
satisfactory but not otherwise specified. (They have fantasy
but not imagination, and this leads to fancy-dress politics.
Che Guevara is, basically, the T. E. Lawrence of the Left.)
Playing with such contentless verbiage gives them the right,
they suppose, to look down upon the philistine lack of vision
of those who at least notice concrete differences between social
forms that are actually found on earth, and who notice that
some achievements and benefits are precarious and cannot
altogether be taken for granted. They simply assume that
prosperity, security, law and order, free speech, will all still
be there whenever the rebel decides to call off, or personally
withdraw from, the amateur dramatics of 'revolution'. This
tacit, largely unconscious confidence is an important clue. In
Arrival and Departure, Arthur Koestler makes the police
officer observe to the hero, before he has him tortured, that
he knows how he feels: he has only just fully realized that this
is for real, that he cannot call the game off now. The situation
of our rebels is quite other. They can run back to mummy
whenever they wish. No one will stop them, and they know it
and trade on it. Contemporary society is so indulgent and
maternal that one has the impression of witnessing *The Possessed* rewritten for production in 'Watch with Mother'.

The techniques and strategy of the movement are also by
now very familiar. One picks some morally important and disturbing issue (the bomb, race, a colonial war). The importance
of the issue, the fact that it is deep and moral, and hence not

suitable for political horse-dealing, clearly warrants the sus-
pension of the ordinary proprieties of political behaviour.
When lives and the deepest principles are at stake, etiquette
hardly deserves much consideration. To be concerned with it
indicates heartlessness at best, and vested interests in camou-
flage at worst. The systematic violation of formal rules which
follows will of course, sooner or later, provoke the authorities
into some repressive measures, however mild. The provocation will in any case simply be repeated until it elicits a response. Then one can mobilize further support in the name of
liberty and tolerance, which are now enlisted on the side of
deep political morality. (One moment, their Walter Mitty
imagination makes them into intrepid revolutionaries, who
expect no quarter and who would evidently take pleasure in
giving none if only they had the chance, and who know that
only revolutionary, unconstitutional, 'direct' action makes
sense against so corrupt and deceitful an establishment; the
next moment, made to suffer some laughably mild penalty –
the least that should be expected from the cornered and terri-
fied guardians of privilege – they suddenly turn into outraged
liberals who, strange to tell, seem to have amazingly high expectations of tolerance, fairness, imagination, generosity and
political wisdom on the part of the authorities. The glory of
the revolutionary, and the well-protected safety of the peaceful citizen of a securely ordered state, are demanded and expected, all at once.) One has already enlisted vicarious infan-
tilism, the conviction of some academics that somehow they
are betraying their deepest values if ever they find themselves
not 'on the side of youth'.

It is noteworthy that the *sursis* occasioned by the deep and
fundamental nature of the initial issues, suspends not merely
the customary properties of behaviour, but also of cognition.
Methodological carefulness or fastidiousness is as suspect as
procedural propriety. On these deep and rousing issues, you
must know with your heart. To invoke complex evidence is as
repellent morally as it is to haggle and compromise over principles. The popularity with leftist students of Thomas S. Kuhn's
remarkable *The Structure of Scientific Revolutions* (1962)

is symptomatic. The central thesis of this book, used by the radicals in a way which can hardly give pleasure to its author, is that scientific thinking is quite unlike its idealized popular image. The individual scientist does not proceed independently from evidence to conclusion, nor does he really test current orthodoxy. At any given time, unless a theoretical revolution is occurring, there is a doctrinal 'paradigm' and the individual researcher or theorist is simply made to go on working until his findings conform to this paradigm. He is made to do this without any awareness of constraint. He simply equates working within the paradigm with scientific competence. This account of science pleases the radicals twice over. It enables them to dispose of all official theories not merely without actually flawing them, but without bothering to learn what they have to say. They are just the official paradigms, and can be discounted as such. At the same time, it enables them to construct their own rival viewpoint with great ease, without bothering about consistency, truth or even content. This is *our* paradigm, and that is good enough. An American student, charged by his teacher with failing to document his thesis, replied simply: my paradigm is different from yours.

Even radical student leaders are liable to find themselves outflanked by their own supporters, and taken further and further into a blind activism by the inherent logic of these ideas. Apparently, during the last and most violent of the L.S.E. 'confrontations', radical student leaders were howled down from their own 'left' when they wished to discuss strategy and tactics: any such calculations of tactical advantage become, in the end, 'opportunism'.

The general recipe for revolutionary 'theory' is as simple as that of revolutionary 'practice'. You start from the fact that the institutions of most societies, including this one, can on the whole be expected to favour their own perpetuation. This trite theory is familiar in the social sciences under the name of 'functionalism'. It is not an altogether true theory, but most certainly it is not altogether false, and plenty of plausible instances can be found to illustrate it, in the educational and cultural realms, amongst others. But the rebels treat these illustrations as the unmasking of a sinister deception: the general social tendency towards continuity and self-perpetuation is treated as a vicious fraud, which quite invalidates the endorsement which most citizens of liberal affluent pluralist societies tacitly accord to them. It places that endorsement, tacit but unconstrained, somehow on the same level as the brutality extorted acquiescence which is found in less liberal political systems.[1] Of course, the rebels do not *call* their theory functionalism-for-infants. They have their own vocabulary, the key term of which is 'alienation'. The effective meaning of this term is, however, simply the obverse of functionalism-for-infants: it designates, generically, the condition of members of all societies which secure a measure of consent from their citizens, without at the same time attaining some total and perfect consummation – in other words, virtually everyone's condition in developed liberal societies. Partial exemption from the condition may be obtained by agreement of the holder of the theory, and is presumably granted to fellow-believers.

These simple devices – made to seem weightier, more complex, by cumbersome terminology – suffice to condemn the present order. But what of the alternative, in the name of which the revolution is supposed to be taking place? Here the rebels are liable to invoke both their supposed intellectual ancestors (Hegel) and their alleged intellectual enemies (Popper) to explain why no specification of the new order need be given. They are not 'historicists', they proudly say – history need not, cannot, should not, be done in advance. So we know nothing whatever about the features of that social order for the sake of which we are to suspend all liberal safeguards, and which would escape infantile functionalism – or, in their language, overcome the estrangement of man from his own generic nature.

But the rebel ideology is not merely in deliberate opposition to the official doctrine: it has also, at the same time, remarkable continuities and similarities with it. The official intellectual climate is marked by three important characteristics:

1. See, for instance, Ralph Miliband, *The State in Capitalist Society* (London, 1969).

(1) *Constitutionalism*; (2) *Pluralism*; and (3) *Auto-function-alism*. These terms are used in a somewhat special sense.

Constitutionalism, in its ordinary and political sense, of course designates a most admirable thing. I am wholly in favour of feelings of respect for a constitution, entrenched in a document or in a set of customs, which enables disagreements to be settled and changes to be made in an orderly and peaceful manner. I am wholly in favour of due process in the conduct of public affairs.

But there is another possible sense of constitutionalism, especially when applied to systems of belief. This other sense is somewhat analogous to constitutional monarchy. A constitutional monarchy develops out of an absolute monarchy by reducing the monarch's powers, but maintaining his symbolic role as an expression of national continuity and unity. A constitutional *faith* is a belief system which has undergone an analogous transformation: it is a belief system which once upon a time was really and near-absolutely *believed*, but whose focus has now shifted to a 'symbolic' role. The assertions contained within it are no longer 'really' believed, they no longer define the effective convictions of the 'believers' concerning the world they live in. Their nominal endorsement in speech, ritual or otherwise, symbolizes loyalty, a sense of national continuity, an aspiration towards stability – but their cognitive import has been eroded, in a manner analogous to that in which the political role of the constitutional monarch has been diminished.

There is, manifestly, a very close parallel between the loyalty of a citizen to a constitutional monarch and his loyalty to the organization and doctrine of a 'constitutional' church (in this sense). But, alas, the analogy is not perfect. The analogy is indeed very nearly complete in terms of the attitude and justification of the subject/citizen or the believer/adherent. But there is a crucial difference in the object of the two loyalties.

The monarchy is primarily an institution and only incidentally a theory. It has beliefs and assertions connected with it, but these are not really of its essence. Men were presumably leaders, rulers, kings first, and only then, if at all, elaborated political theories explaining the fact. At any rate, whatever the historical sequence may have been, it is perfectly possible to conceive kingship without any doctrine. The doctrine is logically an accretion: an accretion which may sometimes be of importance, but it is not the central part of the institution.

The case of religion and faith is different. Here, the doctrine, the content of the faith, is of the very heart of the matter. So a striking contrast becomes manifest between constitutional monarchy and constitutional religion. In both cases, loyalty is combined with a disbelief in the theory. But in the one case, the doubt is only in conflict with something which is marginal and peripheral to the institution. In the other case, the conflict is between a background of disbelief and something which is absolutely central to the institution.

Next to 'constitutionalism' the other important trait of the intellectual scene is 'pluralism'.

Pluralism in the ordinary sense, the view that a plurality of countervailing forces, groups and institutions is the best aid towards the maintenance of both liberty and order, is a view for which I have the warmest regard. Institutional pluralism is an admirable thing: and I have no longing whatsoever for social and political monoliths.

But doctrinal pluralism is somewhat different. It preaches the peaceful co-existence of any and all doctrines, not only within one society or within one person, but within, so to speak, one logical universe of discourse. Everything, or very nearly, can apparently be true all at once: to stress and press home difficulties, incompatibilities and so forth is made into a social and moral solecism.

To express doubts about the desirability of pluralism in this sense is to lay oneself open to the suspicion of intolerance and illiberalism. But this is a terrible misunderstanding. For the distinction between social and logical toleration is crucial. Social toleration is admirable. Logical toleration is by no means obviously admirable and it should not be confused with social toleration.

Social toleration requires that no serious *non-logical* pressures – violence, economic blackmail – be used in support or defence of ideas. But it does not exclude argument. The distinction between the two can perhaps best be highlighted by the most common argument in favour of toleration – to the effect that truth is best sought through a natural selection of ideas. This natural selection can only operate if there is, so to speak, free entry into the market.

But equally, no natural selection will take place if all the entrants cohabit peacefully in an unselective, eclectic, unfastidious mishmash. The selection can only operate if the ideas compete, if there is sensitivity to the implications and incompatibilities between them, and if such logical conflicts lead at least to the eventual elimination of one or other of the competing views. If a sloppy and logically unfastidious syncretism prevails, if ideas live and let live, no advance – at least, no advance by natural selection – will take place. Social tolerance is essential – but so is logical intolerance.

This is the second feature of our intellectual scene: pluralism, in a pejorative sense, the peaceful co-existence of diverse ideas and systems of ideas, logically emasculated and deprived of any rivalry-engendering sense of incompatibility. This kind of pluralism is intimately connected with constitutionalism, which is one of the doctrines invoked for justifying and defending the sloppy logical tolerance. By endowing certain ideas or systems of ideas with 'symbolic' status it exempts them from ordinary scrutiny and criticism, disconnects them from other ideas, preventing any fruitful interaction between them and the rest of our intellectual life and hence, in effect, between them and reality.

In a curious kind of way, intellectual pluralism has become the philosophical orthodoxy, the conventional wisdom of contemporary thinkers. One can find it preached from a variety of viewpoints and premises and in a great variety of idioms. In social theory alone, one can find monism eloquently condemned in Berlin, Oakeshott, Crick, Gallie, Popper, and others. It is easy to conclude, whether or not the authors intended it, that pluralism is good. In a variety of styles, we seem to be told that bridges must be crossed when they are reached, that individual cases must be judged on their merits, and so forth. One might be tempted to answer that when one comes to a river, it is too late to start building a bridge, and that individual cases have no merits in the light of which they could be judged, unless some general standard or norm is tacitly presupposed.

There is a difference between, on the one hand, desiring that there should be a plurality of power-centres in societies, capable of surveying and checking each other (admirable), or the recognition that the world is an extremely complex and diversified place (true), and, on the other hand, the sloppy pluralism which argues because the world is diversified, there-fore our thinking should be untidy, *ad hoc*, use any tool which is to hand, and not even seek any intellectual unification and consistency. The cult of the cognitive or political *débrouillard* or *bricoleur* has no intrinsic merit, and does not follow from the premises which are invoked in its support. It does, how-ever, have a natural affinity with the constitutionalism under discussion. The pluralism in practice enjoins a kind of dis-sociation – 'always disconnect', so to speak – between the intel-lectual tools or vision we use on one occasion and on another.

The third characteristic feature of our intellectual scene is 'auto-functionalism'. This is a special, and currently most popular, manner of validating one's own beliefs and ideas. It appears in a wide variety of superficially diverse forms. It consists not of establishing the soundness of one's beliefs directly, in the ordinary and straightforward way, by showing them to be true, but, on the contrary, of proving their sound-ness by showing them to play an essential role, to be 'func-tional', in the internal economy of one's own personality or society (or tradition, or language, etc.). Of course, the argu-ment needs to be camouflaged and elaborated a little to carry conviction. The first step is to put forward a theory of truth: truth 'really is' the fulfilment of a biological, or social, lin-guistic, etc., function. Then one indicates that certain beliefs do play some such role. The conclusion – the soundness of those beliefs – is then readily available. Modernist theology is a striking example, and has passed through about four or five different styles of such reasoning (though all employed the same basic principle): religious assertions were re-interpreted in biological, psychological, social, linguistic, or existentialist idioms, as fulfilling adaptive, social, psychic, categorial, or commitment-expressing functions.

The morally debilitating aspect of auto-functionalism is that it compels its practitioners to indulge in sustained double-think, to live at two different and carefully separated conceptual levels. The major premise, concerning the functionality of this or that belief or idea, is articulated by a neutral and secularized person, who feeds in the belief as a dispassionately, externally observed datum. The conclusion, on the other hand, is received and read 'from the inside' as a belief true in the real, not just the 'functional', sense. But the supplier of the premise and the beneficiary of the conclusion are the same person, albeit wearing different hats; so one can only have some reservations about the intellectual honesty of this conceptual transvestism. But, so be it.

Auto-functionalism also dovetails with the other two traits. It provides pluralist syncretism with a further and omnibus justification, and it does the same for constitutionalism. 'Latent' justification becomes manifest, though in a selective manner. The only thing which remains latent are the rules concerning when and by whom the latent may be manifestly articulated.

Is our condition a healthy one? It is hard to make up one's mind. The condition described has well-known and well-advertised advantages. The separation of the symbolic from the effective political role has the admirable consequence that a concrete, on-the-ground political mistake does not undermine the confidence and loyalty towards the system as a whole *and*, on the other hand, that concrete successes do not make it easy for the holders of political office to absolutize their rule. The strong emotions, positive or negative, are given multiple and distinct objects: the consequence, one hopes, is relative political stability. The same point may (not quite so convincingly) be applied in the field of knowledge: if the serious business of cognitive exploration of the world is kept distinct from the 'symbolic', identity-conferring and loyalty-expressing 'beliefs', the former is freer, and the latter are more stable, and everyone benefits. I wonder. In the sphere of beliefs, this particular kind of division of labour may, in the end, erode respect for truth and sap the vigour of the drive towards it. If almost everything is true in its own fashion, truth cannot matter very much. Each man can then find such truth as he fancies, and need not fear for its adequate vindication. *Enragé* protest, vacuous and unreasoning, can then easily be the last refuge of the phoney.

But it is not for us to assess our general ideological health. The general intellectual scene was invoked only in order to help us understand the rebels. To a most remarkable extent, they are continuous with it, and exhibit the same traits. They have only inverted the official position at one point, in that they claim to be rebels and critics rather than conservatives. But this inversion is superficial rather than profound. The facile, 'symbolic', disconnected nature of belief, its self-sustaining and circular quality, are the same in both cases. The facility is made possible by the same pluralist, auto-functionalist, symbolic-constitutionalist devices.

Modern liberal society has a two-tier ideological system, a double level of justification. At one level, there are theories which are 'believed' rather than believed. At the other level there are legitimations which are persuasive enough, but which are negative and humdrum. At this level of effective and serious belief, it is idle to pretend that the present social order is a heart-warming ideal. It is not. But it is incomparably better than any realistic and known alternative, it is good enough to make the risks of uncharted change unjustifiable, it has some capacity of self-correction, and it is not altogether a fraud. This is cogent, but it does not warm the blood like wine. Its prosaic nature makes it unacceptable to the ardent young as an avowed theory – it cannot be set to music – whilst the fact that it is only half-articulated and not written out in letters of gold on tablets of marble, enables the rebels to go on relying on it in an unavowed manner. At the same time, in their official proclaimed creed, they take over the facility and the style of the official but non-serious 'belief' system, with its associated self-maintaining devices – only they turn it up-side down. Revolutionary verbiage replaces the other kind.

When, for instance, Sartre announces ponderously, that his central question is 'how is the myth of the French Revolution at all possible?' he intends his question to be understood as some historicized version of the deep Kantian query. But in a way he is asking the right question, if one takes the term *myth* in its daily, pejorative sense: what is at issue is indeed a myth, not a reality. Just as modern constitutional monarchy is pos-sible without anyone for one moment taking seriously the Divine Right of Kings, so this 'revolutionary' movement and rhetoric is possible without anyone really being at all in earn-est. We are in one case, as in the other, dealing with a sym-bolic re-enactment. Just because there is hysteria, it does not follow that there is any seriousness.

Or take a more contemporary figure, closer to the rebels and more prestigious with them, Althusser. On his own admission, the central question which preoccupied him was not one about the world, but a narcissistic, second-order one, about the role of Marxist thought – in effect, the Marxist *thinker* – in the world, a world some of whose crucial features are prejudged by such a *Fragestellung*. 'That passage nonetheless contained *the* crucial question, which our ordeals had irresistibly aroused in us: what of Marxist philosophy? In principle, is it entitled to exist? And if so, what distinguishes it? '[2] This kind of formu-lation and sense of priorities hardly encourages or reflects a genuine inquiry:

Genuine social criticism or questioning does not arrive in this tortuous, self-absorbed way. The preoccupation with the status, the very existence, of 'Marxist' ideas, suggests that the ideas themselves do not inspire all that much interest. This weird formulation presupposes some wider and unquestioned world, in which different styles of thinking, intellectual insti-tutions, etc., have their role, and within which one then sets out to find the specific role of Marxism, or rather, establishes that it does indeed have a specific and distinctive role. (Or does it, on Marxist assumptions, discuss the end of philo-

2. Louis Althusser, *Pour Marx*, 1965, p. 23.

sophy? Either way it is circular.) Sartre's defence of Marxism also characteristically has this form: the argument assumes, as a semi-tacit, and in any case unquestioned premise, a kind of meta-theory which accords to Cartesianism, Marxism, and so on, each its historic role and an epoch in which it alone can fulfil that role. He argues, in effect, not that Marxism is true, but that the Marxist epoch is still with us. What is defended, in the end, is not the truth of a doctrine, but its alleged role. Either a role is found (good), or the search for it is itself the role (just as good), or the role consists of bewailing its own demise, temporary or permanent (just as good). If thou seekest revolutionary theory, thou hast already found it. Modern theology is as happy with the Death of God as it is with God, and likewise the Marxist critic of society wobbles happily between a Marxist critique of society, and a critique of society for its lack of Marxist critique. You certainly cannot lose on this.

Coming closer to the local rebels and their intellectual sources, the same underlying logic can be found in the thought of the late Isaac Deutscher. In a lecture brilliantly delivered at the L.S.E. in 1965 (*Listener,* 28 August 1969), his defence of Marxism has exactly the same logic as Sartre's. Neither the poverty of Western Marxist thought, nor the social realities of Eastern Marxist societies, is denied. But Deutscher gives himself a blank cheque on the future, in which the 'real' social structure of the Eastern European societies will assert itself against the present distortions, and in which Marxist thought will flourish again and fulfil its destiny. That it has such a destiny to fulfil is taken for granted. What it will have to say we do not know. Yet the more devoid of content, the more rigidly is such Marxism held. The author announces with evident pride that he cannot think in any but a Marxist way: were you to kill him, he says, still he could do no other. Of course one would do no such harsh thing; one merely wishes to point out to him that his Marxism has no defensible content. But, in the case of the *verkrampte* leftists, there simply seems to be no mental capacity even to contemplate such a possibility.

It does not seem to enter their heads that the radical socialist critique of liberal democracy loses all its force today if you do not even attempt to give reasons why, or how, future revolutionary socialist regimes should succeed in being less repulsive than those already found in Eastern Europe. The reasoning offered would have to be a little more serious than the unbelievably facile predictions, such as Deutscher's, to the effect that nationalism or racialism will disappear in Eastern Europe because these traits are incompatible with the basic structure of socialist society. One is happy to hear this, but at the moment the evidence seems to point to a different conclusion. One can only shudder at the arrogant self-confidence of people who would willingly lead others to a similar fate, if only they had the power, simply on the strength of their own private revelation, and who actually take a pride in their rigidity, in the fact that, were you to kill them, they would still (they say) be unable to think in any other manner.

Or again, consider a remarkable essay by Mr Perry Anderson in which he diagnoses the current cultural condition of England, including the protest movement itself. The poverty of ground-level, first-order revolutionary thought is not denied. (In down-to-earth terms: no one can think of any good general social criticism – as opposed to the 'alienation' gibberish.) But, as in the case of Sartre or Deutscher, he gives himself a *carte blanche* for the future (by tacitly drawing on a meta-theory guaranteeing the availability, in some platonic heaven, of a 'revolutionary theory', waiting only for a suitable midwife to bring it to earth):

British culture ... is a deeply ... stifling force, operating against the growth of any revolutionary Left. It quite literally deprives the Left of any source of concepts and categories.... History has tied this knot; only history will ultimately undo it. A revolutionary culture is not for tomorrow. But a revolutionary practice within culture is possible....[3]

The parallel with auto-functionalist logic on the other side is again perfect. We have no defensible propositions, only a

3. *New Left Review*, No. 50, July–August 1968, p. 57. Republished in *Student Power*, edited by A. Cockburn and R. Blackburn, Penguin, 1969, p. 277.

woolly meta-theory, guaranteeing that some are required and will be available, some time.

The mirror image is not completely faithful at all points. The rebels demand total fulfilment and eschew sordid compromise, and to that extent they do not go in for praise or practice of pluralism. But within their system of belief and action, the cult of spontaneity performs the same role as do pluralism and the cult of the *ad hoc* in the Establishment. If the promptings of your ardent, generous and revolutionary heart are sovereign, no pedantic requirements of consistency are likely to inhibit you very much.

On the rebel side, we find facility and totality – but the total picture is empty. A blank cheque is drawn on the future. On the Establishment side, facility and fragmentation. The logical devices which cover up or justify the emptiness on one side, are similar to those which on the other side make the fragmented hotchpotch serviceable and palatable.

In some measure, these affinities of logic are even half-recognized. Various observers have noticed that this revolutionary movement is remarkably free of any anti-religious element. Indeed, there seems to be an instinctive sympathy between modernist, symbolic believers of various kinds, and they are eager to engage in 'dialogue'. The *mot* is *juste*, for they could hardly indulge in *argument*. (I understand that the application by the Communist Party to join the World Council of Churches is at present under consideration.) They also accord each other, and are generally accorded, what might be called Believer's Licence. A certain fashionable art critic sometimes begins his expositions with some such phrase as: 'But, of course, I am a Marxist.' What this means intellectually, no one knows. But socially speaking, the meaning is perfectly clear. One is meant to look solemn and feel too embarrassed to carp. It could be spelt out as follows: 'What I am about to say records my particular deep vision and commitment. Hence to subject it to sharp criticism would be a solecism, like criticizing a funeral oration. Always disconnect.'

Successful careers and reputations can be built on facile spiritual pilgrimages between these various positions – which can also be occupied simultaneously – and all held in an auto-functionalist spirit. The practitioners do not care whether those with whom they indulge in 'dialogue' are believers or not; they can't really tell the difference. There isn't one. All they want and require is that one should take the historical role of their creed solemnly and seriously. Perhaps a grand International of easy credulity will emerge from the dialogue.